The European Union and South East Europe

This book explores the interaction of the EU in Greece, Slovenia, Croatia and Macedonia in three key policy sectors – cohesion, border managements and the environment – and assesses the degree to which the European Union's engagement with the democracies of South East Europe has promoted Europeanisation and multi-level governance.

Although there is a tendency to view the Balkans as peripheral, this book argues that South East European states are central to what the EU is and aspires to become, and goes to the heart of many of the key issues confronting the EU. It compares changing modes of governance in three policy areas which have been selected as they represent contentious issues in domestic politics; issues which have potential transboundary policy consequences and in which there is significant EU involvement.

The book draws on over a hundred interviews conducted to explore actor motivation, preferences and perceptions in the face of pressure to adapt from the EU and uses Social Network Analysis. Timely and informative, this book considers broader dilemmas of integration and enlargement at a time when the EU's effectiveness is under close scrutiny.

The European Union and South East Europe will be of interest to students and scholars of European politics, public policy, and European Union governance and integration.

Andrew Taylor is Professor of Politics at the University of Sheffield.

Andrew Geddes is Professor of Politics at the University of Sheffield.

Charles Lees, formerly at the University of Sheffield, is now Professor of Politics at the University of Bath.

Routledge/UACES Contemporary European Studies

Edited by Federica Bicchi, London School of Economics and Political Science, Tanja Börzel, Free University of Berlin, and Mark Pollack, Temple University, on behalf of the University Association for Contemporary European Studies.

Editorial Board: Grainne De Búrca, European University Institute and Columbia University; Andreas Føllesdal, Norwegian Centre for Human Rights, University of Oslo; Peter Holmes, University of Sussex; Liesbet Hooghe, University of North Carolina at Chapel Hill, and Vrije Universiteit Amsterdam; David Phinnemore, Queen's University Belfast; Ben Rosamond, University of Warwick; Vivien Ann Schmidt, University of Boston; Jo Shaw, University of Edinburgh; Mike Smith, University of Loughborough and Loukas Tsoukalis, ELIAMEP, University of Athens and European University Institute.

The primary objective of the new Contemporary European Studies series is to provide a research outlet for scholars of European Studies from all disciplines. The series publishes important scholarly works and aims to forge for itself an international reputation.

The European Union and South East Europe

The dynamics of Europeanisation and multi-level governance

Andrew Taylor, Andrew Geddes and Charles Lees

Routledge
Taylor & Francis Group

LONDON AND NEW YORK

First published 2013
by Routledge
2 Park Square, Milton Park, Abingdon, Oxfordshire OX14 4RN

Simultaneously published in the USA and Canada
by Routledge
711 Third Avenue, New York, NY 10017

First issued in paperback 2014

*Routledge is an imprint of the Taylor & Francis Group,
an informa business*

British Library Cataloguing in Publication Data
A catalogue record for this book is available from the British Library

Library of Congress Cataloging-in-Publication Data
Taylor, Andrew.
 The European Union and South East Europe: the dynamics of
 Europeanization and multilevel governance/Andrew Taylor,
 Andrew Geddes, and Charles Lees.
 p. cm. – (Routledge/uaces contemporary european studies; 21)
 Includes bibliographical references and index.
 1. European Union – Balkan Peninsula. 2. Balkan Peninsula –
 Foreign economic relations –European Union countries.
 3. European Union countries – Foreign economic relations –
 Balkan Peninsula. 4. Balkan Peninsula – Foreign relations –
 European Union countries. 5. European Union countries – Foreign
 relations – Balkan Peninsula. I. Geddes, Andrew. II. Lees, Charles.
 III. Title.
 HC240.25.B28T39 2012
 341.242'209496 – dc23
 2011052529

ISBN: 978–0–415–66906–1 (hbk)
ISBN: 978–1–138–82220–7 (pbk)

Typeset in Times New Roman by
Florence Production, Stoodleigh, Devon

Contents

Figures

Tables

Acknowledgements

A considerable number of people and institutions provided help and support for the three-year research project and during the writing of the book drawing on that research and we have accumulated a large number of debts over the years.

First, we would like to thank the Economic and Social Research Council for their support. The research on which this book is based was funded by grant RES-062–23–0183, *Multi-Level Governance in South-East Europe, Institutional Innovation and Adaptation in Croatia, Greece, FYR Macedonia and Slovenia*. The Principal Investigator was Andrew Taylor and the co-investigators were Ian Bache, Andrew Geddes and Charles Lees, all from the Department of Politics at the University of Sheffield.

Second, we would like to record our thanks to the many individuals – some 120 – in Greece, Slovenia, Croatia and Macedonia, as well as the European Commission in Brussels, who kindly gave up their time to be interviewed and complete questionnaires for the project. Our interviewees were unfailingly helpful and open in their responses to our questions and for their contribution to the project we cannot thank them enough. That they remain anonymous does not detract from their role; without them there would have been no project and no book. Every effort has been made to trace all the copyright-holders, but if any have been overlooked the publishers will be pleased to make the necessary arrangement at the first opportunity.

We were particularly fortunate in our fieldworkers George Andreou, Gorica Atanasova, Darko Fercej, Elena Lazarou, Kumjana Novakova, Danjel Tomsic and Simona Zavratnik. They displayed not only considerable enthusiasm for the project, but also undertook the arduous work of collecting documents, conducting interviews, collating material and preparing interview transcripts with great efficiency and commitment. Our fieldworkers also played an important role in contributing to the intellectual evolution of the project.

Christina Miariti and Nicos Zaharis of the South East Europe Research Centre (SEERC), a joint initiative of the University of Sheffield and City University, Thessaloniki, played an important role in providing a 'base' for the project in the region. Christina's management skills were vital in helping us recruit the fieldworkers and manage the research, and in organising a flawless dissemination event for practitioners. In this context we would also like to thank the staff of the *Zythos* bar and restaurant in Thessaloniki for providing so congenial a space for informal meetings on the project. The Sheffield end of the project was managed by Margaret Holder, who, like her counterpart in Thessaloniki, was a tower of strength. Also in Sheffield, we would like to thank Rob Collins who managed the project's funds.

Papers relating to aspects of the research were presented before various audiences, including UACES (Plymouth and Angers), Zagreb, DeMontfort University, Sussex European Institute, CES (Montreal) and the Free University of Berlin. We would like to thank these audiences for their constructive criticism of our work. Particularly important were two dissemination events, one in Thessaloniki and one in Sheffield. The first was hosted by SEERC (2 June 2009) and was directed at practitioners (civil servants, NGO representatives, and so on), both those who had been interviewed for the project as well as individuals invited from across the region. The event attracted some thirty participants. A second event was held at the in the Department of Politics, University of Sheffield (18 September 2009). In addition to the empirical findings, this event focused on the conceptual and theoretical aspects of the project and the participants were academics who were experts in the region, policy sector experts and Europeanisation. This event attracted some 25 invited participants. We would like to thank all those who participated and contributed to what were extremely valuable and productive events.

Finally, we would like to thank our families for their support.

Andrew Taylor
Andrew Geddes
Charles Lees
Sheffield, August 2011

Abbreviations

AFSJ	Area of Freedom, Security and Justice
CARDS	Community Assistance for Reconstruction, Development and Stabilisation
CEE	Central and Eastern Europe
CSF	Community Support Framework
DIS	Decentralised Implementation System
DPA	Democratic Party of Albanians
EA	Europe Agreement
EAGGF	European Agricultural Guarantee and Guidance Fund
EAS	European Administrative Space
EB	Eurobarometer
EC	European Commission
ECB	European Central Bank
ECJ	European Courts of Justice
EEA	European Environment Agency
EEC	European Economic Community
EMU	European Monetary Union
ERDF	European Regional Development Fund
ESF	European Structural Fund
EU	European Union
FYROM	Former Yugoslav Republic of Macedonia
GDP	gross domestic product
IBM	Integrated Border Management
ICTY	International Criminal Tribunal for the former Yugoslavia
IMF	International Monetary Fund
IMP	Integrated Mediterranean Programme
IOM	International Organization for Migration
IPA	Instrument for Pre-Accession Assistance
ISPA	Instrument for Structural Policy for Pre-Accession
LAU	Local Administrative Unit
LEAPs	Local Environmental Action Plans
MLG	multi-level governance
NATO	North Atlantic Treaty Organisation

NEAP	National Environment Action Plan
NEIS	National Environmental Information System
NGO	Non Governmental Organisation
NPAA	National Plan for the Adoption of the Acquis
NRSD	National Strategy for Regional Development
NSRF	National Strategic Reference Framework
NUTS	Nomenclature des Unités Territoriales Statistiques
OFA	Ohrid Framework Agreement
OP	Operating Plans
PHARE	Poland and Hungary: Assistance for Restructuring their Economies
RDA	Regional Development Agency
ROP	Regional Operating Programme
SAA	Stabilisation and Association Agreement
SAP	Stabilisation and Accession Process
SAPARD	Special Accession Programme for Agricultural and Rural Development
SDF	Strategic Development Framework
SEE	South East Europe
SIGMA	Support for Improvement in Governance and Management in Central and Eastern European Countries
SIS	Schengen Information System
SNA	social network analysis
TAIEX	Technical Assistance and Information Exchange
UN	United Nations
UNDP	United Nations Development Programme
WGI	World Bank Governance Indicators

Note: This list does not give abbreviations of country-specific institutions and organisations. These are explained at the relevant point in the text. To do otherwise would merely expand further an already lengthy list.

1 Introduction

This book is about how states adapt as a result of their engagement with the European Union (EU). It analyses adaptation to the requirements of the EU in four states of South East Europe (SEE) states (Greece, Slovenia, Croatia and Macedonia) in three policy areas (cohesion, environment, and migration and border security) between 1995 and 2010. We analyse one relatively long-standing member state (Greece, which joined the EU in 1981), one newer member state (Slovenia joined in 2004), one state that will join in June 2013 (Croatia) and one with a more distant prospect of membership (Macedonia).

There is a long-established tendency to view the Balkans as a peripheral region, as an 'other' that defines Europe but, we argue, that SEE is central to what the EU is and aspires to become. Through its close assessment of specific forms of engagement in three key policy areas, the book also goes to the heart of many of the key issues confronting the EU. What can experiences in SEE tell us about the interconnected evolution of domestic and supranational governance? What types and forms of policy and politics are generated by engagement with the EU? We do not, therefore, regard SEE as 'exceptional'. Rejecting 'Balkan exceptionalism' reframes SEE as central to the EU's development. The EU's future will be determined by events in SEE, events that have the potential to make or break the EU. The crisis in the Greek political economy occurred during the final stages of our work and while we study neither it nor European Monetary Union (EMU), the types of institutional (and other) pathologies that were revealed were evident in our research.

SEE provides a test-bed for the operationalisation, interrogation and development of existing theories drawn from the established European governance and integration literatures. The book compares changing modes of governance in three policy areas – cohesion; migration and border security; and environment – and it covers the period after 1995. These policy areas were selected because they are all highly salient political issues and important to the development of the region. Second, they are all transboundary policy areas and thus disposed to multi-level governance (MLG). Third, they are all policy areas in which there is a significant EU dimension. Engagement with the EU is our independent variable and changes in the modes of governance our dependent variables. However, we also isolate and identify intervening variables to explain variance across time and space.

The research involved extensive desk-based analysis of policy and legislative developments in all three policy areas and in all four case countries, and 120 semi-structured interviews conducted in Brussels, Greece, Slovenia, Croatia and Macedonia that were designed to acquire insight into actor motivation, preferences and perceptions in the face of adaptational pressures from the EU and other sources. We worked with six field researchers in each of our case countries to help secure access to relevant policy-makers and officials and to help to overcome linguistic issues.

The research that we present is timely for a number of reasons. The first is the centrality of our three policy areas to the contemporary EU. The second is that EU engagement in SEE demonstrates broader dilemmas of integration, enlargement and adaptation to the *acquis* at a time when the EU's effectiveness and that of key institutions such as the European Commission is under scrutiny. While we keep a close eye on supranational governance, our main analytical focus is adaptation at state level. The state is the essential layer between society and the supranational, the filter through which EU policies flow and which is chiefly responsible for implementation, shaping these polices in the light of national traditions. We also consciously seek to add territory and territoriality to the analytical triptych of power, authority and legitimacy because the sovereign national state remains the essential building-block of the EU and the default container for policy and politics. In each of our cases the EU has significant territorial consequences, transcending and reinforcing borders within a complex multi-level context. We also see the distinction between formal compliance with EU requirements and the scope for more complex on-the-ground patterns of adaptation when domestic political processes in each of the three policy areas are factored into the analysis.

The prime theoretical and conceptual orientations for this book are debates about MLG and Europeanisation. In all our cases we are interested in MLG as an *outcome* of the wider process of Europeanisation. We use a top-down view, which requires adaptational pressure for Europeanisation to occur. However, we also recognise that the presence of 'misfit' is not a sufficient condition for Europeanisation and acknowledge the role of intervening variables, notably the state and other key domestic actors, so according agency its due. Engagement with the EU has been analysed in terms of 'sovereignty bargains' that impact on a state's autonomy, policy control and legitimacy. States strike 'sovereignty bargains' in the expectation they will be better able to secure national goals, which then implies an improvement in capacity. In the analysis that follows we seek to specify and utilise this notion of a capacity bargain in order to explore how and why Europe 'hits home', so to speak, in the domestic politics of adaptation.

The following chapter provides a close and detailed discussion of what we mean when we discuss capacity bargains, how we use and employ the term, and how we understand the implications for policy and politics across three policy areas in all four of our case countries. Our argument is not that the capacity bargain can be likened to some simple process of 'filling' a state with capacity as though it were a previously empty receptacle. Our core idea is that the EU *acquis* raises very specific, sectorally focused issues of adaptation and change, and that we can understand these as possessing functional, political and administrative dimensions, as we discuss more fully in Chapter 2. The point is that, while the meaning and content of policy can be contested, each of our policy sectors has its own capacity bargain (which we see as the mix of resources and actors derived from the requirements of EU policy and the demands of national implementation). These sectoral capacity bargains then address issues of output legitimacy, misfit and policy style. The capacity bargain can then be understood as an essential component of the wider sovereignty bargain addressing the potential misfit between the EU and the domestic, as well as the gap between formal compliance and implementation. As implementation tends to be most likely at the centre, this implies the extension of capacity to all levels of the polity with attendant scope for non-adaptation and contestation of the 'meaning' of Europe in domestic politics. The capacity bargain therefore has a distinct territorial dimension relating to a state's ability to act within the EU. Europeanisation and multi-level governance must be seen in relation to this dimension. The EU both de- and re-borders states, it challenges and reinforces sovereignty, which remains the constitutive principle of territorial organisation in the EU and SEE. Only sovereign states may join, so aspirants must demonstrate their sovereignty prior to pooling it in a sovereignty bargain intended to improve their capacity. Engaging the EU therefore promotes 'state-ness'.

In all four case countries and in each of the three policy areas we would expect to see extensive Europeanisation as a result of *acquis* transposition and the efforts of national authorities to address misfit. We would also expect the scale of adjustment to vary according to the scale of the misfit and be influenced by domestic factors (both historical and contemporary) as well as by the tensions between established and emerging constellations of power and interest. The character of the politics in each sector is also likely to be influenced by policy type – regulatory, distributive or a mixture of the two – as well as by EU governance principles such as subsidiarity, transparency and partnership, and specific policy requirements. All polities, even the most unitary, are multi-level and our three policies have multi-level attributes and consequences. We now briefly specify the key characteristics of each of our three policy areas.

Cohesion policy is the foundational policy for analysis of MLG. We would expect to see the development of new tiers of administration and the development of horizontal and vertical network governance. Cohesion is not only explicitly multi-level but also has a distinctive 'European' governance (programming, partnership and regionalisation). Because of the politics generated – distributive – we would expect to find scope for substantial conflict. This mix, we hypothesise, will place the initiative with the centre.

In contrast, the multi-levelled-ness of migration and border security will differ from cohesion (while both differ from environment). Migration and border security is certainly 'multi-level', involving as it does centre-periphery relations, the supranational and other states, but relationships are likely to be more hierarchical and managed from the centre. In border management, however, we would expect to see a fairly simple network dominated by relatively few actors with power concentrated in the central state. This, it must be emphasised, does not rule out the involvement of other actors (a structural feature of cohesion and environment) but does raise questions about their influence in all our policy areas. We would also expect to see a key role for other international organisations, such as the International Organization for Migration (IOM) in helping states build capacity in this policy area. Finally, each of our case countries is a relatively 'new' country of migration and/or is represented as exposed to the effects of irregular migration across the EU's external frontiers.

Similarly, in environment policy we would expect complex internal and external multi-level networks, reflecting the transboundary and technical complexity of environmental issues. The state's gate-keeper role in cohesion and the essentialist nature of migration and border security in defining a state (as well as the potential political sensitivity of the issues) will reinforce the centre's power; the same broad expectation applies to the environment but here the centre's dominance is reinforced by the sheer technical complexity and range of interests and actors involved at multiple levels. In all three, however, capacity is needed to implement policy, and to aggregate and coordinate different and conflicting interests. Engagement with the EU, therefore, has a general tendency to reinforce the centre. In polities with a history and tradition of centralised governance, and where a major concern of the Commission has been to create (or endow) states with the capacity to undertake and sustain the duties and obligations of membership, we would expect to see the resilience of the centre and a concentration of power in each policy network.

In each chapter we identify the relevant European-level processes that imply some measure of domestic change to ensure compliance. We explore 'goodness of fit' between the European-level processes and domestic institutions and practices. The degree of fit leads to varying degrees of adaptational pressure on member states: poor fit implies strong adaptational pressure; good fit implies weak pressure. Pressure for change to domestic structures can either come directly from external processes that require institutional change or indirectly through a 'policy misfit', placing pressure on underlying institutions. Each chapter then examines the extent to which adaptational pressure, filtered by the national authorities, leads to domestic change. An external process is most likely to produce domestic structural change when it generates significant adaptational pressures; and where facilitating factors are present that enable domestic actors to promote change, highlighting the extent to which ideas are embraced or opposed by domestic actors; the mechanisms of change; the strategies and tactics used by various actors; and their consequences. Thus, as already noted, we provide a dynamic conception of Europeanisation that allows for political agency.

Organisation of the book

Each chapter addresses the following questions. First, do the concepts of Europeanisation and MLG adequately link theory and method in explaining how engagement with the EU changes domestic governance? Second, what do developing modes of governance tells us about the explanatory power of MLG? Third, to what degree does engagement with the EU lead to convergence in governance? The case study chapters explore these questions through an examination of institutions and policies, specification of the nature of the policy network, assessment of the nature and direction of change, and an analysis of the extent to which change challenges established distributions of power.

In Chapter 2 we explore the book's conceptual and theoretical framework, beginning with a discussion of the book's core concepts – Europeanisation and MLG – and how these relate to and influence governance in our states and policy sectors. Central to the relationship between the EU and a state (whether a member or not) are sovereignty bargains and capacity bargains. These concepts are specified and used to assess the policy-sectoral consequences of Europeanisation. The third section discusses institutional change and, in particular, the relationship between supranational, national and subnational government, and their consequences for territoriality. This is then widened to include a discussion of historical institutionalism and the question of change. These are very broad, macro-analytical issues and need a more nuanced, fine-grained approach to Europeanisation and MLG in politics, polity and policy. To penetrate politics, polity and policy we deploy social network analysis (SNA) to map and represent the architecture of each sectoral capacity bargain and outline the network of actors in order to understand the dynamics and to form the basis of a more systemic analysis. In each chapter we then use extensive interview material to explicate the underlying distributions of power and resources within these networks. Finally, the chapter discusses the issue of incentives. These are usually seen as being more directly relevant to states subject to direct conditionality via enlargement, and three of our four cases have been subject to 'external incentives'. We would argue, however, that all states are subject to active and passive leverage. Certainly, the mix varies between countries and policy sectors but manifests itself in the measures adopted (or not) to resolve misfit; in our cases we identify a relatively active and rapid transposition and compliance at the centre, with a more passive and partial implementation becoming the further away from the centre.

Chapter 3 discusses a range of issues that are intended to provide the necessary background for the case study chapters. Central to these chapters is the historical issue of state building in SEE and the EU's current role in building state capacity and developing the capabilities essential for EU membership. Despite variation we contend, first, that historical state-building projects sought to emulate directly the process and outcomes of state building in Western Europe; and second, that state building is both historically and contemporaneously a dialectic of border creation and transcendence. In this sense, then, engagement with the EU is the latest, and perhaps final, stage of state building in SEE. The chapter then broadens by examining the different national paths to Europe with an emphasis on critical junctures in relation to each state's engagement with the EU. These critical junctures are balanced by resilient historical patterns that continue to influence polity, politics and policy and within which (paradoxically) engagement with the EU can strengthen the state. The most resilient of these patterns is the tendency towards centralised power in these states. The third part of the chapter returns to the broad issues of governance and its contours in our four cases; it also considers the 'input' side of Europeanisation, namely the attitude of populations to the EU and its various impacts. The overall picture is of a group of states with embedded weaknesses in governance and variation in the impact and effectiveness of their responses. Public opinion remains (generally) favourably disposed to the EU albeit with specific complaints and grumbles which, however, prompts the question: what is the alternative to the EU for these states?

The next three chapters are the book's core: the policy sector case studies. The common theme is the degree of misfit between the EU and the domestic and the measures taken to address that misfit, measures that constitute Europeanisation. Each chapter addresses the specifics of adaptation and the consequence of adaption for governance, with MLG as the primary analytical frame. Each chapter addresses the book's three core questions (see p. 5) and is organised around three themes: institutions and policies, the policy network (which utilises SNA) and the sources of change impacting on the network. The chapters conclude with observations on the sectoral consequences of engagement with the EU.

Cohesion policy's significance (Chapter 4) as an EU policy and the essential role in it of MLG allied to its wider implications for governance, as well as its obvious financial attractions for governments means we would expect to see rapid transposition and very significant domestic efforts to reduce misfit in order to benefit from the policy. Not surprisingly, this is exactly what we find. Extensive and rapid Europeanisation and very obvious MLG effects are plain to see, but of itself this is of little interest. What is of real interest are the consequences of this for domestic governance and politics. Cohesion can be seen as representing a markedly different style of governance and governing to that characteristic of a unitary 'simple' polity and there is no doubt that features such as multi-annual programming, civil society participation, partnership and so on, encourage the development of a more pluralistic policy process. Moreover, cohesion has marked territorial consequences. However, and reflecting a finding common to the wider cohesion literature, the decentralisation and pluralisation of process is compatible with a continued, and even strengthened, centralisation of power. In all our cases the evidence of cohesion policy is that it strengthens the central state. Our evidence also shows considerable potential for *radical* change in governance via cohesion policy (both in the specific policy sector and through spill-over and social learning), but even the crudest historical institutional approach would urge caution in all cases because a combination of national history, political calculation and the pressures of accession and membership means that a radical shift is unlikely without a powerful exogenous shock.

Migration and border security (Chapter 5) have ascended the EU policy agenda and have become key components of adaptation pressure for new and candidate countries. Chapter 5 assesses both the EU *acquis* and explicates it in the context of the underlying perceptions of SEE as a new migration region viewed as exposed to the 'threat' of illegal immigration. We see that this has led to a strong EU focus on what is sometimes represented as the EU's 'soft underbelly', i.e. states with relatively weak migration control and border security capacities. In such a setting we can see the analytical value and utility of the capacity bargain as we look at the form and content of policy, but also explore underlying meaning and conceptualisations of policy dilemmas and challenges. This helps to avoid simplistic notions of capacity that are devoid of consideration of scope for the contestation of the meaning of policy and also of the important differences that can emerge between formal compliance and on-the-ground implementation. In the context of capacity, the chapter also demonstrates the key role played by a range of international organisations in delivering migration management services in pursuit of 'Integrated Border Management'.

In our analysis of environmental policy (Chapter 6) we find that the nature of the environmental problems facing SEE, the demands and logic of environmental protection as a transboundary policy problem, and the technical demands inherent in the transposition and implementation of the environmental *acquis* lend the capacity bargain framework particular analytical power. We found significant misfit in all of our case countries but variance in the apparent enthusiasm of elites for tackling it and different distributional consequences when they did. Elites were faced with an implicit conflict in which the efficient transposition of the *acquis* generated centralising tendencies that were at odds with the EU's parallel objective of encouraging open and pluralistic governance networks within the sector. Variance in levels of socio-economic development, as well as existing administrative capacity and know-how, impact on the manner and extent to which these conflicting demands were addressed, and this is evident in the quite distinct constellations of actors found in our four case countries.

Chapter 7 provides an analytical synthesis of our policy-focused chapters. This is done because of the need to avoid an over-specification of particular sectoral dynamics with the consequent lack of attention to the broader dynamics of Europeanisation and MLG that are also central components of the analysis contained within this book. In this chapter we specifically address the questions identified earlier in this chapter as we assess the utility and value of Europeanisation and MLG as organising concepts in explaining domestic adaptation and their implications for polities, politics and policy in our three case countries.

2   Europeanisation and multi-level governance in South East Europe

Introduction

This chapter establishes the analytical framework that we employ to explore interactions between European and domestic politics and the adaptation that occurs in polity, politics and policy as a result of engagement with the EU in three policy areas in four SEE countries. Methodologically, it adopts an approach that starts at the domestic, explores the nature of EU policies and expectations, and then assesses the domestic political consequences (Börzel 2002: 193) or what Graziano and Vink and describe as a 'bottom-up-down' design (2007: 10). Our aim is to account for the EU's domestic impact using well-established concepts and theories within four countries – Greece, Slovenia, Croatia and Macedonia – that have experienced differing relationships over time with the EU. We do this by examining three policy sectors – cohesion, migration and border security, and environmental policy – and the nature of these differing relationships (two member states and two candidate states) with the EU.

The key puzzles that underpin this book are: does political engagement with the EU promote MLG, of what type(s), and through what mechanisms and processes? What are the implications for the distribution of power in the domestic polity of engagement with the EU? Europeanisation and MLG are our two core concepts and we explore these in the first section of this chapter. This chapter focuses on the theoretical underpinning of the policy chapters (Chapters 4, 5 and 6) and poses three questions.

Our first question is: how has political engagement with the EU changed domestic modes of governance (structures, practices/standard operation procedures, norms and beliefs)? While our *primary* empirical and theoretical focus is on MLG, which we conceive as an *outcome* of the wider process of Europeanisation, it is clear that responses vary by state and by policy sector. To explore this question, and to link theory and method, we develop the idea of the 'capacity bargain' in the second section, which we use to link state adaptation with our analyses of the policy networks.

Our second question is: what do the developing modes of governance tell us about the explanatory power of MLG? All polities, even the most centralised, have more than one level, so what actually does multi-level mean? We argue that if 'multi-levelness' is to be more than a metaphor for complexity, then networks have to be mapped and understood from the perspective of those who constitute the network and then analysed. In the third section we consider the nature of institutional change. We use SNA supplemented by extensive material from interviews with key policy-makers and officials to understand how institutions operate that are subject to downward pressure and adaptation pressures. The chapter's fourth section explains how SNA was applied and with what purpose, its strengths and weaknesses, and how it can enhance our understanding of Europeanisation and MLG.

The third question is: to what degree does engagement with the EU lead to convergence in governance across sectors and countries? While these states and policy sectors are subject to a capacity bargain and downward pressure from the EU, both of these are profoundly influenced by intervening domestic variables and political agency. In the final section we consider the question of incentives. Two of our states (Croatia and Macedonia) are subject to the EU's post-2004 conditionality process, which differs from that to which Slovenia was subject and both differ totally from the accession process undergone by Greece. Incentive structures have obvious implications for domestic change. Institutional change and adaptation, and, in particular, the interplay between path-dependence and our core concepts are discussed in the third section.

The core issue in each of these questions is the capture and use of resources, which involves reconciling competing interests and pressures in ways specific to each policy sector. In the Introduction we introduced the idea of the 'capacity bargain' as a way of understanding various dimensions of adaptation in each of our countries and policy areas to the requirements of EU integration. As we discuss below, these bargains have 'functional', 'political' and 'administrative' dimensions, and are focal points for engagement with the EU. Each sectoral capacity bargain is located within a dense matrix of influences and characterised by a complex calculus, again unique to that network. The networks – mapped by SNA – constitute, therefore, what our respondents identify as being the key institutional channels linked to, influenced by and reflective of Europeanisation and MLG. They constitute what network actors themselves regard as the arenas for the capture of resources and the reconciliation of competing, complex and, at times, contradictory interests operating at the supranational, national and subnational levels. Permeating the network metaphor is the issue of how to achieve compliance and implementation in complex systems characterised by extended policy delivery chains.

The core concepts

In this section we discuss our two core concepts: Europeanisation and MLG. We explain how we seek to derive insight from both these important areas of analysis within EU studies and apply them to our specific cases of policy development in three policy sectors in four SEE countries.

Europeanisation

We define Europeanisation as 'the domestic adaptation to European integration' (Graziano and Vink 2007: 7; see also Vink 2003: 63), which makes this the dependent variable in our study. This definition also covers the development of linkages (formal and informal) and does not conflate Europeanisation with 'EU-isation', although the EU is the most significant actor (Radaelli 2005). Adaptation embraces institutional change, policy shifts and changes in behaviour congruent with engagement with the EU. The analytical and empirical focus is on the domestic and the primary direction of influence is downwards from the EU as well as from the central state to subnational tiers, and from the state to civil society. A major theme of the book is that Europeanisation promotes and sustains centralisation, and that centralisation is often mistaken for Europeanisation. While the three policy sectors constitute the core of the book, we use these as platforms to understand broader and variegated impacts within the four polities and we do not make an a priori argument for convergence (Jordan 2005). We do not suggest that convergence and harmonisation are not aspects of Europeanisation, but in our sample of countries, of greater interest are the specific network dynamics and how these fit into the wider process of European integration and domestic politics (Kassim *et al.* 2000; Börzel 2005b; Kassim 2005).

So, our concern is with changing patterns of governance in three policy areas and four states, and whether change is the consequence of engaging with the EU. This avoids falling into the trap of overstating the importance of the EU for domestic change. Avoiding this trap also requires sensitivity to the narratives and stories of actors dealing with the EU's influence. Grabbe (for example) identified how both EU and Central and East European (CEE) policy-makers exaggerated the influence of the EU for domestic political management purposes (2001, 2003). Europeanisation has affected our four states differently according to the intensity, timing and length (and type) of engagement with the EU. Radaelli (2004) identifies three generations of Europeanisation research. The first saw Europeanisation as a synonym for integration, while the second generation had a 'top-down' focus. Our work, however, owes more to the third generation of Europeanisation research, which asks how politics (the policy-making process), policy (content and nature) and polity (domestic institutions) adapt to top-down pressures generated by engagement with the EU (Cowles *et al.* 2001; Jordan and Liefferink 2003; Bulmer and Radaelli 2005).

The first significant attempt to define Europeanisation was Ladrech's 1994 article, in which he defined Europeanisation as 'an incremental process reorienting the direction and shape of politics to the degree that EC political and economic dynamics become part of the organisational logic of national politics and policy-making' (Ladrech 1994: 69). Yet if the starting point was to understand Europeanisation as a top-down process in which the EU impacted on states, research revealed a more complex interactive dynamic: member states did not simply or passively 'download' policies from the EU, but also actively 'uploaded' their preferences to the EU level: the greater their influence on the EU position, the less the subsequent problems of adapting. It is reasonable to assume that our non-member states (Croatia and Macedonia) are more likely to be policy-takers rather than policy-shapers compared to the two member states (Greece and Slovenia). From a research perspective, however, we remain open to the possibility of a two-way influence in the EU-state relationship and assess the flow of influence empirically, state by state and sector by sector.

Kassim (2003a, b; 2005) argues that both accession and membership states coordinate policy in response to EU pressure but this common stimulus produces varying national responses. The systemic implication is a rebalancing of institutions as a result of EU pressure coupled with distinctive national administrative styles that are profoundly influenced by history. Wessels (1996), Rometsch and Wessels (1996) and Wessels *et al*. (2003) see engagement with the EU as triggering institutional adaptation but an adaptation *conditioned* by national histories and traditions. This is one of our major concerns. We are also interested in the role of the core executive and its relationship with subnational government and civil society, and the policy networks directly inspired by EU requirements. However, it is important to remember that in some policy areas, including migration and border security and environment policy, international organisations other than the EU are closely involved. Their involvement is based on different roles and attributes (for example, their moral authority or technical expertise) but their involvement does deliver important resources to the policy networks (Barnett and Duvall 2005). The EU is a unique type of international organisation and is central to our analysis, but it is not the only international organisation operating in SEE (Cameron and Kintis 2001).

Much of the Europeanisation literature is institutionalist by nature (Knill and Lehmkuhl 1999; Börzel 1999; Knill 2001; Radaelli 2003) and, indeed, Bulmer has argued that 'an awareness of the new institutionalisms is indispensable for understanding how Europeanisation is theorized' (2007: 51). New institutionalist approaches are the theoretical means through which we assess the degree of Europeanisation. In particular, a useful contrast is made between rational choice, sociological and historical variants, and particularly on the claims of the *logic of consequentiality* versus the *logic of appropriateness* (Hix and Goetz 2000; Börzel and Risse 2003; Vink 2003).

The book's focus is on what is transmitted from the EU and the degree of fit/misfit between this and the domestic arena (Börzel 2005a: 52–3) and how this is mediated by domestic actors. The key assumption made is that the greater the misfit, the greater the degree of adaptive pressure, although specific responses (and therefore effects) will vary (Börzel and Risse 2007: 69–70). Studies of institutional adaptation generally adopt either a logic of consequentiality (rational, goal-driven action) or a logic of appropriateness (a complex process of social learning). While these logics are analytically distinct, it is often impossible to disentangle them empirically (March and Olsen 1989: 10). In the logic of consequentiality policy networks composed of actors making strategic choices are the core drivers of adaptation and this interaction between and within networks generates new opportunities for actors to pursue goals. There is a tendency to see power as zero-sum with Europeanisation, which redistributes domestic power, creating winners and losers.

The analysis presented here, and that of classic network theorists (Rhodes 1988 and 1997, for example), disputes this zero-sum assumption. The evidence we deploy tends to suggest that network interaction is based on the exchange of resources and bargaining for mutual gain as no single actor is in a position to dominate or achieve outcomes without the cooperation of others. Power is, therefore, a positive sum even though the configuration of winners and losers may shift as a result of Europeanisation. An analysis drawing on the logic of appropriateness retains the network as an organising device but sees interaction as an activity encapsulating a potential for significant shifts in values and preferences through the development of trust, cooperation and mutual gain (Kohler-Koch 1996: 359–80). For instance, Thielemann's (2001: 181–97) focus on the partnership principle, a principle of cohesion policy, but which has wider relevance (in, for example, environment policy) provides a good starting point for bridging rational and social learning approaches within the overall framework of the policy network. Network governance may encourage a shift to problem-solving behaviour, but it can also encapsulate decision-making based on the control of power resources or 'difference-splitting'.

These two logics and approaches to Europeanisation have different ontologies, but in terms of empirical political analysis they can be accommodated if not reconciled by reference to the style of governance advocated by the EU and which is inherent in individual policies. Placed alongside empirical complexity it is unclear to say the least that rationalist and sociological interpretations are mutually exclusive or generate radically different hypotheses about power (zero sum/positive sum), interests (fixed/changeable) or whether Europeanisation redistributes power or promotes social learning. Interviewees at the Commission emphasised that interaction was essential to developing knowledge but that the closer a country came to membership, the more nuanced became its view of the EU (interview, DG Enlargement, 31 March 2009). Radaelli's distinction between 'thin' and 'thick' learning suggests that over time an actor will adjust their strategy(ies) to preserve established goals in a new context (thin learning) but interaction (longevity, intensity and frequency) in networks modifies values and preferences (thick learning) (2003: 27–56). The trinity of longevity, intensity and frequency brings us to the role of history, which will be discussed in a later section, but first we need to consider our second core concept: MLG.

Multi-level governance

Multi-level governance is one of the most widely used concepts in the analysis of the EU and its domestic effects (Piattoni 2010: 17–31). In the context of the analysis of European integration, Marks (1992) first applied the term MLG to capture developments in EC structural policy after it was reformed in 1988. Subsequently, Marks and others developed MLG to apply more broadly to EU decision-making (for example, Marks *et al.* 1996; Hooghe and Marks 2003; Bache 2008). The approach draws insights from both the study of domestic and comparative politics as well as the study of international politics. In particular, it has connections to the work by Scharpf and others on German federalism and *Politikverflechtung* (Scharpf 1988, 1997, 2003; Benz and Eberlin 1999) that resembles aspects of neo-functionalism and is replete with network metaphors.

MLG was developed as a counterview to the state-centrism that dominated the study of the EU from the 1960s to the 1980s, and which subsequently found a more contemporary voice in the post-SEA (Single European Act) period through the work on liberal intergovernmentalism of Moravcsik (1991, 1993, 1994, 1998). Moravcsik argued that the control of state executives at the agenda-setting stage of EU policy-making conferred on them 'gatekeeping' power: 'the power to veto proposed policies, permits executives to block negotiation or agreement at the international level, thereby imposing a *de facto* domestic veto' (1994: 9). Yet MLG does not reject the central role played by state executives in EU decision-making; rather, it acknowledged them as 'the most important pieces of the European puzzle'. However, 'when one asserts that the state no longer monopolises European level policy-making or the aggregation of domestic interests, a very different polity comes into focus' (Hooghe and Marks 2001: 3). On this issue, MLG makes three claims: first, decision-making competences are shared by actors at different levels rather than monopolised by state executives; second, collective decision-making among states involves a significant loss of control for individual state executives (notably, through qualified majority voting in the Council); and third, political arenas are interconnected rather than nested. Subnational actors operate in both national and supranational arenas, creating transnational associations in the process (Hooghe and Marks 2001: 3–4).

We assume the existence of MLG in each of the policy sectors but that decision-making is manipulated by state executives and policy arenas are nested rather than interconnected. The MLG literature's focus has tended to be on states not subject to a conditionality regime remotely comparable to that applied in CEE and SEE. Flowing from this is a failure to give appropriate weight to the complexity, intensity and intrusiveness of engagement with the EU in Slovenia (until 2004), Croatia and Macedonia. This is why we use a range of countries with different and varying relationships with the EU to explore variation over time. This is only a starting point. For example, we need to know *which* competences are (or are not) shared by actors at different levels and the significance of and the explanations for this. To do so we must consider power and its relation to the relationship between the EU and the domestic polity, questions addressed empirically in the policy chapters.

Central to MLG and Europeanisation are debates over authority linked to the organisation and meaning of territory. Territorial politics centre on 'fixed and mutually exclusive enclaves of legitimate domination' (Ruggie 1993: 151). So European integration can be seen as part of what Ruggie calls the 'unbundling' of territory, but we prefer to think in terms of 're-bundling' territory within a new form of 'bounded space' that possesses a strong EU dimension (Taylor 1994; Ansell 2004). We thus reject notions of the end of territory (Badie 1995), of 'loss of control' (Sassen 2007) or of a borderless world (Allen and Hamnett 1995). In short, 'territory matters' and we explore how the meanings of both territory and sovereignty have changed under the impact of the EU (Krasner 1988). Challenges to state sovereignty are not new, but sovereignty remains a constitutive principle for the organising of territory within the EU and SEE.

Territory is closely linked to sovereignty through the control of bounded space that 'displace personal relationships, between controlled and controller, by relationships between people and the law of the place' (Sack 1986: 57). This relationship is particularly relevant to our study where a paradox appears in which some states are in the process of recovering their statehood while at the same time apparently eager to cede aspects of this statehood to the EU. The process of finding or recovering statehood is closely associated with European integration, which becomes part of the process by which nationalism is 'reframed' and 'contained' (Brubaker 1996; Hechter 2000). With enlargement, the EU has become a – if not the – critical actor in a whole range of activities covered by the *acquis*. The EU's 'stick-and-carrot' approach, or what Vachudova (2005) describes as 'active' and 'passive' leverage, compels elites to focus attention on state effectiveness. This can be understood as a paradox rather than a contradiction if we accept that European integration changes the meaning of statehood and sovereignty without eviscerating them. Others have viewed sovereignty (or the uses to which it is put) as being 'rebundled' as Ansell (2004) puts it or 'redefined' (Bartolini 2005). Engaging with the EU might promote stateness, an argument that echoes the thesis that European integration rescues and strengthens the state. We discuss this at greater length in the next section.

Power – its location and degree of concentration – is central to MLG and Europeanisation, but 'multi-levelled-ness' per se does not automatically produce a dispersion of power or a single pattern of governance. As already touched upon, even the most centralised polity has more than one level of government so we need some conceptual apparatus that conveys how multi-levelled-ness develops and that accounts for variations in the distribution of power. Schmidt (2006) distinguished between the ideal-type of the *compound* polity (characterised by proportional representation, corporatist policy-making, and regionalised or federalised subnational government) and that of the *simple* polity (with majoritarian electoral system, centralised decision-making and a unitary state structure). The EU can be conceived of as a *highly compound* regionalised polity that pulls applicant and member states towards the compound end of the continuum and states furthest away from this pole will be under the greatest pressure to change with the effect of weakening the unitary state and the centralisation of power. In our four states, therefore, we would expect to see the 'pluralisation' of policy and power with the political process opened up to greater involvement by international organisation, interest groups, regional interests, subnational government and civil society (Schmidt 2006: 34, 227).

'Federalising', 'regionalising' and 'pluralising' are not synonymous, but this is not the place to explore the distinctions between these terms (Grasse 2001). All, however, evoke images of MLG and the growth of increasingly complex vertical interaction between territorial levels and horizontal interaction between the public, private and third sectors. MLG points to a form of governance based on a matrix within which central power is challenged. The classic formulation, which we adopt, by Marks and Hooghe (2004) identifies two ideal-types of MLG (Figure 2.1).

In the real-world elements of both Type I and Type II modes will often co-exist but the balance between the two will be influenced by a state's location on the simple-compound continuum with Type I focused on state structures (for example, federal, devolved, decentralised) and Type II on the conduct of policy-making (for example, statist, corporatist). In the policy chapters we will consider the degree to which state structures have been 'regionalised' (none of our cases are 'federal', with the partial exception of Macedonia) and Type I MLG has developed, and the degree to which centralised policy-making has weakened and redistributed power from the core executive. The two formulations of MLG say little about intensity and frequency of interaction, or actor perceptions of the network(s), and to address these questions we employ SNA and our extensive interview material in each of our policy-focused chapters. This is discussed more fully in a later section of this chapter.

The pursuit of 'good' governance

Europeanisation and MLG were developed as analytic concepts to explain and understand the nature of and consequences of EU governance to which there is a strong normative element (SIGMA 1998a, b, 1999; CEC 2003). The literature on MLG, in common with much of the governance literature, elides between analytic and normative concerns, which has raised suspicions that governance (often prefaced by 'good') is a neo-liberal agenda. Through a range of World Bank, International Monetary Fund (IMF) and United Nations (UN)

Type I MLG	Type II MLG
General-purpose jurisdiction	Task specific jurisdiction
Non-intersecting membership	Intersecting membership
Jurisdiction at a limited number of levels	No limit to the number of jurisdictional levels
System-wide architecture	Flexible design

Source: Hooghe and Marks 2004: 17.

Figure 2.1 Types and characteristics of multi-level governance

programmes, 'good governance' has been equated with the imposition of neoliberal economics and Western models of liberal democracy, irrespective of their 'fit' with domestic cultures and capacities (Taylor 2002: 35–53). While such 'conditionality' has historically been a feature of policies towards Africa, it was also seen as a feature of the EU's enlargement process to include the former communist states of central and eastern Europe, and is seen as embedded in a raft of EU policies currently aimed at its near neighbours (Börzel *et al.* 2008). The concept's specific application and relevance to SEE has been questioned by, for example, Stubbs (2005), who summarily dismisses MLG as 'rehashed pluralism'. This accusation might be reasonable, if one assumes that MLG embraces a cosy consensual set of arrangements in which power is dispersed and conflict is absent. As such, it is an easy target at which criticisms of ideal-type pluralism can be thrown. It is a charge that does not, however, enhance our understanding of the EU's impact on a polity or the growing complexity of policy (Knill 1998).

The European Commission itself has stated in relation to the EU's external relations policy:

> As the concepts of human rights, democratisation and democracy, the rule of law, civil society, decentralised power sharing, and sound public administration gain importance and relevance as a society develops into a more sophisticated political system, governance evolves into good governance.
>
> (CEC 2003: 4; see also CEC 2001a)

The Commission has fluctuated over time and by context in its emphasis on good governance as efficient policy-making (particularly in relation to economic development) and good governance as a political concept. In either view, the promotion of civil society actors in public decision-making is seen as beneficial, as is the existence of effective governing capacity at subnational levels. In this sense, the EU often equates good governance with MLG.

Much of the extant work on MLG has reported the difficulties of challenging established patterns of governance, invariably characterised by asymmetric power relations, through exogenous incentives and pressures. Patterns of MLG exhibit considerable variation and Hooghe (1996), for example, demonstrated the emergence of varying patterns of MLG on its 'home ground' of cohesion policy. Many of the arrangements characterised as MLG are elite and state-dominated, forming part of state strategy to bypass stubborn local institutions or as a means of addressing deficiencies in capabilities and capacities.

In summary, MLG has proved a useful and durable heuristic device, providing hypotheses concerning the impact of the EU on domestic institutions. However, broadening MLG away from its 'home' territory of cohesion does prompt the question whether or not it can bear the analytical weight being placed on it. All polities, even the most centralised, are multi-level, so analytically what matters are the functions undertaken at different levels, their autonomy and the distribution of power between levels. The research design underpinning this book was intended to penetrate further into these issues than has usually been the case while methodologically our concerns about MLG crystallise around whether or not MLG is actually a theory. If all polities are multi-level, is MLG nothing other than descriptive and case determined? Is MLG a metaphor for complexity and, given its origins in one policy area, can it be deployed in others? These questions are addressed in the policy chapters.

The capacity bargain

While Europeanisation and MLG constitute our core concepts, we need to find a more specific way of linking theory and method and, in particular, integrating the question of state adaptation with the analysis of the networks that are subject to institutional change (see the next section) and adaptation. To this end we develop the notion of the 'capacity bargain' to go beyond the logic of regional integration and assess the ways in which integration changes or affects domestic political logics for the management of transboundary issues (Menon and Weatherill 2006).

The idea of a capacity bargain derives in part from Mattli's concept of the sovereignty bargain (1999a, b, 2002) allied to ideas drawn from Weiss (1998) and Mann (1984, 1993). Essentially, Mattli argues that states will voluntarily accept limitations on their sovereignty in exchange for benefits but – and this is a key point – the content of a bargain will vary according to historical circumstance and its specific policy concern. Sovereignty bargains have three dimensions: *autonomy* (the degree of independence in policy-making), *control* (the ability to produce an effect) and *legitimacy* (recognition of a right to make and implement rules), and these three interact in each policy sector. So, a state might cede autonomy to improve control over a policy but at the cost of weakening its legitimacy; these permutations are a major reason why sovereignty bargains are so useful to states. The sovereignty bargain also points to the fact that state sovereignty is frequently reconfigured as a result of pressures from outside as well as from within the state. The key point is that a sovereignty bargain does not necessarily diminish sovereignty and, even in those cases where a high price is paid, decision-makers think this worthwhile because of the gains made in other areas, such as economic growth.

The sovereignty bargain provides the basic building-block of the state–EU relationship, but securing the benefits of such a bargain depends on the state's capacity and its ability to translate potential into actual gains. 'State capacity' implies a *general* capacity, but states are not monolithic and not uniformly effective across all the activities they undertake. Any discussion of state capacity must, therefore, be *sectoral* (Weiss 1998: 4). While we agree with Weiss's points on heterogeneity and sectoral variation in capacity, we argue that engagement with the EU does have implications for a state's *general* capacity because of the obligation to implement the *acquis communautaire*.

Hence, in part, our focus on distinct and autonomous policies – cohesion, borders, environment – where the specific capacities, mix of actors and combinations of resources vary but which are subject to a common downward pressure from the EU.

Weiss's focus is on industrial policy and the global political economy, while ours is on cohesion, border security and the environment, and the influence of the EU thereon, but after allowing for obvious differences all have in common a concern with a state's transformative capacity, or its ability to adapt, and the contours of specific domestic adjustment strategies. States pursuing enlargement, for instance, may have

> neither the infrastructure nor the expertise to keep up with regulatory developments in the Union, but as a candidate country it would receive extensive financial and technical support to establish a modern administrative and judicial apparatus capable of implementing and enforcing Union Rules.
>
> (Mattli 2002: 153)

The purpose of developing these capacities is to coordinate and mobilise resources under the rubric of the *acquis* or accession conditionality; this capacity is not easy to measure (although obvious sources are the Worldwide Governance Indicators, the EU's Internal Market Scoreboard, European Court of Justice (ECJ) rulings and annual country progress reports), but it is a domestic phenomenon with supranational connections and as such is both multi-level and reinforces the role of intervening variables. The state constitutes the central actor.

To explore further the politics of domestic adaptation Weiss uses 'political crystallization', a term originally developed by Mann to describe the development of adaptation and the different constellations of actors and resources that coalesce into diverse policy networks undertaking adaptation. We explore these networks (or political crystallisations) in the policy chapters using SNA. Our cases, and this is where we depart from Weiss, are embedded in a general capacity framework engendered by the *acquis* interacting with national political and administrative traditions. As the range of tasks undertaken by the state broaden, the number of political crystallisations diversifies; they are seldom in either direct conflict or in harmony, their normal state is to differ from each other, but they have in common a direct relationship with the state for which they are crucial. These political crystallisations, or networks, constitute one of the vehicles whereby a state promotes its infrastructural power.

Infrastructural power is a state's capacity to penetrate civil society (Mann 1984: 185–213) and enforce policies by providing central services (these are not necessarily concerned with direct *delivery* but may involve the central *co-ordination* of service delivery), boosting the quantity and quality of collective goods and increased legitimacy through civil society participation in the making and delivery of policy. Infrastructural power is not bureaucratic power, though the two co-exist in any polity, the distinction between the two is a state having power *over* a society as distinct from having power *through* society. Infrastructural power is territorially bounded and therefore intimately related to sovereignty, but engagement with the EU and the resulting sovereignty bargain constitutes an admission by a state that its infrastructural power depends in part on supranational, transboundary cooperation and resource mobilisation – a capacity bargain. The capacity bargain produces governed interdependence (Weiss 1998: 38) in which public and private actors maintain their autonomy in a relationship governed by broader goals set and monitored by the state which, in our case, is also engaged in a close relationship with a supranational organisation exercising downward pressure on the domestic polity to achieve common agreed ends. The capacity bargain, therefore, implies an increase in the state's institutional depth (the degree to which state actions define a public sphere distinct from that of wider society) and institutional breadth (the diversity of the links between the state and other actors) and as such represents an important aspect of infrastructural power, or what has been termed 'the catalytic state' (Weiss 1998: 19; Lind 1992: 3–14).

The capacity bargain has an affinity with an influential strand in the integration literature: namely, that the EU (or its antecedents) 'rescues' and 'strengthens' the member state (Milward 2000; Moravcsik 1994, for example). As we shall see in the case study chapters, the effect of engagement with the EU has been to strengthen the state and that all four states have developed a capacity bargain as part of the wider sovereignty bargain in order to achieve objectives they could not achieve with their current resources and capabilities. Such a finding is also quite common in discussions of the value of multilateral institutions (Keohane *et al.* 2009), but we broaden the discussion by identifying three key dimensions (Menon and Weatherill 2006). Capacity bargains are *functionally* significant for the EU and the state as they compensate to some degree the perceived weakness of the 'input' side of integration and EU rule-making by balancing increased policy effectiveness against the perceived democratic deficit (Sharpf 1997). Output legitimacy is clearly important in all our cases in that a capacity bargain can be justified by the prospect of 'better' policy than could be achieved in the absence of a capacity bargain. A capacity bargain, therefore, offers potentially significant *political* benefits by seeming to address the gap (or in Europeanisation's terms, 'misfit') between (sovereign) national capabilities and the commitments a state is required to undertake as a part of the EU (Poiares Maduro 2003: 86). By addressing directly the gap/misfit between sovereign/national capabilities and those required for EU membership, the capacity bargain may reduce significantly the domestic costs of adaptation and resolving misfit. In our three policy areas it is relatively easy to see how a capacity bargain could deliver gains that outweigh its costs in, for example, greater social solidarity, improved environmental regulation and better border management, while enhancing citizen rights. In *administrative* terms, the capacity bargains mesh neatly with the EU modus operandi of seeking the adaptation, not replacement, of national administrations, when dealing with 'domestic' (e.g. cohesion) and 'transboundary' (e.g., environment and border management) policies, coupled with the expectation that hitherto un- or poorly-represented interests secure access to the policy-making process and domestic actors are incorporated into 'trans-governmental networks' (Menon and Weatherill 2006: 408). The capacity bargain adds political breadth and depth to a state's infrastructural power, but this could entail a redistribution of resources from the status quo to new sets of winners and losers. Whether or not this redistribution erects obstacles to adaptation or eases adaptation is an artefact of the domestic political process.

The capacity bargain is significant for two reasons: first, it aspires to make states 'stronger' or more effective; and second, it explains in part differences between states and between policy sectors within states. The capacity bargains between states and the EU have, as we have noted, functional, political and administrative dimensions that impact directly on both the degree and nature of 'multi-levelled-ness' and the distinctive changes flowing from engagement with the EU. This enables us to look more closely at the significance of variations within our three policy cases and the resulting change in domestic governance so paying attention to the specific modes of governance in each policy area. This enables us to use the capacity bargain to look more closely at the variation between our cases and the consequences of this for domestic governance while paying due regard to the specific governance of each policy. This variation means that some ways of doing things change, while others do not; some actors may be empowered, others weakened.

We would expect, given different policy content and therefore different political crystallisations to find the effects of the change flowing from engagement with the EU to be substantial but unevenly distributed (Harmsen 1999). The capacity bargain is valuable in drawing attention to the significance of politics and domestic decision-making through which engagement with the EU is filtered and processed. This domestic process also encourages variation between policy networks and implies that states exercise substantial control over policy and its coordination, but this greater domestic control mediated and articulated through a specific political crystallisation could change the meaning of the policy and privilege different actors to those originally envisaged by the EU and Commission. The significance of the domestic raises another important question, namely the possible reversal (or stagnation) of change. Evidence cited elsewhere in this book (Chapter 3), drawing on research undertaken by SIGMA into civil service and public administration reform in the 2004 enlargement states in Eastern Europe (including Slovenia), found regression in openness and accountability after a decade of EU membership. Greece demonstrates the resources available to a member state and denied to the EU and Commission, in resisting, neutralising or capturing downward pressure from the EU to protect the domestic status quo. Analysing this problem is reflected in our use of SNA maps that show the interrelationships between key domestic (and non-domestic) actors in each policy domain and delineate the relevant policy coalitions. These constitute the arenas in which the final contours of policy are determined.

Institutional change

Of the three policy areas that we analyse, cohesion is the sector where MLG effects will be most likely. MLG predicts territorial changes in which subnational governments will organise and mobilise around cohesion issues and challenge the state as gate-keeper. Subnational governments will develop strong relationships with civil society organisations, forge and operate cross-border alliances, and establish a separate supranational presence. MLG will feature prominently in environment policy because of the policy's technical complexity, transborder effects and dependence on multiple actor (governmental and non-governmental) networks operating at the supranational, national and subnational levels.

Migration and border security demand a multi-level response but one that is qualitatively different from those evident in the cohesion and environment sectors as border security goes to the heart of what constitutes 'state-ness' and sovereignty. EU border policy entails clear policy requirements of states which requires cooperation and coordination but which is dominated by state-to-state relations. This is a complex multi-level network with little civil society involvement but with the potential for a great deal of political mobilisation because of the political sensitivity of immigration in domestic politics. The network's internal power structure is likely to be centralised and dominated by the state. Neither Europeanisation nor MLG necessarily generates a plural power structure.

In contrast, as a highly salient territorial policy, but with non-territorial consequences, environment policy will involve substantial mobilisation in which subnational governments and environmental groups often challenge the central state in pursuit of stricter regulation. This implies subnational and supranational alliances directed against national government and, as a policy type, this is primarily regulatory but also involves some redistribution.

In all three sectors the EU has a determining role and the state mediates between the supranational and the domestic. In both cohesion and environment, MLG implies that the state is one of many actors in complex networks, whereas in migration and border security complex networks exist but the state plays a central and determining role, thereby simplifying organisational complexity. Conceptually and theoretically these differences imply that MLG is not a theory but a description of political and organisational reality. That the EU has domestic effects is incontrovertible, but Olsen notes that EU developments

> do not dictate specific forms of institutional adaptation but leave considerable discretion to domestic actors and institutions. There are significant impacts, yet the actual ability of the European level institutions

to penetrate domestic institutions is not perfect, universal or constant. Adaptations reflect variations in European pressure as well as domestic motivations.

(2003: 356)

Both as a theory and as a component and consequence of Europeanisation, MLG implies a weakening of the central state, but our empirical work strongly suggests the opposite and a central concern of this book is to assess how Europeanisation (and European integration) exert functional, political and administrative pressures for adaptation and change that alter the distribution of power and resources within the central state. We also explore specific dynamics in three policy sectors and cannot assume a priori that each policy sector possesses some simple, objective meaning that makes sense in all countries and across time. That would be absurd given the varying relationships with the EU. 'Weaker' and 'stronger' are relative and imprecise terms, and obscure the nuances of governing. The capacity bargain strengthens states through its functional, political and administrative aspects but it also *changes* states. Capacity can be seen in terms of 'weaker' or 'stronger' but also, and more importantly in engagement with the EU, in promoting difference. The capacity bargain, with its focus on policy sectors, allows us to explore the nature of those differences.

The nature of institutions is contested within political analysis. The 'thinnest' accounts are provided by rational choice scholars. Although institutions do impose constraints on the actions available to actors in pursuit of their preferences, preferences are exogenous to the institutional setting and their content is of little or no interest. The changes to governance structures and practices envisaged and explored by this book are, in this perspective at least, relatively unproblematic, being a function of strategic action and collective choice. The assumption that preferences are exogenous to institutions is, however, inappropriate as the relationship between Europeanisation and MLG is not linear, but often indirect and a relationship where intervening domestic variables matter greatly, and which are not exogenous to institutional settings.

By contrast, social constructivist, sociological and normative institutionalist approaches privilege the impact of established practices, beliefs and values that limit the scope and scale of change. Institutions monitor their environment and adapt to changes, threats or opportunities in that environment. However, in any context the range of policy alternatives will be restricted and some alternatives are 'unthinkable' for the institutions and actors. This is an intuitive and plausible assumption, but has two drawbacks. First, the emphasis on values as endogenous to institutions imposes a priori limits upon the potential for change and, second, while values, practices and beliefs are given prominence, this does not itself explain the processes through which these practices and beliefs become dominant or the resources they confer on actors.

Europeanisation is not a theory but a phenomenon, hence our focus on how the process affects domestic political institutions. Institutions are:

the rules of the game in a society or, more formally, are humanly devised constraints that shape human interaction . . . they structure incentives in human exchange, whether political, social, or economic. Institutional change shapes the way societies evolve through time and space and hence is the key to understanding historical change.

(North 1990: 3)

We adopt a broadly rationalist institutionalist approach even though the fit between this and the empirical work is not exact, while allowing room for sociological institutionalism's notion of learning, as a result of actor interaction within networks. The time-span of the project, the intensity and extensiveness of engagement with the EU, the range of countries and policy sectors allows to consider time (when?), timing (sequence?) and tempo (speed?) (Goetz 2000: 223; Goetz and Meyerr-Sahling, 2009) and follow the path mapped by Börzel and Risse (for example, Börzel 2005a, b; Börzel and Risse 2003). This enables us to avoid over-formalism and 'snapshots' by exploring the adjustment over time of domestic politics but taking into account 'stickiness' (the institutional and policy legacies) that sustain state centralisation and how this is (temporarily?) reinforced by engagement with the EU.

So, the change brought about by engagement with the EU is complex, non-linear and shaped by intervening variables. Governance evolves, a process marked by 'complex causality' (Saurugger 2005) and in which the relationship between independent, intervening and dependent variables is contingent and so the causal claims we can make are probabilistic at best. This point reinforces the importance of SNA in mapping governance architectures. Such a nuanced environment requires a method of contextual analysis that captures the scope and scale of institutional change and the *process* of emergence and evolution, which points to historical institutionalism (see, for example, Krasner 1988; Hall 1989; Skocpol 1992).

In our reading of historical institutionalism, institutions evolve and are occasionally marked by 'punctuations' or junctures in which 'rapid bursts of change [are] followed by long periods of stasis' (Krasner 1988: 242). The policy choices made at the time of institutional formation have a persistent impact in the long run. 'Standard operating procedures' (SOPs) develop and, under normal circumstances, inhibit anything more than incremental change. SOPs can lead to suboptimal institutional performance and policy failure, which can lead to further critical junctures, in which the ideas that underpin policy-making, policy choices and governance undergo rapid change. Despite a bias towards inertia, institutions adapt and policy choices change over time because of changes in the external environment and changes in perceptions of the performance of institutions in the context of that environment. Institutions constitute the arenas within which agency is practised but are more than passive settings for agency. They are *not* 'political actors in their own right' (March and Olsen 1984: 738) but they are *composed of* highly political actors that may deploy veto power (Tsebelis 2009: 19).

Path dependence means that initial decisions can become 'locked in' through a process of 'positive feedback' that re-enforces the suboptimal outcomes associated with them. The following example gives an idea of path dependency's likely power. Macedonia's administrative system is (obviously) crucial to satisfying EU conditionality and implementing the *acquis* but institutional legacies pose serious obstacles. Despite the amendment in 2008 of the *Law on General Administrative Procedures*,

> The law in general still reflects the authoritarian understanding of the public administration of the past, provides highly formalised and protracted procedures, perpetuates the absolutely hierarchical structure of decision-making processes, and it goes into regulatory details that should be dealt with by secondary legislation or internal administrative rules.
>
> (SIGMA 2009a: 5)

There is disagreement in the literature about the extent to which instances such as this are examples of lock-in, poor decision-making, or a lack of political will. Although lock-in implies suboptimal collective *outcomes*, it does not necessarily imply suboptimal individual *choices*. Given the importance of the specific context this is an interesting analytical and intellectual puzzle but is not insurmountable. However, it becomes a thornier problem if these early adoption choices have a disproportionate impact on later choices.

A 'vulgar' reading of path dependence underpinned the criticism of historical institutionalism as static and over-deterministic, and unable to adequately explain institutional change. A second, 'positive' definition (David 2000) is that such processes are 'stochastic' (non-deterministic) and therefore probabilistic. Past decisions are crucial but there is nothing inevitable about the scope and scale of their impact and much depends on the contingencies of time, timing, speed and sequencing of efforts to modify the present consequences of past decisions. We adopt this 'positive' definition of path dependence: feedback effects exist and the case studies demonstrate how structures, principles and practices have evolved and, where appropriate, what effects these may have had on institutional performance and policy outcomes.

Bebchuck and Roe (1999) distinguish between 'structure-driven' and 'rule-driven' path dependence. Structure-driven path dependence is where existing governance structures impact on the choice and evolution of subsequent structures. Rule-driven path dependence occurs when the emergence of rules and practices is shaped by existing power relationships and path-dependence is grounded in veto group politics. This distinguishes between formal institutions and governance structures and the principles and practices associated with modes of governance. This has three advantages. First, the division between structures and rules permits a more nuanced notion of preferences in which there is no a priori judgement about the exogenous or endogenous location of preferences. Second, institutional performance can be assessed without making any a priori assumptions about the impact of goodness of fit or adaptational pressures on institutions; and third, it permits the factoring of the impact of intervening variables and, in particular, agency in institutional change promoting, for example, either 'shallow' and 'deep' Europeanisation as well as 'policy transfer' and 'policy resistance'. This is consistent with the transformation of modes of governance being probabilistic and contingent upon timing and sequencing.

The danger of focusing on the sequence of decisions is infinite regression in which early moves in the sequence are given inordinate weight. Timing and sequencing are central to our analysis, but it is a matter of analytical judgment as to the relative significance of these events. This is consistent with our 'positive' definition of path dependence, characterised by non-deterministic processes and probabilistic outcomes, but the enduring analytical power of such an approach is derived from analytical judgements about what constitute the critical junctures. These are discussed in the next chapter. A focus on long-term political processes has two obvious analytical implications. The first is that it is harder to isolate causal variables and, more importantly, more difficult to generate reliable accounts of *cumulative* causal factors. The second difficulty is in identifying the effects generated by our putative causes. The initial impact of the casual variable may be negligible until the cumulative impact reaches a critical threshold, beyond which causality is much easier to identify (Pierson 2004: 83).

Longevity is only one consideration. As important is the nature – the intensity and intrusiveness – of the engagement; this is particularly relevant for Slovenia, Croatia and Macedonia who were (or are) subject to the explicit conditionality and monitoring of enlargement. In Greece's case the length of engagement is of greater significance, implying limited intensity and intrusiveness. The bulk of the causality attributed to our historic junctures is inferred analytically through the intervening variables. Does this difference in experience mean we will be able to identify sufficient variance on the dependent variable in order to identify effects? Different degrees and combinations of longevity, intensity and intrusiveness, allied with the range of policy sectors, gives us confidence that we will identify variance on the dependent variable, the extent of which can be either directly attributed to the independent variable or, alternatively, mediated through our intervening variables.

The state mediates upward pressure to the EU and downward pressure from the EU and Commission, and this has two aspects: the transmission and implementation of political conditionality (the rules of the game) and institutional design (*acquis* conditionality). Greece, however, experienced a far weaker conditionality regime than did Slovenia, while the conditionality regime experienced by Croatia and Macedonia is even more rigorous than that experienced by Slovenia. Governments must handle simultaneously domestic and supranational pressures, mediating between levels and networks. All four states are responding to a 'European state model', the essence of which requires states to be capable of meeting the obligations of EU membership. Adaptation is, however, neither instantaneous nor straightforward. While domestic elites may agree on the desirability of EU membership because of the benefits to be gained, consensus does not exclude conflict between national governments and policy networks, or between domestic governments and the EU. Networks generate (and are also a manifestation of) complexity, complexity generates the need for coordination, and coordination enables the preferences of interdependent actors to combine and achieve a higher aggregate level of welfare. Networks are particularly good at reconciling interests to produce robust solutions (Scharpf 1997: 28). This applies at the supra-, national and subnational levels and all the networks engage in multilateral resource exchanges in multi-level networks (Ansell 2006: 86). Once the process is underway, defection ('exit') is unlikely because of sunk costs (Hirschman 1970).

Penetrating politics, polity and policy

How do domestic actors respond to Europeanisation pressures (Olsen 2002: 923–24)? To what degree does Europeanisation affect the stability and coherence of domestic institutions and processes (Kohler-Koch 1996; 1999)? These are important questions but, as already noted, there is a danger of ascribing all change to Europeanisation and the EU. The two elements on which we focus are the degree of fit/misfit between European and domestic institutions and the degree of pressure for change generated by engagement with the EU. The second component is the convergence of factors that mediate between the EU and the domestic level, including formal and informal institutions and veto groups (which may or may not act). This locates the focus of our work firmly in the politics of institution-building over time, which produces complex patterns of adaptation and interaction, patterns that can also take into account ideational factors, sense making and normative judgements, and their articulation (Börzel and Head-Lauréote 2009). SNA offers a technique to explore relationships, thereby linking sociological and rational choice institutionalism with policy networks; it offers a counter to the small-N problem associated with studies of this type.[1] SNA offers the possibility of systematic analysis and 'thick description' across networks and countries, and over time.

   With the exception of a limited use of descriptive statistics, the data on which the research is based is largely qualitative, the 120 semi-structured interviews with policy-makers, officials and other actors concerned with each of our three policy sectors and four countries, and supplemented by interviews in Brussels. While conscious of the limitations of interview data, we contend that interviews, if carefully constructed, can provide data to provide significant insights into actor behaviour, motivation and preferences. In addition, interviewees were also asked to complete a short, structured questionnaire in which they identified those institutions and organisations with which they interacted and estimated the frequency of that interaction. This data was then collated to construct networks maps to explore interaction.

The policy chapters use SNA to visualise the networks associated with our three policy areas and identified from the interviews. 'Nodes', a term originating in computer science, constitute the individual actors within the policy networks, and 'ties' are the relationships between them. These nodes and ties can be presented as 'webs' that can be graphically complex, but visual representation is important to understand the data and convey the result of the analysis. In its simplest form SNA maps all the relevant ties between all the nodes being studied but the result can be analytically intractable, which points to the importance of research design (Berkowitz 1982; Wellman 1988; Scott 1991; Freeman 2004; Tilly 2005). A social network is a structure composed of, in our case, organisations (nodes) that are tied (connected) by the relationships established by actors to satisfy the requirements set out by the EU in that specific policy sector. There can be many kinds of ties between the nodes but we are concerned with the exchange of resources and the development of interorganisational dependencies directed at the achievement of outputs or outcomes. SNA helps to understand which actors play a critical role in determining the way problems are handled, political relationships managed, and the degree to which goals are achieved.

In political science, network theory has enjoyed something of a vogue but its use has often been primarily as a metaphor (Wellman 1988: 19–61). While not decrying this, we are concerned to penetrate, as Dowding (1995) advocated, the nature of the ties and not just the nodes. Rather than treating organisations as the unit of analysis, SNA focuses on how the structure of ties affects relationships between nodes and resulting outcomes and so moves away from a 'black box' approach to studying the policy process. Moreover, the network itself is influenced by, and influences, actor behaviour and their norms. Although SNA takes actors seriously, it focuses not on personal attributes but on relationships in the network; 'success' depends on the network's components and their interaction. The analysis of the policy sectors uses our extensive interview data to 'bring agency back in' to the analysis.

Coupling SNA with data derived from our extensive interviews allows us to examine the politics of organisational interaction by focusing on the ties between nodes and question the assumption that an actor's power is associated with a central position in a network. Rather, we see power and influence flowing from the network relationships that are influenced, perhaps even determined, by the environment in which the network is located. The influences structuring that environment constitute a proximate determining influence on a network's composition, activity and even beliefs. Networks provide ways for organisations to gather information, learn, manage and, conceivably, resist pressure for change from inside and outside the network (Wasserman and Faust 1994; Breiger 2004; Brandes and Erlebach 2005; Carrington *et al.* 2005). We explore *whole (*or *complete) networks*, identifying the ties expressing specified relations in defined and discrete areas (policies) by interviewees. No attempt is made at achieving 'comprehensive' coverage of policy networks, in part because of the need to manage complexity and in part because of the 'reputational method' we used in the interviews (Polsby 1980: 144–5).

As noted, the interview schedule was 'reputational', asking interviewees who *they* considered to be the most influential and with whom their organisation interacted most frequently. We did not specifically ask about European integration in order to avoid 'leading' respondents in a way that could potentially over-emphasise the EU's role as a driver of change and crowd out other relevant actors at subnational, national and international levels. Where no other interviewee subsequently mentioned an actor, that actor was excluded on the grounds that it had no influence in the *network*, otherwise long lists of 'network' participants would have been generated. The aim was to distinguish how actors *perceived* the influence (or lack of influence) of the EU on their activities; the second part of the questionnaire asked about day-to-day interaction. This produced a very interesting result. The EU may not be a highly visible *participant* in that network even though actors *perceive* it to be an influential, or even a determining influence, on a network's activities.

When using SNA to map a network we must be careful not to assume too much from physical shape. It is, for example, easy to assume that a large, complex map with many participants indicates a diffuse power structure and pluralistic politics. Equally, smaller, tighter networks do not necessarily indicate an elite, or oligarchical, power structure because the ties between the few members could be weak and sporadic but nonetheless real. An SNA chart with a dense network may reflect the ease with which interviews could be secured. Central to the interview schedule was 'cascading', asking interviewees who *they* considered to be the most influential and with whom their organisation interacted most frequently. No attempt was made to map relationships *between* networks in the three policy sectors because our interview evidence suggested that these networks were isolated from each other because of their specific concerns even though they were, overall, subject to a wider set of influences flowing from engagement with the EU. We do not explore whether there are actors who constitute 'brokers' bridging these networks. This would require us to delve deeply into the nature of each core executive. Inevitably, there are some shortcomings in the data used in the SNA, but these are not, we believe, of a sufficient magnitude to invalidate the networks maps, which were triangulated against other sources, notably the interviews with participants and extensive analysis of primary and secondary documentary material.

We applied the union rule for symmetric data (if one organisation identified contacts with a second but the second did not mention the first or was not interviewed, we assume that the contact is reciprocal). This is an assumption commonly made in SNA. However, because more than one interview was conducted with an organisation, or where the answers differed between two organisations regarding the nature and frequency of their contacts we opted for the following solutions: in cases where two entries on one questionnaire, or various questionnaires produced different answers, the average was coded, and where the two same entries appeared on various questionnaires, the highest answer mentioned was used. More serious issues are data gaps, the correspondence between interviewees and network actors, as well as the non-appearance of the European Commission as a network actor.

Data gaps Some central actors were not interviewed. The main reason was an inability to arrange a mutually convenient time for the interview to be conducted. If other actors regarded a non-interviewed actor as influential, however, this would be picked up. It is in the nature of SNA that one only finds out about the relationship between actors interviewed and not about the relationships of actors not interviewed. SNA is likely to show a dense network between actors interviewed which might (or might not) correspond with 'reality' depending on the interviews conducted. However, in presenting and discussing our results in a number of fora involving both academic experts and participants in the networks we were reassured by comments that the relationships we identified were, by and large, the most significant.

Correspondence of interviewees with actors on questionnaires Since every interviewee represents an organisation that is of some importance to the policy field, each of the organisation's interviews ought to be present on the list of organisations. This was not always the case as interviewees added contacts that did not overlap with those identified by other interviewees. If no other actor mentioned these contacts, we must assume no other actor is linked with them. This was to avoid the generation of very long lists of network participants who are not linked with one another.

The European Commission In some cases the Commission was notable by its absence. In the interview schedule we sought to distinguish how actors *perceived* EU (or Commission) influence (or lack of) on their activities and so the second part of the questionnaire asked about day-to-day interaction in the policy networks. This means that the EU may not be a highly visible or regular *participant* in a network even though actors *perceive* it to be influential, or even a determining influence, on the network's activities. The EU is the single most critical influence on networks as the agenda setter, proximately influencing the behaviour of the domestic actors responsible for the implementing policy. The EU can appear therefore as an 'isolated' actor, or even not appear at all in the SNA, but this is what we would expect as it is the domestic networks that are responsible for the implementation of policy.

External incentives and conditionality

We now move away from methodological considerations to discussing the role of incentives and conditionality. Radaelli and Pasquier (in Graziano and Vink 2007: 39) raise the pertinent question of how far Europeanisation can be stretched as a concept. Can it, for example, cover enlargement? Our answer is, as one might expect, 'yes', but we also stress the process of refraction. Our evidence points to some degree of convergence but little in the way of homogenisation and this reinforces Goetz's (2002) point that Europeanisation is a journey not a destination. Our research, in common with all Europeanisation research, is vulnerable to prejudging the EU's impact and assuming that if change occurs comparable to that sought by the Commission then this must be a case of Europeanisation at work. We have discussed how research design on Europeanisation often involves a debate between 'top-down' and 'bottom-up' approaches, and our research design has a strong top-down element given the importance of political and *acquis* conditionality in three of our four cases and Greece's reputation for poor compliance with EU policies, reflected in the crisis in the Greek political economy and increased policing role adopted by the Commission and IMF. We see downward adaptational pressure as crucial for the long-term redistribution of resources (including power) in all four polities. Börzel presents Europeanisation as a process combining elements of up-loading (bottom up) and down-loading (top down), with the former concerned with constructing EU governance and the latter with its domestic impact on states so that states, given their preferences and abilities to act on them, may try to upload preferences to avoid later adjustment (2002; 2005a, b).

A complication is that this only applies to member states, so candidate and accession states are subject to a far greater degree of down-loading and top-down Europeanisation. An adequate exploration of this requires a nuanced and fine-grained analysis of the domestic impact, especially as a theme in the Europeanisation literature (and this book) is that engagement with the EU strengthens (but also changes) domestic governments. Comparison is central to the research design to show how the sequencing of accession influenced Europeanisation's scope and impact. This leads ineluctably to comparing the stages of accession in their historical context to expose the different dynamics of engagement with the EU. Three of our cases had, like their CEE predecessors, declared 'the return to Europe' and membership of the EU as central foreign policy objectives; three of our cases were, during the course of the project, either new or candidates for membership and were therefore subject to, or had been subject to, extensive conditionality.

Schimmelfennig and Sedelmeier (2004, 2005) note conditionality's central-ity when 'studying the impact of the EU on domestic change in the CEECs' and define conditionality as

> a strategy . . . in which the EU sets its rules as conditions that the CEECs have to fulfil in order to receive EU rewards. These rewards consist of assistance and institutional ties ranging from trade and co-operation agreements via association agreements to full membership . . . Under this strategy, the EU pays the reward if the target government complies with the conditions and withholds the reward if it fails to comply.
>
> (2004: 663)

This external incentives model (Figure 2.2) was developed to analyse the 2004 enlargement that included Slovenia, applies with even greater force to Croatia and Macedonia. As conditionality developed in the 1990s, it widened and deepened (interview, DG Enlargement, 31 March 2009). Elements such as a

Determinacy	'the effectiveness of rule transfer increases if rules are set as conditions for rewards and the more determinate they are'
Rewards	'the effectiveness of rule transfer increases with the size and speed of rewards'
Credibility	'the likelihood of rule adoption increases with the credibility of conditional threats and promises'
Adoption costs	'the likelihood of rule adoption decreases with the number of veto players incurring net adoption costs (opportunity costs, welfare and power losses) from compliance'

Source: Schimmelfennig and Sedelmeier (2004) 664, 665, 666, and 667.

Figure 2.2 The external incentives model: an outline

commitment to liberal democratic institutions and processes, human (including minority) rights, and the creation of market economies became more stringent; at the heart of this were the Copenhagen Criteria (1993), Madrid Criteria (1995) and Santa Maria de Feira (2000) conclusions. Once accession negotiations start the focus moves from political to *acquis* conditionality whereby candidate countries are required to accept the *acquis communautaire* and transpose it into domestic law. Combined these aspire to create states capable of undertaking the duties and obligations of membership and conditionality's effects reverberate through politics, policy, and polity.

During and after the 2004 and 2007 enlargements scholars began to consider the effectiveness of conditionality in bringing about sustained change compared, for example, to social learning and whether or not conditionality had the effects intended or predicted. In Brussels the view was that most of the *acquis'* content would have to be implemented in order for a country to modernise, so the EU was not requiring anything particularly radical (interview, DG Enlargement, 31 March 2009). Vachudova (2005) sees the EU's passive leverage (the material benefits of membership) and active leverage (the conditionalities derived from the Copenhagen Criteria), coupled with the power asymmetry inherent in a country seeking membership that generates considerable EU influence. This inevitably imposes great strains on a polity. Sceptics (Hughes *et al.* 2004, 2005, for example) argue for the essential redundancy of conditionality given the recent history of CEE countries and the absence of any model other than liberal-democratic market capitalism (for a survey of the literature, see Haughton 2007). In fact, as we will argue, these perspectives are not incompatible given the complexity of the undertaking and the range of activities covered by conditionality. These and the region's complex history mean that variation is inevitable, which is reinforced by the Commission's decision that enlargement into SEE will be on a case-by-case basis. Moreover, conditionality is directed not only at modernisation but at EU membership, which renders it far more specific and intrusive (Renner and

Trauner 2009: 449–65). Our understanding of conditionality in Slovenia, Croatia and Macedonia follows broadly the external incentives model. Conditionality works because of a highly asymmetric relationship favouring the EU and the Commission. This asymmetry existed in CEE states but is even stronger in SEE as a result of the proportionately greater weakness of these states (including Slovenia); the desire to join the EU reinforced the asymmetry and bolstered the conditionality process as Europeanisation.

An important aspect of Europeanisation, which is also central to MLG, is the transposition of policies and norms and their enforcement. Following earlier comments about domestic variation our exploration of implementation in the policy chapters considers the gaps flowing from weaknesses in capacities and the dynamics of domestic politics that are likely to result in compliance. The fate of EU decisions lies in the hands of domestic governments, so it makes sense to see domestic actors subject to bounded rationality; given the complexity of the tasks confronting them, limited resources and (sometimes) major opposition actors engage in only a limited search for responses, addressing new problems with established methods (Cyert and March 1963).

The (as yet) unanswerable question at this point is the extent to which Europeanisation has been embedded via conditionality and/or membership, but this is of secondary importance given our concern with politics, policy and polity. The evidence from Eastern Europe indicates the persistence of formal compliance and even the re-emergence of pre-conditionality attitudes and behaviours, amplified by real shortages of capacities and capabilities (Jacoby 1999, 2002, 2004; SIGMA 2009a). Schimmelfennig and Sedelmeier contend that 'in the absence of high conditional external benefits [and by implication, costs], domestic structures . . . which were superseded in the conditionality context, will again have a causal impact (2005: 95). One consequence of the 2004 enlargement was to strengthen the tendency towards technocratic top-down policy-making processes. A former member of the Slovenian accession team emphasised that transposition was easier than implementation, which involved a great deal of domestic negotiation. Moreover, often capacity had to be created to ensure coordination between levels and that this – coordination – was the key form of institution building (interview, 31 March 2009). As Greece, Slovenia, Croatia and Macedonia are 'simple' polities, an important question is the degree to which, and in what areas, engagement has mitigated these historic patterns of governance.

The Europeanisation taking place in SEE is 'different' from that in Eastern Europe in both form and content, if not objective. Moreover, both differ substantially to pre-2004 enlargements. SEE states are carrying a more problematic historical legacy and are entering an enlargement process influenced by the shortcomings of the 2004 and 2007 enlargements as well as 'enlargement fatigue' among member states' and concerns about cost and absorption capacity. These considerations lengthened the process and rendered it more intrusive and more heavily policed. It is therefore reasonable to conclude that accession conditionality has major consequences, the most important of which is how, and to what degree, external incentives have impacted on the politics, polity and policies of candidate states and pushed them towards 'European' forms.

The tenor of our evidence is to confirm that the adoption of EU rules and transposition of the *acquis* under pre-accession and accession conditionality constitutes high adaptive pressure, producing often rapid institutional and policy adaptation. Whether this produces rapid socialisation into new norms and values, and disrupts attitudes and behaviours influenced by the past is far less certain, as we can see particularly in the case of Greece. The endorsement of membership inhibited veto players without necessarily reducing the adoption and adaptation costs; more significant (in *all* our cases) were shortages of capabilities and capacities that tended to produce compliance. National traditions, historical legacies and institutions retained considerable vitality and had the potential to reassert themselves. To categorise these variations Radaelli, for example, identifies inertia, absorption, transformation and retrenchment (2003: 37) while Börzel and Risse offer absorption, accommodation and retrenchment (2003: 69–73). Which of these, if any, characterise the situations discussed in the policy chapters will be explored more fully in Chapters 4, 5 and 6.

Conclusions

Engagement with the EU reshapes domestic politics which, in turn, reshapes the relationship with the EU. The EU has articulated a progression through successive stages coordination and harmonisation (pre-accession → candidate → accession negotiations → membership) that focuses on building the state capacities and capabilities of members and applicants.

We define power as 'the production, in and through social relations, of effects that shape the capacities of actors to determine their own circumstances and fate' (Barnett and Duvall 2004: 3). Barnett and Duvall identify four types of power, and engagement with the EU has consequences for all of them. *Compulsory power* is where one actor has direct control over another. The enlargement process is the most obvious example of this. Second, *institutional power* is where actors exercise indirect control over others and this is represented by, for example, the relationship between the Commission and governments. Third, *structural power* is the constitution of social capacities reflected, for example, in the redistribution of power (of the absence of redistribution) as a result of engagement with the EU. Finally, *productive power* is the production of meaning and signification, which shapes actor perceptions (Barnett and Duvall 2004: 3–4). This implies that engagement with the EU has pervasive effects on the polity but that these effects are not felt equally in all areas.

To achieve its goals we see the EU wielding compulsory, institutional, structural and productive power and influencing two of the fundamentals of 'stateness': territoriality and sovereignty. A member of the Council of Ministers' secretariat emphasised that EU expectations of how politics should be conducted and the transposition of EU rules into domestic legislation constitute new 'rules of the game' but states decided the specifics (interview, 4 April 2009). Policy coordination between levels is integral to this and requires substantial investment in monitoring and enforcement to ensure the development of appropriate and effective policy networks (for example, Knill 2005).

Our notion of the capacity bargain is important because it connects theory and method. It constitutes the mechanism that connects our core concepts of Europeanisation and MLG to the three policy networks that shape the functional, political and administrative dimensions of adaptation. It is also the vehicle for extending the state's infrastructural power. Despite common influences, each of the networks is autonomous and has its own characteristics flowing from its unique policy focus. However, the function of the capacity bargain and the objects of each network's activities are the same: the capture and use of resources and the reconciliation of competing interests and pressures. With its functional, political and administrative dimensions, the capacity bargain (and its complex decisional calculus) becomes the focal point for engagement with the EU.

Fundamental to our top-down approach is the contention that the greater the misfit, the greater the adaptational pressure that is mediated via the specific relationship with the EU and history. While Croatia and Macedonia are accession states, the former has a much more developed state than the latter, but Croatia's progress was disrupted by cooperation with the International Criminal Tribunal for the former Yugoslavia (ICTY). Macedonia, on the other hand, with a far higher degree of misfit, made rapid progress after 2001 and the Ohrid Agreement, slowing thereafter over EU concern about, for example, the politicisation of the judiciary and corruption. Misfit and adaptational pressure combine elements of rational and social institutionalism.

Europeanisation emerged as a concept before CEE enlargement, which led to the rapid expansion of the literature. These states had less established democratic politics and market economies, but relatively effective states; in SEE the weaknesses of polity and economy are joined by concern over the effectiveness of states. How Europeanisation is manifested within individual polities will vary in accordance with national histories and institutional settings, something that also applies to MLG as a general phenomenon. Additionally, MLG as a general governance trait will vary by policy type – regulatory, redistributive or a mix – and over time. Central to these effects is the impact of the EU as a highly compound polity on highly centralised polities. The EU's good governance principles, political conditionality and, in some cases (such as cohesion policy) stipulations that policy will be made and implemented via participation and engagement, seek to redistribute power away from the centre. The effect of this general aspiration will, however, vary from policy sector to policy sector and from state to state.

We have noted that MLG effects are most likely to be found in cohesion policy, the policy area in which MLG was originally theorised and on which a substantial literature exists. In cohesion we would expect to find that subnational governments will mobilise around cohesion issues and where these structures do not exist, they will be created. These subnational governments will challenge the central state's gatekeeper role and eventually establish cross-border links with other subnational governments to resolve common problems. In addition, they will ally with civil society and NGOs, forming new patterns of governance and power.

While migration and border security have obvious multi-level elements, extending from the supra to the local level, it has one major difference to cohesion and environment policy: borders and their management are quintessentially state functions and can be highly politically sensitive issues. As a result we would expect subnational government to mobilise to resist the consequences of migration while the state's gatekeeper function would not be challenged. In contrast to cohesion and environment policy, we expect civil society and NGOs to have only a limited role in the integration and the care of migrants, advocacy and the provision of expert advice to policy-makers.

Environmental policy has obvious territorial/multi-level implications for a polity because environmental problems can be cross-border and require considerable social and resource mobilisation for their resolution. As a policy area it has both redistributive and regulatory elements, in common with cohesion, and we would expect to see subnational governments playing a key role in alliance with central government and civil society. A tension within this sector will be between those trying to boost environmental regulation and those seeking to evade the costs of that regulation. Also of critical importance will be the possession of, or access to, technical and scientific expertise in addition to political resources.

As capacity bargains, each of these will have unique features but they represent significant political crystallisations. Within a broadly rationalist explanation of domestic change and adaptation, with actors responding to EU pressure, adaptation must involve social learning if only as a by-product of interaction over time (longevity). However, longevity is by itself insufficient (as the Greek case demonstrates) and longevity has to be placed alongside capacity and history. These are powerful countervailing forces and suggest EU policies and practices are implemented but power distributions are not altered significantly. So, two key issues to be explored are first, the historical legacy of centralisation and the degree to which Europeanisation challenges this historical legacy. The second issue is the effectiveness of states, their capacities and capabilities (particularly subnationally and in civil society) in meeting the obligations of EU membership. MLG evokes two images: the dispersion of power but also the potential for the concentration of power at the centre. Multi-levelness implies hierarchy, which implies inequalities of power and in much of the literature the problem of levels and the relationship between them is reduced to the proposition that 'all levels are equal but some are more equal than others'. There is, as we noted earlier, no reason why multi-levelness cannot coexist with the centralisation of power; indeed, a history of centralisation and weaknesses in capacities and capabilities would preserve centralisation in the face of contrary pressures from the EU. When the Commission downgrades the promotion of decentralisation in favour of effectiveness, the preservation of centralisation is certain.

Despite their differing relationships with the EU, this suggests that our four states may have much in common in terms of their governance. The differences between candidate and member states are obvious, but in both cases engagement with the EU brings about changes in governance, which, at its most basic, means the development of elements of the compound polity. We have observed that all our states are at the 'simple' end of the continuum, with a substantial gap with the hyper-compound EU polity, but engagement has sustained a characteristic feature of the simple polity: the centralised state. This common outcome has occurred for different reasons: in Slovenia, Croatia and Macedonia it was the result of conditionality but in Greece the cause was the *absence* of conditionality. In all four cases this outcome was underpinned by a historical tradition of centralisation. Exploring the empirical effects of this is the task of the policy sector chapters; in the next chapter the evolution the four states' relationship with the EU is explored in order to understand the historical legacies influencing engagement with the EU and its domestic effects.

3   History and governance

Introduction

This chapter provides context for the examination of cohesion, borders and migration, and environmental policy in Greece, Slovenia, Croatia and Macedonia, and thereby elaborates further on the case selection. As such, the chapter takes time and place as its major concerns, informed by a broadly 'historical theory', an approach that seeks to explain a state's governance through interaction with major historical transformations (Tilly 1975, 2006). We are not attempting a comparative historical-sociological analysis of the development of 'the' Balkan state (Jelavich and Jelavich 1977; Jelavich 1983a, b; Wachtel 2008; van Meurs and Pippidi 2010) but we do see engagement with the EU as an epochal historical transformation, reflecting 'an ontology of constant and profound change' (Todorova 1997: 184). The chapter has three parts: the first places the process of EU member-state building in the wider experience of state building in SEE and elsewhere, arguing that engagement with EU is characterised by separate but interconnected processes of boundary creation and transcendence. The second part outlines the process whereby each of our cases 'came to Europe'. It adopts a broadly historical institutionalist approach to explore legacies, and especially the critical junctures that influenced engagement with the EU and its predecessors. The final part examines patterns of governance and compares these with the aggregate pattern in the EU, and then considers how citizens perceive their relationship with the EU. The aim here is to provide some estimate of the 'misfit' between our cases and the EU before embarking on the case studies.

Member state-building

State-building is an often vague and seldom uncontested term which, in SEE, covers diverse historical experiences embracing (*inter alia*) the emergence of Greece (an archetypal nation-state) in the 1830s, the two multi-nation Yugoslavias (1918–41 and 1945–91), and international protectorates (Bosnia and Herzegovina, and Kosovo). There are important differences in state building in our three ex-Yugoslav cases. Slovenia and post-1995 Croatia are largely mono-ethnic with more effective state institutions when compared to Macedonia where power sharing was established under the direct influence of the EU. Macedonia's power-sharing institutions also differ markedly from the 'simple' polities of Croatia and Slovenia. In Macedonia state-building was, in a large part, concerned with promoting political legitimacy and stability through the accommodation of the Albanian minority; in Slovenia and Croatia state building was, as in CEE, primarily concerned with institutional capacities and capabilities. Greece has been a continuously recognised sovereign state for some 180 years and, like Slovenia and Croatia, is mono-ethnic and a 'simple' polity; it also has the longest engagement with the EU and its predecessors. Despite Greece's long engagement with the EU, downward pressure from the EU level has been insufficient to address long-established weaknesses in the Greek state as well new ones flowing directly from its engagement with the EU.

The comparative analysis of state-building raises complex issues that go far beyond the scope of this book, which is primarily about public policy, and there is a further problem: the danger of a 'Yugoslav-centric' analysis as three of our states are former Yugoslav republics. In the aftermath of the Second World War each state had to industrialise to create work for growing populations and to catch up with Western Europe, which led to a further expansion in the role of the state on both sides of the Iron Curtain where patterns of growth, but not growth rates, diverged. The urbanisation and industrialisation of peasant societies added a further twist to already clientelistic patterns of politics, but both Yugoslavia and Greece became urbanising, industrialising and modernising societies. The oil shock of 1973 impacted on both: in Greece's case it stimulated democratisation and after 1981 EU membership mitigated and postponed crisis, whereas in Yugoslavia the oil shock exacerbated serious structural weaknesses and triggered, in part, the interrepublic tensions that led to the break-up of Yugoslavia (Gallagher 2001, 2003, 2005).

Socio-economically, these four states have elements in common. In 2009, using the Purchasing Power Standard (PPS) measure with the EU27 = 100, Eurostat assessed Greece at 93, Slovenia 87, Croatia 63 and Macedonia 34; these are all poorer than the EU average, Macedonia significantly so. In terms of inequality, Greece had a Gini coefficient of 33.0 (2005), Slovenia 28.4 (2008), Croatia 29.0 (2008) and Macedonia 39.0 (2003). With the exception of Slovenia, a majority of their populations are urbanised: in 2008 Macedonia and Greece were 61 per cent urbanised, Croatia 57 per cent and Slovenia 48 per cent. The estimated urbanisation rate (2005–10) was 0.8 per cent for Greece and Macedonia, 0.4 per cent for Croatia and –0.6 per cent in Slovenia. These states enjoy high levels of literacy: Greece 96 per cent, Slovenia 99.7 per cent, Croatia 98.1 per cent and Macedonia 96.1 per cent. Infant mortality (deaths per 1,000 live births) is sometimes used as a surrogate for social development and state effectiveness: for Greece the infant mortality rate is 6.37 (188th in the world), Slovenia 4.25 (206th), Croatia 6.37 (178th) and Macedonia 9.10 (158th). Life expectancy is 79.6 years in Greece, 76.9 in Slovenia, 75.3 in Croatia, and 74.6 in Macedonia.

We must avoid over-generalising from the Yugoslav experience while not diminishing its significance either for the region or the EU (Ramet 2005, 2006). In three of our cases, state formation, the creation of free markets and democratisation accelerated after 1991 and 1995, and overlapped with EU enlargement and European integration. Irrespective of national variation it is legitimate to identify historical continuities. The legacy of the Ottoman Empire provided a powerful and profoundly negative 'other' for all states in the region, including Slovenia and Croatia, which were part of the Habsburg Empire. This raises the question of which legacy or legacies we should privilege (Kitromilides 1983, 1989, 1996). We believe two are directly relevant to our study: boundary creation and boundary transcendence.

Stein Rokkan saw nation and state-building as a dialectic of order (boundary creation) and movement (boundary transcendence) so '[T]he history of each territory is essentially the history of success or failure in this conflict between boundary reduction and boundary accentuation' (Flora 1999: 101, 103). This focuses on the process whereby geographical spaces and membership spaces are constructed and reproduced: geographical space requires strong boundaries to secure control of transactions, but the history of the modern state is largely determined by its interaction with other states and the degree to which sovereignty is compromised. The membership space is concerned with determining which social groups are defined as full members of that geographical space. The interaction between geographical and membership space constitutes the modern state (Flora 1999: 104, 106).

Conflicts over boundaries and membership are competitions between groups for scarce economic and political resources, not the result of primordial ethnic loyalties, and are often exercises in integration (and exclusion) through the redistribution of resources. History demonstrates that redistribution and resource competition in conditions of scarcity and mal-distribution promotes centrifugal politics (Banac 1984; Hardin 1995; Farley 2007). For Rokkan, a successful state is one that has successfully overcome boundary building/ boundary transcendence and centre/periphery conflicts, elevating centripetal over centrifugal forces (Flora 1999: 147). The EU's solution is a geographical and membership space that does not define membership by language or ethnicity but through shared values, political cooperation and economic integration. Translated into the concerns of this project, successful member state-building requires the creation of effective multi-level governance within and between polities. Europeanisation and the EU are the latest attempt to resolve and manage successfully boundary building and transcendence, and the tension between geographical and membership space.

Boundary creation

The most powerful Ottoman legacy is demographic (Todorova 1997: 174–8), a legacy that influences both geographical and membership space. By the mid-nineteenth century the nation-state was the default option of political organisation and modernisation in Western Europe (Tilly 1975: 27); Creveld sees the 'modern' state as 'an almost purely West European development', the product of the rise of the central state bureaucracy; the definition of borders and the ability to tax those within the borders; the establishment of a monopoly over the use of legitimate violence; and the development of a political theory to legitimise the state's domestic hegemony and international sovereignty (1999: 127–8). When constructing states, elites looked to the 'advanced' models of Western Europe, of states characterised by the 'emergence of specialized personnel, control over consolidated territory, loyalty, and durability, permanent institutions with a centralized and autonomous state that held the monopoly of violence over a given population' (Tilly 1975: 70). Events in the 1990s led many to see 'ethnic cleansing', or political violence more broadly, as a typically Balkan phenomenon rather than intrinsic to the wider European state-building process (Rae 2002: 165–211; Mann 2005: 353–81). In terms of ethnic and religious fragmentation (Table 3.1) our states, with the exception of Macedonia (where ethnic fragmentation does translate into politics), do not appear to be dangerously fragmented societies.[1]

There is also little evidence that SEE is uniquely violent or lawless. The homicide rate (excluding attempted homicide) per 100,000 people is 2.10 in Macedonia, 1.62 in Croatia, 1.00 in Slovenia and 0.98 in Greece; the EU27 average is 1.68, in the United States it is 5.00. The prison population (per 100,000) is 100.1 in Macedonia, 90.9 in Greece, 84.1 in Croatia and 65 in Slovenia. In the UK it is 145.1. Nationalism in the historic context of multilingual and multiethnic empires meant that political violence and ethnic cleansing was never

> the spontaneous eruption of primeval hatreds but the deliberate use of organised violence against civilians by paramilitary squads and army units; it represented the extreme force required by nationalists to break apart a society which was otherwise capable of ignoring the mundane fractures of class and ethnicity.
>
> (Mazower 2001: 144)

Table 3.1 Ethnic and religious fragmentation (2010 estimate)

	Ethno-linguistic	Religious
Greece	0.13*	0.039
Slovenia	0.29	0.60
Croatia	0.19	0.22
Macedonia	0.52	0.47

* The Greek census does not collect data on ethnicity as Greece recognises religious, not ethnic, minorities.
Source: Calculated from data in *The CIA World Factbook*. Available from: www.cia.gov. (accessed 15 September 2010).

Boundaries are the result of interaction between pre-Ottoman and Habsburg administrative boundaries, the administrative needs of the Ottoman and Habsburg empires, nationalist movements, the politics of self-determination, and the interests of outside powers. The conception of the national boundary held by independence movements was strongly influenced by West European ideas and developments based on impeccably liberal and progressive notions of self-determination organised around ethnicity and language as the basis for citizenship within a geographic space. Self-determination cannot resolve nationality problems as the right of self- determination cannot be extended to every group within a state's borders. In theory, majority (ethnic) rule, coupled with guarantees for individual rights, would encourage assimilation and homogenisation, but theory and reality never corresponded. In SEE and Western Europe the demographic legacy of 'mixed' populations encouraged continuous attempts at homogenisation that often exacted a terrible price in emigration, assimilation, ethnic cleansing and genocide, but all states retained their minorities and 'lost' populations (Todorova 1997: 167–8). The imperial demographic legacy is pervasive and continues to influence contemporary politics.

State formation in SEE is a complex mix of factors internal to a country and external intervention by the Great Powers and engagement with the EU continues this pattern (Glenny 2000: 39; Mazower 2001: 86, 101). The historical pattern of geopolitics in SEE is often pejoratively referred to as 'Balkanisation', the division of an area into small antagonistic states. As a term, Balkanisation dates from the Russo-Turkish Wars (1877–78) but

> It was not until the end of the Great War that a new layer of meaning was imposed on the term. 'Balkanization' was first used by journalists and politicians not to describe the political fragmentation of the Balkan peninsula but the emergence of several small new states.
>
> (Glenny 2000: xxiii)

Balkanisation implies a peripheral region at the intersection of competing powers or blocs whose attempts to resolve instability provide the starting point for the next cycle of instability. In the nineteenth century SEE sat at the intersection of three empires (the Habsburg, the Romanov and the Ottoman) and from 1945 to 1991 it lay between the Western and Soviet blocs. In this historical perspective the EU represents the latest attempt to fold the region into a single geopolitical entity in an effort to end instability.

State-building was triggered by different causes in different historical contexts: by nationalist movements supported by external powers in the nineteenth century, the Balkan countries' destruction of Ottoman power in Turkey-in-Europe in the wars of 1912–13, by imperial collapse after 1918, by the German and Italian invasions, and the onset and then the end of the Cold War but the direction of development always favoured the centralised state. State building in SEE involved, as elsewhere, the centre attempting to monopolise power which, when combined with façade democracy, produced a state seeking to dominate society while remaining autonomous (Mazower 2001: 147). The geopolitical structure laid down at the end of the 1914–18 war was re-established after 1945 as the vehicle for Titoist communism (Fine 2007: 269–318). The extended pre-war Greek political and economic crisis was seriously exacerbated by war and occupation (Papacosma 2007). After liberation, Greece became a constitutional monarchy but was deeply and profoundly divided between left and right. A vicious civil war resulted, followed by a hardening of politics as a result of the Cold War and US support for conservative Greek politics (Kofas 1989; Blinkhorn and Veremis 1990; Iotrides and Wrigley 1995). The region, a potential flashpoint after Tito broke with Stalin, was neutralised by the USSR and USA, with the most likely conflict being between NATO members, Greece and Turkey. This history influences profoundly the EU's approach to a region whose recent bloody past suggests the EU, itself a creation of, and reaction to, violent conflict, is an appropriate response to antagonism between states. From the 1830s, therefore, the region's politics have been dominated by the same issues that dominated state building in Western Europe, 'issues of self-determination versus inviolable status quo, citizenship and minority rights, the problems of ethnic and religious autonomy, the prospects and limits of succession, the balance between big and small national nations and states, the role of international institutions' (Todorova 1997: 188). Comparable issues fuelled the post-war drive for integration so the EU and its members are products of, and responses to, the complexities of state building. As Tilly reminds us, 'West European history revealed repeated crises, constant struggle, numerous collapses [and] far more states disappeared than survived' (2006: 419).

Thus, in SEE 'The search for a form of government suitable to the social and economic conditions of each country has always been characterised by a constant interaction between internal and foreign affairs' (Woodward 2001: 3). State-building is the core of Balkanisation, not its antithesis; its cause and consequence. Nationalists drew their inspiration from West European state-building:

> The notion of the complete cultural isolation of the Balkans, from the European mainstream because of the lengthy Ottoman rule and Byzantine legacy and the widespread stereotype of the Balkans having skipped the crucial formative stages of European/Western civilization have been seriously challenged.
>
> (Todorova 1997: 179)

From the 1830s to the 1990s in every episode of border creation states 'appealed to the principle of nationality to claim their neighbour's lands: irredentism lived on, and few Balkan borders were uncontested. Moreover, the nationality principle cut two ways. All the new states had ethnic minorities whose existence undermined their claim to rule in the name of the Nation'

(Mazower 2001: 117). The crisis of the 1990s was the product of the collapse of the most ambitious effort to deal with Balkanisation and, as in the past, failure produced external intervention. The major change in the geopolitics of the SEE was the EU, which took on an increasingly prominent role in the political reconstruction of the region.

State formation was primarily endogenous but conditioned by engagement with exogenous actors. All the states considered here are deemed by the international community and the EU to be sovereign states and functioning liberal-market democracies able to meet the requirements of membership under the Copenhagen Criteria. The 1993 European Council agreed, as a statement of basic principle, that states could, if they so wished, 'become members of the European Union. Accession would take place as soon as the associated country is able to assume the obligations of membership by satisfying the economic and political conditions required.'[2] The adaptational pressures flowing from engagement with the EU continue and extend a process that is over 150 years old: promoting regional stability via legitimate and effective states. However, the EU's core objective is not that of the nineteenth-, or even late-twentieth-century nationalist:

> The EU integration paradigm views the political challenges in the Balkans in terms not of state-building, but in terms of *building a member state*. The institutional environment in the region is perceived exclusively in terms of its compatibility with EU norms and standards. The integration paradigm is the only long-term policy vision for the region and this explains its growing significance.
>
> (Krastev 2002: 5, emphasis added)

Although the EU does promulgate a normative definition of what it is to be European, this is not necessarily an *ex ante* imposition of Western European values on the region. Article 6(1) of the Treaty of the European Union states that, 'The Union is founded on the principles of liberty, democracy, respect for human rights and fundamental freedoms, and the rule of law, principles which are common to the member states.' Any European state respecting these principles may apply for membership but enlargement will not take place at the expense of integration and, as we saw in the last chapter, progress is closely monitored and the process can be slowed or even stopped. The Commission and member states decide when these criteria have been satisfied and when the Union is in a position to accept a new member(s) (CEC 2007a: 6).

The EU differs from other international organisations in two ways: the intensity of interaction and the requirement that policies will be downloaded from the supranational to the domestic. Being a member state involves extensive *vertical* (with supranational institutions) and *horizontal* engagement (with other members) and Ladrech conceptualises 'the nature of the EU "member state" as a condition of embedded interaction in which boundaries are permeable depending upon the specific linkage that is in question' (2010:

20). How the domestic state responds is, of course, determined by the specific mix of endogenous and exogenous factors. An interviewee at DG Enlargement captured the EU's role in member state-building, arguing that the core capabilities and competencies required from a state by the Commission were to win money, spend it and account for it. If a state could do all three, it was a functioning, effective state (interview, 31 March 2009). A characteristic feature of member state-building is, therefore, the relationship between the supranational and the domestic, which involves modifications to notions of the sovereign territorial state. As the history of state-making is largely concerned with territorial (re)definition, this implies that engagement with the EU entails a reordering of sovereignty.

Boundary transcendence

A characteristic feature of the Westphalian system are the limits placed on sovereignty, and EU membership has major implications for its members and those aspiring to be members. At its simplest, for three of our cases the culmination of boundary creation in the 1990s was the transfer of state sovereignty from Yugoslavia by its constituent republics; and for Greece, long-term membership of the EU meant penetration of the polity and modified sovereignty. Bartolini (2005; see also Ferrera 2005) argues, using Rokkan's work, that enlargement and integration represents a further phase in state-building, following on from centre formation, system building and political structuring.[3]

In state formation, the inadequate resolution of identity issues increases the potential for conflict (Flora 1999: 310 , 398). Stabilising social and political relationships by anchoring individual life chances to national institutions failed in Yugoslavia and came under severe strain in Greece, resulting in civil war and military rule. After 1991 many internal boundaries were redefined as external but most remained unchanged and the basic organisational unit remained the sovereign state responding to an EU governance that entails, in part, the restructuring of political space as well as institution building. European integration has a paradoxical consequence for Rokkan's theory: the creation of sovereign states that then surrender (or 'pool') that sovereignty as part of a supra-national body via a sovereignty bargain. When a state joins the EU it voluntarily accepts limits on its sovereignty, composed of *autonomy* (independence in policy-making), *control* (the ability to produce an effect) and *legitimacy* (a recognised right to make rules) in exchange for benefits, but to obtain these benefits a state may pay a high price. This is the sovereignty bargain (Mattli 2002: 149–80) discussed in the last chapter. Sovereignty is not fixed but is frequently reconfigured as a result of pressure from within and outside the state so a sovereignty bargain need not diminish a state's sovereignty. European integration is an incremental process of transforming nation-states into a more integrated system by addressing both boundary maintenance and transcendence (Bartolini 2005). The EU is, in these terms, a complex process of boundary removal to promote internal integration and boundary creation to delineate the European space at the national, regional and global levels. At any historical point the EU is the contingent product of a complex process of enlargement and integration, abolishing and redrawing boundaries that were the result of state formation. The EU is a product of Europe's historical state-building in that it is a response to bloody conflict between West European states. The sovereignty bargain, which is fundamental to integration, is the EU's solution to regional and national instability and is central to the EU's conception of member state-building.

The transcendence of state boundaries was fundamental to integration, but going further, as the critical reaction of public opinion to the slowness of enlargement into SEE indicates, may jeopardise the legitimacy of the elites promoting enlargement and integration. Between the 1860s and 1960s the triad of nation, cultural identity and social sharing dominated what is meant by a state. This triad also underpinned the devastating competition between states that eventually fuelled the original impetus for European integration (Bartolini 2005: 366). As integration widened and deepened, a paradox became apparent: democratic governance, social sharing and cultural identity are grounded on nationally bounded communities, but integration hinges on the removal (or weakening) of boundaries and national control. The EU lacks the resources and capacities to engage in imperial system-building and territorial consolidation, but it has sufficient power through enlargement and integration to influence domestic politics. Aspiring and member states are subject to de-differentiation and boundary transcendence that may presage a critical juncture. With the eventual benefit of hindsight, the EU's response to the eurozone crisis may come to be seen as such a juncture.

Integration inevitably expands the capacities of intrastate actors and their access to external resources so states no longer monopolise the production of collective goods. The production of collective-public goods depends increasingly on controlling the boundaries between different levels of authority so the extent of boundary transcendence is no longer determined by domestic politics. Some actors have the capacity and knowledge to transcend borders, others do not and territorialised oppositions may use domestic political resources to limit boundary transcendence. Some political resources cannot be 'locked into' the domestic polity and are less subject to territorial influences and exchange pressures, which links to the development of MLG that can be conceptualised as offering the opportunity for 'partial' exit from territorial political production. MLG creates multiple access points and varying coalitions of actors and interests, many of whom will be drawn to the European/non-state level (Bartolini 2005: 378–80).

The EU exerts significant influence on centre formation and boundary redrawing not by abolishing boundaries but functionally transcending them. Europeanisation and MLG, based on horizontal and vertical networks and resource exchange between actors, may operate at the expense of more conventional political representation and legitimacy flows, however territoriality remains a (perhaps the) key factor (Bartolini 2005: 384). Integration, enlargement and European centre formation are challenged by domestic resistance to the concentration of resources and capacities at the centre, and to perceived threats of cultural standardisation and power centralisation. This has been characterised as isomorphic functional political restructuring in which territorial structuring combines with cross-border coordination by national actors with (broadly) similar interests (Lodge 2000: 89–107). This generates both vertical and horizontal cross-border linkages, so isomorphic functional political restructuring is at the heart of Europeanisation and MLG. Such functional restructuring undermines territoriality and increases the number of decision-making sites, encourages organisational fragmentation, network complexity, and problems of political legitimacy. Bartolini suggests 'stratarchic territorial representation, based mainly on the interaction between substate elites, national rulers, and centre-builders at the EU level seems more likely than the new formation of European wide cross-territorial functional alliances' (2005: 394). The policy sectors considered in this book – cohesion, migration and the environment – all display conflicts generated by the competition between boundary transcendence and control. The collapse of communism and long-term engagement with the EU posed the same basic set of challenges to our four states,

> the dismantling of tariffs and protected state industries as well as the exposure to global competition meant the triumph of neo-liberal forces. The traditional Balkan nation-state is no longer challenged by the old empires; it is not even challenged by the rivalry and hostility of its neighbours; its main threat comes now from the international economy.
>
> (Mazower 2001: 142)

The common strategic response was a sovereignty bargain with the EU: the EU seeks to enhance Europe's global competitiveness, provide safety in numbers and offer protection against some aspects of globalisation. This results in parallel processes of boundary removal and building in which

> the success of the reforms needs a stable and durable policy consensus based on the long term goals of development [but] the very process of transformation polarizes society, producing winners and losers. Governments do not have a lot of room for manoeuvre.
>
> (Krastev 2002: 9)

In this process the capacity bargain identified in the last chapter plays a critical role. All the states are exposed to this parallel process and the strains generated by multiple and often incongruent boundaries. Historically, boundary creation entailed the stabilisation of complex social and political relationships, anchoring life chances to state-national institutions but now national social and political integration is independent of and conditioned by the EU.

Boundaries have been, and will continue to be, redefined and reordered but the state will remain.

National paths to Europe

The realities of power are such that enlargement and integration have unleashed more adaptive pressures on prospective members than on the member states. As a proposition these adaptive pressures are most visible in the accession process and adaptive pressures on candidates and members have increased over time. This is reflected in Héritier's distinction between processes of 'Europeanisation East' and 'Europeanisation West'. Héritier notes the relevance of historical institutionalism and contrasts the two processes, arguing that path dependence limits Europeanisation West to the extent that 'only under exceptional circumstances would member states completely substitute policy instruments or engage in innovation' (2005: 202). There is, on the contrary, ample evidence of 'Western' EU members engaging in voluntary adoption and in social learning; the accession of the CEE states (including Slovenia) has been described as a triumph for

> A set of institutional mechanisms powerful enough to bring a diverse group of states, each undergoing highly destabilizing changes, to a single destination. European-style market based democracy. It was neither natural nor inevitable that all of these states would meet the rigorous political and economic criteria for EU accession – rather, it was the outcome of a very deliberate set of state-building processes.
>
> (European Stability Initiative 2005a: 2)[4]

The analytical problem here is distinguishing between the effects flowing from modernisation and those from Europeanisation, both of which influence the nature of the capacity bargain, but this does not conflict with the contention that Europeanisation's effects have been greater in the 'East' than in the 'West', because of conditionality, the greater adaptive pressures and the degree of 'misfit'. In South East Europe, sovereignties, boundaries and identities are challenged by the European project, changing and influencing preferences while enhancing state capacities and capabilities to negotiate, implement and sustain the required changes. Member state-building and integration are two sides of the same coin, which places a tremendous weight on national political elites who are in a complex political position: building state sovereignty, institutionalising national identities and building a state capable of joining the EU and sustaining the obligations of membership while managing the domestic consequences of these processes.

Existing sovereignties, boundaries and identities are challenged by the EU's constructivist project (Noutcheva 2006; Papadimitriou 2001: 69–94). The EU's solution to Balkanisation is pooling sovereignty, but in SEE the Westphalian system is alive and well. Institutional change entails a dynamic of punctuated equilibrium in which 'there are brief moments in which opportunities for major institutional reforms appear, followed by long stretches of institutional stability. Junctures are "critical" because they place institutional arrangements on paths or trajectories, which are then very difficult to alter' (Pierson 2004: 135). Contemporary politics in SEE are the product of critical junctures and in order to understand them we must examine the recent experience of state formation in our four countries.

Greece

The Karamanlis government sought an association agreement with the EEC which, because of the development gap between Greece and the EEC and differences of opinion among the Six, meant that agreement was not finalised until 1961. The 1967 coup halted implementation and EEC-Greek relations were frozen until 1974. The Greek colonels are often remembered for their attempt to ban mini-skirts and beards, but this was no comic opera regime, but a vicious military dictatorship. It had little ideology; its propaganda rhapsodised about *Ellas Ellinon Christianon* ('Greece of the Christian Greeks') and 'Helleno-Christian civilisation', contrasting sturdy Greek traditions with decadent Western liberalism. Back in power after the fall of the military regime (the period of *metapolitefsi* or regime change) over the Cyprus debacle, Karamanlis prioritised Greek membership, applying for membership in 1975 (Woodhouse 1985; Papadimitriou 2007: 393–424). Despite Commission doubts, the Council of Ministers accepted Greece's application and negotiations began in 1976. The Treaty of Accession was signed in Athens on 28 May 1979 with Greece joining on 1 January 1981. Membership was seen by its advocates, particularly conservatives in the New Democracy, as stimulating Greece's political and economic development and modernisation. PASOK (the socialists) and the wider left was broadly (some virulently) anti-membership, and in the October 1981 elections PASOK came to office. PASOK's suspicion slowed Europeanisation but it won several transitional concessions and in 1985 PASOK shifted position. Greece became a net beneficiary of the budget but Europeanisation and integration revealed serious weaknesses in the ability of the Greek state to implement and administer programmes, leading to major reform programmes in the 1990s that stimulated considerable opposition limiting the reforms' impact (Kazakos and Ioakmidis 1994; Tsalikoglou 1995; Featherstone 1998; Spanou 1998, 2000).

Greece is frequently presented as a critical case for the Europeanisation hypothesis, having a history of centralisation and statism in which successive governments of left and right have failed to achieve significant reform despite pressure from the EU. Featherstone and Papadimitriou, for example, argue that

Greece is an EU member state that has had a reputation for being the 'black-sheep' – standing aside from common declarations on foreign policy, failing to meet agreed targets, and misusing EU funds. Further, it has had one of the poorest records in implementing and upholding EU legislation.

(2008: 5)

Shortcomings in implementing EU programmes, up to and including the Growth and Stability Pact and the Lisbon Agenda, revealed severe short-comings in the capabilities and capacities of the Greek state. Despite a history of, and continuing public support for the EU, euro scepticism and even unrest grew as governments attempted to implement EU-inspired reforms revealing the weakness of the state, the power of veto groups and even cultural resistance to 'foreign' ways. The statist, populist and clientelistic strains in Greek politics remain strong and inimical to Europeanisation.

Promising monetary stability and a Greek presence in the core integration process, as well as powerful exogenous support for domestic reformers, EMU and its adjustment process nevertheless imposed great (and continuing) strains on the polity. The content and scope of reform caused Greece considerable difficulties in implementation, administration and legitimisation. Privatisation proved highly controversial and the proceeds were used to fund the public sector deficit, not investment, and reforms (for example, labour market and pension reform) either failed or produced modest results in comparison to the unrest generated by their attempted implementation. This was made worse when temporary improvement was followed by a sharp deterioration, reflecting persistent structural rigidities in Greece's political economy (Blavoukos and Pagoulatos 2008). In governance terms, the Greek state has been neither hollowed out, nor have its core capacities hardened and 'the track record of structural reform suggested that the domestic system was structured in a manner that appeared to militate against consensus and delivery' (Featherstone and Papadimitriou 2008: 16). This is the context to the explosion of unrest in December 2008 (Kalyvas 2008), which preceded the eurozone crisis of 2010.

Yugoslavia's break-up and the political–economic transition of Bulgaria and Albania represented both a threat and opportunity for Greece. Despite the Cold War, it is important not to overstate Greece's isolation from its SEE hinterland. From 1974 Greece was diplomatically active and trade, tourism and infra-structure links developed with Bulgaria and Yugoslavia, with only the Albanian border sealed. Albania's collapse, the emergence of Bulgaria from communism and Greece's sympathy for Serbia during NATO's Kosovo intervention, and, most visibly (and inexplicably to outsiders), the name controversy with Macedonia led to Greece playing an important regional role as the only EU member in the Balkans (Koliopoulos 2002: 25–38; Huliaras and Tsardanidis 2006: 1–19). The turbulence generated in the region (for example, popula-tion movement, people trafficking, smuggling and organised crime) had, however, implications for Greece's domestic tranquillity as well as offering an opportunity for Greece to take a leading role in reconstructing and modernising SEE (Monastiriotis and Tsamis 2007). Greece was well placed geographically and politically to benefit from the opening up of SEE, but failed to exploit its geopolitical advantage as fully as it might. The dispute with Macedonia and support for the Milošević regime, for example, promoted Greek isolation within the EU and NATO. Greece failed to develop and advocate a comprehensive development programme for the region via the EU and other international institutions. Under PASOK, Greek policy towards SEE remained largely bilateral, but Greece was a prime mover in the revival of the South East European Cooperation Process (the first regional summit was held in Crete in 1997) and in pushing the EU further along the road to enlargement in SEE via the Thessaloniki Agenda (2003).

That the EU has shaped Greece's recent history and politics is incontrovertible, and can be seen in both the domestic reform and foreign policy agendas. Pro-European and reform rhetoric and attitudes (except in the case of Macedonia) were articulated by elites, but compliance was problematic, as was implementation, in a society where internal divisions and entrenched interests supported by political elites, dissipated the reform effort. Moreover, weaknesses in state capacities and capabilities in the face of powerful veto groups points to *systemic* features that resist the adaptation of the domestic model towards a liberal state-economy relationship. The EU stimulus in this regard challenges embedded domestic norms and interests. At the same time, the domestic tension remains and even grows as a 'Europeanising' elite defines reform as an essential development priority and fears what the alternative path of its opponents will mean for the national interest (Featherstone and Papadimitriou 2008: 19). As a member state Greece cannot by definition be subject to this conditionality and it joined the Community at a time when membership conditionality did not exist. During its accession Greece was not subject to a regime remotely comparable to that undergone by Slovenia, Croatia and Macedonia, and this did not, as recent events show, change the trajectory of the Greek state. This is reinforced by the absence of any implementation *acquis* binding on all members; members have by definition satisfied conditionality. Member states are highly unlikely to agree to any extension of conditionality to themselves except, as the Greek eurozone crisis showed, in extreme situations threatening the stability of the entire EU, which revealed a power asymmetry comparable to that inherent in the accession process.

Member states are required by treaty to apply Community law as they would national law and to ensure the fulfilment of their treaty obligations. The Commission and ECJ monitors and sanctions non-compliance on their own initiative and via complaints relating to breaches of treaty provisions, regulations and decisions, failure to transpose directives, incorrect legal implementation, improper application of directives, and failure to comply with ECJ rulings. Infringement procedures embrace a letter of formal notice, a reasoned opinion and a reference to the ECJ, but a settlement can be negotiated at each stage. Enforcement relies on the ability of central EU institutions to secure domestic compliance, which implies a central capacity to impose, if necessary, domestic change through 'hard' (e.g. fines) or 'soft' (e.g. naming and shaming) measures and instruments. The point is, however, that the EU's enforcement capacities over member states are (or were until the eurozone crisis) limited, and this shifts the focus to the dynamics of domestic politics. The calculus involves the benefit derived from the EU's rules and regulations, reduced transaction costs and the resolution of coordination problems but none eliminate domestic variations in implementation. Minimally, this involves recognising that membership entails conformity with a club's rules, but implementation may be limited by a lack of legal and administrative capability and capacity, and the Commission is in no position to micro-manage programmes (interview, DG Enlargement, 31 March 2009).

As already touched upon, even before the eurozone crisis of 2010, Greece enjoyed a poor reputation as an implementer of EU policy. Two sets of indicators are useful: the Single Market Scoreboard that details the percentage rate of non-implementation of single market rules and data from the ECJ. Greece has a problematic record with implementing the single market directives since 1997; the higher the ranking, the worse the record. Up to July 2009 states were expected to achieve a 1.5 per cent implementation deficit and Greece only achieved this once, in July 2008. Subsequently, the implementation deficit target was reduced to 1 per cent. In December 2005 Greece was described as performing 'poorly on a consistent basis [and] the situation has not improved [Greece] combines a poor transposition record with an equally poor record as regards the application of internal market legislation' (Internal Market Scoreboard 14: 11, 21). Five years later, in 2010, Greece was described as 'the worst offender' at failing to transpose directives (Internal Market Scoreboard 20: 22). An equally dismal picture emerges from ECJ data on new actions brought against a country for failing to meets treaty obligations and the infringements of which a country is found guilty. Greece does not have the worst record of infringements declared. Italy was first in 2001, 2002, 2004 and 2005, and first equal with Greece in 2003 and 2007. Spain had most infringements declared in 2003 and France in 2008. Nevertheless, Greece was first (or first equal) or second in infringements declared in 2000, 2001, 2002, 2004, 2006, 2007 and 2008. Its best placing was fourth worst in 2003.

These data indicate serious weaknesses in the Greek state and an unwillingness by the political elites to confront the status quo that persisted until the eurozone crisis exploded in early 2010. The Commission noted, for example, that major revisions of official statistics were 'extremely rare in other EU Member States, but have taken place in Greece on several occasions'. This was symptomatic of a lack of quality and capability, but more seriously reflected 'inappropriate governance ... poor cooperation and lack of clear responsibilities between several Greek institutions ... which leave ... fiscal statistics subject to political pressures and electoral cycles' (CEC 2010a: 3–4). Despite the EU's requirements that its members implement European law and Greece's poor record in this respect, the Commission has been unable and unwilling to take action against Greece of the sort it would take against a candidate country. Between 1997 and 2003, for example, Greece consistently misreported deficit and debt data, and on six occasions after 2004 EUROSTAT expressed reservations about Greece's economic statistics but nothing effective was done. The efficient and accurate gathering of statistics to enable a government to 'map' and render society legible and governable is one of the core markers of 'stateness', so failings here are of major significance (Scott 1998: 11–52; Anderson 2006: 163–70). Only with the onset of the eurozone crisis and the near collapse of the Greek economy did the EU's members and the Commission agree on a far more interventionist role for the Commission and imposed conditionality on Greece (CEC 2010b). The Greek polity displays deeply embedded tensions and inertia that have a long historical provenance but which are grounded in contending interests and identities given expression by Greece's long relationship with the EU.

Slovenia

Slovenia is often presented as the Goldilocks, as it were, of regional politics: the state in which everything was 'just right' for it to take advantage of enlargement and integration. Slovenia's success has been attributed to its central European heritage as part of the Habsburg lands, its Catholic Western-oriented political culture and ethnic homogeneity (Vodopine 1992: 220–41; Fink-Hafner and Robbins 1997; Gow and Carmichael 2000; Cox 2005).[5] Slovenia appears to be the only component of Yugoslavia that followed the classic West European pattern of state-building but it did so in the mid-twentieth century (Bibič 1993). Slovenia's borders (with some exceptions) and national identity are essentially the product of the nineteenth century, reflecting its location in the Austro-Hungarian Empire and the cultural awakening represented by intellectuals such as the philologist Jernej Kopitar (1780–1844) and the poet France Presersen (1800–49). For contemporary politics, however, the most significant figure is Edvard Kardelj (1910–79). Kardelj was a leading Slovenian communist in the 1930s. After narrowly escaping death in Stalin's purge of foreign communists he returned to Yugoslavia in 1937, and after the invasion in 1941 helped create the partisan resistance. Kardelj was a leading ideologist of Titoism. One of his most influential (and controversial) works was *The Evolution of the Slovene National Question* (1939) and in the 1950s he helped to develop the workers' self-management system, beginning with the 1953 Constitution; he also had close connections with Yugoslav military intelligence (Kardelj 1982). Eclipsed in the 1960s, he re-emerged after Tito's purge of the Croatian, Serbian and Slovenian reformists in 1973. Of greatest significance was his role in drawing up the 1974 constitution that entrenched decentralised decision-making in the republics, placing them under the direct leadership of their respective 'national' communist leaderships. This provided the basis of Slovene statehood, using the protective umbrella provided by Tito's Yugoslavia and its increasingly decentralised constitutions to build a de facto Slovenian state (Hribar 1993: 43–9). Beginning in the 1950s, this process was largely completed by the mid-1980s and 'Slovene success lay in creating first a state then a nation, endogenously within Yugoslavia, and finally during 1990, turning the full force of this national unity against Yugoslavia and for independence' (Woodward 2001: 5).

During the 1980s the internal political crisis triggered by Tito's death in May 1980 and the economic crisis flowing from the first and second oil crises and the onset of globalisation encouraged the Slovene Communist Party to regard European integration as a 'win–win' opportunity. Dimitrij Rupel, a Slovenian intellectual and the first post-independence foreign minister, argued that the EU as 'a collection of nation-states sent a clear signal to Slovenia that only a fundamentally transformed Yugoslavia could be accepted into its ranks' (Rizman 2006: 27). A Yugoslavia dominated by Serbia, which evinced little interest in European integration and which could not sustain internal reform on the required scale, meant that if Slovenia was to embark on the European path, Slovenia would have to recover its sovereignty from the Federation, which it was entitled to do under the 1974 constitution as a constituent republic. Slovenia's historic and geographic proximity to Italy and Austria (Grams 1991: 331–40), its high standard of living and cultural homogeneity made integration the obvious path (Inotai and Stanovnik 2004: 353–66).

The more pluralist internal politics of the Yugoslav federation made Slovenia's path to democratic consolidation less fraught than in CEE with its Soviet-style political institutions. Slovenian nationalism, in contrast to Serbia's or Croatia's, tended to embrace universalistic norms and values, and regarded European integration as complementary to Slovenian sovereignty. This did not, however, preclude actions such as depriving non-Slovene Yugoslavs of citizenship rights after independence, actions that were contrary to the letter and spirit of the EU accession process. After independence some 18,000 individuals who were citizens of other Yugoslav republics and who had emigrated to Slovenia were compelled to register as foreigners, were removed from the population records, and as a result lost their residency rights. In 2004 citizen rights were restored to 'the erased' but a referendum in May 2004 rejected the law: only 4 per cent voted in favour, albeit in a turnout of 31 per cent. After years of internal protest, as well as pressure from the Vatican, the UN and the Commission, and in response to an ECJ ruling in July 2010, an amendment was pushed through parliament ending the 18-year-long saga.

Slovenian nationalism and democratisation had their dark side but were intertwined in such a way that between 1990 and 2004 the construction of a sovereign state able to take on the demands and obligations of EU membership in a capacity bargain was achieved with relative ease. Rizman describes Slovenia as 'a stable democracy that is vulnerable and uncertain only to the extent that this holds true for other, more advanced and older democratic establishments in Western Europe' (2006: 75–6).

In 1989, fearing Serb domination of the Federation, the Slovene parliament amended the republic's constitution to pave the way for independence. Multi-party elections took place in April 1990 and in a referendum (23 December) 88 per cent voted for independence. The *Basic Charter on Independence and*

Sovereignty for Slovenia was adopted on 25 June 1991 and precipitated the Ten Day War (26 June–6 July 1991) for independence. Slovenia's location and very effective resistance, together with the small number of Serbs affected by independence, meant Milošević was not willing to expend resources on reversing secession (Bucar and Brinar 2005: 93–133). Even before Yugoslavia's collapse Slovenia, always the most affluent Yugoslav republic, was keen to develop a relationship with the EU and benefited from the 1980 EC–Yugoslavia cooperation agreement. In 1989 Slovenian politicians adopted *Europe 1992*, which explored what a new relationship with the EU would require. Slovenia was recognised by the EU on 15 January 1992. In February 1992 Slovenia sought a revised agreement and aid to restructure and consolidate the economy. The EU–Slovenia Cooperation agreement (modelled on the 1980 agreement) came into force in 1993, and the government then sought negotiations on a formal (and broader) European Agreement. This was signed on 10 June 1996 but subsequent negotiations were slowed by disputes with the Berlusconi–Fini governments over the rights of Slovenia's Italian minority and compensation for property expropriated by the communists in 1945. Faced by a possible Italian veto, Slovenia bowed to the inevitable. Slovenia's European Agreement came into force on 1 February 1999, four and a half years after those of Czechoslovakia, Hungary and Poland and three years after Bulgaria and Romania (Potocnik and Lombardero 2004: 367–80).

The Slovenian reform process, which began in 1989 and accelerated after independence, was designed to both modernise the country and prepare it for EU membership, always the primary objective. EU assistance was provided under PHARE between 1997 and 1999 but the reform drive generated both reform fatigue and internal resistance. SIGMA, for example, noted that political pressure for reform 'faded away rapidly. No government was willing to tackle reforms in earnest because it was risky and politically unrewarding. There was no reform constituency strong enough to apply pressure. The political momentum of 1996 was lost' (2002: 1). Key stakeholders – parliament, political parties, trade unions – were reluctant to alter the status quo despite a commitment to EU membership. Some external stimulus was required and this was provided by the Commission's 1998 Progress Report. Although described as 'well prepared', Slovenia's National Plan for the Adoption of the Acquis (NPAA) was subject to a litany of criticism, including inconsistent quality, a short-term focus, information gaps, a failure to cover all the *acquis*, a poor timetable and unclear implementation. It required, in other words, drastic revision (CEC 1998: 47–50). As a result 'the Slovene political class realise[ed] that EU membership was conditional on administrative reform and more serious endeavours for reform started to be discussed' (SIGMA 2002: 1). The government, a multi-party coalition under Janis Drnovšek (Liberal Democracy of Slovenia) made reform a priority but the demands of coalition politics and the scale of change meant his government had to proceed by consensus, winning over parliament and the National Economic–Social Council, a corporate chamber composed of social, economic and professional interests that can propose laws and force a re-examination of legislation and oblige government to call a referendum. Slovenia's reform process was characterised by constant negotiation and trade-offs, which explains both the reform fatigue and, after the exogenous shock from the Commission, its effectiveness.

Although the last CEE state to sign a Europe Agreement (EA), the gap between signing and applying for membership was the shortest – Slovenia submitted its membership application on the same day. The Commission's opinion on the ten CEE states defined Slovenia as a stable democracy, which satisfied the political and economic aspects of the Copenhagen Criteria, but that implementing the *acquis* would require considerable effort. In December 1997 Slovenia was invited to begin negotiations. Accession was akin to adjustment but there were some problems. The Slovenian government was variously criticised by the Commission for the slow pace of privatisation and a failure to bring down high production costs at the required speed, but overall the accession process was, in the final analysis, neither politically nor economically disruptive. By 1999 Slovenia had the highest per capita income of any transition state and its economic strength was reflected in that it never called on the IMF for stand-by credits. The international context played a crucial role in the consolidation of democracy and the free market, developments that underpinned Slovenia's accession to the EU (Ramet 1993, 1997, 1998). After 1991, building on the pluralistic tendencies established within Yugoslav politics and Kardelj's exploitation of the 1974 federal constitution, state-building in Slovenia after 1991 provided the back-drop to, and foundation of, convergence with the EU whose conditionality requirements reinforced a modernisation process already underway and which enjoyed popular legitimacy (Frane *et al.* 2002: 133–47). In the referendum on whether Slovenia should accept the offered treaty of accession, 90 per cent voted to join the EU.

Since joining the EU Slovenia has developed a reputation as an effective member state. The Commission Internal Market Scoreboard, for example, noted that in its implementation and application of internal market rules Slovenia was one of the best performers, being consistently above the EU average. Slovenia had a 0.5 per cent non-transposition rate, had no unimplemented directives and transposition took, on average, 3.1 months (the EU average was 7.1). In terms of infringements Slovenia had 17 pending cases (the EU average was 46) and there had been a decrease of 26 per cent in infringement cases compared to 2009 compared to a fall of 11 per cent for the EU as a whole (Internal Market Scoreboard 21: 2010). In January 2007 the euro was successfully introduced, in December 2007 Slovenia joined the Schengen zone and between January and June 2008 it cemented its reputation when it became the first of the 2004 enlargement countries to hold the rotating EU Presidency (Republic of Slovenia 2008).

Croatia

Croatia was a sovereign republic of the Federal People's Republic of Yugoslavia founded in 1945 (Bartlett 2002; Magas 2007; Tanner 2010).

Croatia's economy, as in Slovenia and Macedonia, was based on workers' self-management, which was first introduced in Croatia. This initially produced better growth and levels of prosperity than in CEE, and Croatia industrialised rapidly in the 1960s and 1970s. Croats, the second largest ethnic group after Serbs, benefited from Tito's policy of balancing Serb and Croat interests, but both nationalism and reformism were frowned upon (Uzelac 2006). The 1963 Yugoslav constitution was widely interpreted as an attempt to restrict further Serb dominance and Croats enjoyed a substantial federal political presence – for example, five of the nine federal prime ministers were Croats.

The Croatian Spring was triggered in 1967, initially by intellectuals, notably poets and linguists, seeking greater cultural autonomy, but which inevitably widened into a movement seeking economic and political reform. Up to the end of 1971 Tito still regarded Serb domination as the greatest threat to Yugoslavia so Croat cultural nationalism offered an important counterweight. Monitoring the Croatian party's 10th Plenum, Tito sanctioned support for those in the Croatian party advocating cultural distinctiveness, so triggering the Croatian Spring. The dispute soon widened to embrace the distribution of resources in the Federation, the management of the economy and even the absorption of Herzegovina into Croatia. The Croatian Spring culminated in December 1971 in a student strike and demonstrations. As the 'Maspok' ('mass movement') seemingly ran out of control opposition from unitarists in the Croatian party (led by Vladimir Bakarić) and in other republics (including Kardelj), in the military and from those who, while sympathetic to greater decentralisation feared resurgent nationalism, coalesced. By this time Tito needed little persuading that the time had come to act and the result was a purge and repression. This forced Croatian nationalism underground but the original goals of the Croatian Spring were largely achieved by the 1974 constitution (Cuvalo 1990). After Tito's death in 1980, growing political and economic difficulties undermined Yugoslavia's coherence. Croatia was the second most-prosperous (after Slovenia) of the constituent republics and increasingly resented the transfer of wealth to poorer areas and what was perceived as growing Serb political domination in the Federation. However, economic problems in the West, domestic inflation and declining productivity reduced Croatia's competitiveness and undermined confidence in the framework provided by Yugoslavia. This was amplified by the rise of Serb nationalism under Milošević (Cohen 2007: 425–74).

At the 14th Congress of the League of Communists of Yugoslavia (1990), the Serb delegation, led by Milošević, demanded the revision of the 1974 constitution to give, in effect, control of Yugoslavia to the Serbs, the largest ethnic group. The Slovenian and Croatian delegations walked out. Ethnic Serbs (some 12 per cent Croatia's population) rejected Croatia's secession and Serb politicians stoked fears that a new Ustaša regime would be instituted; these sentiments were reciprocated by some Croatian politicians, notably Franjo Tudjman (1922–99).[6] Tudjman was president of Croatia from 30 May 1990 until his death on 10 December 1999, after his nationalist HDZ (the Croatian

Democratic Union, founded in 1989) won the first post-communist multi-party elections in 1990. A year later he proclaimed Croatian independence. Tudjman fought with Tito's partisans (his brother was killed in 1943) and after the war he worked in the Federal Ministry of Defence and after military academy he became one of the youngest JNA (Yugoslav People's Army) generals. Leaving the military in 1961 Tudjman founded the Institute for the History of Croatia's Workers' Movement, remaining director until 1967. As a result of a series of articles questioning Yugoslavia's socialist elite, Tudjman was eventually expelled from the party. After the Croatian Spring Tudjman, found guilty of subversion, was imprisoned for two years but served only nine months of his sentence. He was also subsequently to be charged with spreading anti-socialist propaganda in 1981 after an interview with Swedish television. This time, sentenced to three years in prison, he served eleven months. Tudjman's dissidence focused on Serbian nationalism, the centralisation of power in Belgrade and the concept of Yugoslavism, which he interpreted as a drive for Serbian hegemony. Tudjman saw himself as expressing Croatia's historic identity (Schöpflin 1973: 123–46); he was less concerned about one-party authoritarian rule per se as long as Croats were doing the ruling.

In the late 1980s, like his Slovenian counterparts, Tudjman formulated a national state-building programme. Aware that the realities of international politics meant a sovereign Croatia would not be recognised, he sought ever greater autonomy and decentralisation (Pusić 1994: 389–404). Tudjman's HDZ was, however, virulently nationalist and as Yugoslavia destabilised his aim became independence. Tudjman's original constitution did not recognise the Serb presence in Croatia, and the police and security forces, the media and economic management were purged of Serbs. Croatia's secession in 1991 precipitated the war with Serbia but secured independence. However, the privatisation programme was disastrous economically and stimulated corruption; unemployment surged to 20 per cent, economic growth slumped and the budget deficit grew. Tudjman and the HDZ attracted international criticism for its equivocal attitude to the pro-Nazi Independent State of Croatia and for war crimes, particularly during Operation Flash in Slavonia and Operation Storm (July–August 1995) that resulted in the ethnic cleansing of the Krajina's Serb majority. In contrast to Milošević, Tudjman disguised his nationalism somewhat, although this became much more difficult after the end of the fighting in 1995, benefiting from Western sympathy while maintaining a façade of democracy. Death saved him from indictment by the ICTY.

Democratic transition was slowed by Tudjman's presence, compounded by the legacies of war and Tudjman's authoritarianism; these also determined Croatia's relationship with the EU. Initially, Tudjman felt able to largely ignore the EU's disapproval, seeing himself, and being seen by many Croats, as Croatia's George Washington, but even at the height of the war neither he nor the HDZ were unchallenged. Post-war unemployment remained high and Croatia was criticised for corruption, democratic shortcomings, inaction over the return of displaced persons, threats to press and individual freedom, and its reluctance to cooperate with the ICTY. Matters began to change after the 1995 Dayton Accords and the start of Slovenia's negotiations in 1997. Croatian elites tended to compare themselves with Slovenia not the remnants of Yugoslavia, and Croatia enjoyed the support of some major EU states, notably Germany. This meant that 'Croatia was slowly working its way toward the EU by the mid-1990s joining the Phare programme in 1995 and stating negotiations on a cooperation agreement [however] the expulsion of ethnic Serbs that same year . . . set Croatia off track, after which the country was removed from Phare and cooperation negotiations were halted' (Fisher 2006: 191–2). The EU made it clear that Croatia's 'return to Europe' would not be possible with Tudjman in power and by the time of Tudjman's death pressure for change, reflected in the 2000 elections, was increasing.

Tudjman's conception of Croatia's identity was always subject to challenge and his regime never established a secure democratic legitimacy and remained corrupt and morally questionable. Post-Tudjman governments subsequently engaged simultaneously in nation and state-building, which were reflected in their

> near total preoccupation with Europeanisation – rejecting Tudjman's nationalism in regard to cooperation with European and international organisations and norms, from cooperation with the [ICTY] to funda- mentally different signals and policies toward Bosnia and pushing the European integration agenda with great speed and gusto.
>
> (Woodward 2001: 8–9)

After the 2000 elections a coalition led by the Social Democratic Party held office until 2003. With Tudjman dead and the HDZ out of office, the party underwent a reformation and after the 2003 elections returned to office under Ivo Sanader, whose government focused on EU membership.

Croatia's accession relationship dates from the formation of the Ministry of European Integration in March 1998. Croatia signed a Stabilisation and Association Agreement (SAA) in October 2001 as part of the Stabilisation and Accession Process (SAP) launched at the Zagreb Summit in November 2000. The SAP's aim was to provide support to strengthen democracy, promote the rule of law and a market economy and regional cooperation. The SAA sought domestic reform as a prelude to the accession process and in return for beginning the alignment of domestic legislation with the *acquis*, Croatia was recognised as a potential candidate. The SAP was strengthened at the Thessaloniki Summit that created the SAA, a contractual relationship, whose fulfilment depended on a positive evaluation by the Commission of the progress made, the granting of trade preferences and a new financial instru- ment, the Instrument for Pre-Accession Assistance (IPA) for 2007–13. SAA discussions began in November 2000, an agreement was initialled in May 2001 and signed in October. This was ratified by the Commission and Croatia on 30 January 2002, coming into force three months later. The SAA then had to be ratified by all the EU's members, which took until December 2004. The SAA came into operation on 1 February 2005, a total of sixty-three months from start to finish.

The rapid progress of Romania and Bulgaria towards accession led the Croat political elite to believe that if those countries could achieve membership so quickly, so could Croatia. Sanader isolated the nationalist right and formed a minority HDZ government that pushed forward despite a major crisis with the ICTY that led to the freezing of negotiations on 16 March 2005. The Commission and members states had frequently expressed concern about Croatia's approach to the ICTY and on 20 December 2004 the European Council had set 17 March as the starting point for negotiations conditional on full cooperation with the ICTY. On 16 March the ICTY criticised Croatia's failure to cooperate fully. The UK, Netherlands and Sweden made the surrender of General Ante Gotovina, who had led Operation Storm and was accused of responsibility for war crimes, a precondition for reopening talks. Gotovina was arrested by the Spanish in Tenerife on 7 December 2005 and transferred to the ICTY where, on 24 April 2011, he was sentenced to 24 years' imprisonment for war crimes. Border disputes with Slovenia caused further problems. In December 2008 Slovenia stalled negotiations for ten months over a number of border issues but notably over the sea border with Croatia in the Piran Bay. This was despite the fact that a majority of EU members wanted the chapter negotiations to continue and Croatia had agreed to scrap its Ecological and Fisheries Protection Zone in the Adriatic. The dispute was eventually resolved by both sides agreeing on 26 October 2009 to submit outstanding border issues to international arbitration, a decision approved in a referendum in Slovenia in June 2010.

On 21 February 2003, Croatia submitted its application to join the EU and in April 2004 the European Commission delivered its assessment that Croatia was ready to begin negotiations, which were opened on 4 October 2005. The official EU position is that negotiations continue until *both* sides are satisfied with the arrangements and agreements necessary for entry but the inherent asymmetry of the process (the Council of Ministers is the primary decision-maker and decisions on enlargement have to be unanimous and approved by the parliaments of each member state or in some cases by referendum) means that it is the EU's degree of satisfaction that really determines the outcome. Thus,

> The EU wishes Croatia to become its member, but eventually this decision will be taken by Croatia's citizens . . . Becoming a member of the European Union can be compared to joining a club which has a number of its rules and regulations. Each country wishing to join the club has to fulfill the rules . . . but final decision depends on citizens' will . . . Croatia is already a European country and belongs to Europe by its tradition, history and culture. Therefore membership in the European Union would represent just a political confirmation of what Croatia has always been.[7]

There was no timescale or target date. For two of the chapters (Chapter 34 Institutions and Chapter 35 Other Issues) Croatia had to undertake no action. Screening was initiated on 20 October 2005 (Chapter 25 Science and Research was the first to be opened) and ended on 13 October 2006 (Chapter 23 Judiciary and Fundamental Rights). Negotiations on 21 chapters were opened and provisionally closed and 5 were delayed by Croatia's failure to cooperate with the ICTY. The time this process takes is considerable. Taking *only* the 19 chapters, as of January 2011, in which negotiations were not frozen for any reason the shortest gap between ending screening and starting chapter negotiations was 10 days (Chapter 10, Information, Society and Media) and the second shortest was 7 months (Chapter 20, Enterprise and Industrial Policy and Chapter 25, Science and Research). The longest was 53 months (Chapter 8, Competition Policy) and the second longest was Chapter 23 (Judiciary and Fundamental Rights), a gap of 44 months. The average gap between closing screening and opening chapter negotiations was 20.5 months. The average negotiation time was 22.7 months; the longest (Chapter 32, Financial Control) lasted 37 months and the shortest (Chapter 30, External Relations) lasted 12 months. In June 2011 the Commission recommended closure of the accession negotiations, a recommendation approved at the 23–24 June European Council in Brussels. On 9 December 2011 Croatia signed the Treaty of Accession, becoming the 28th member state by 1 July 2013. Close monitoring (particularly of judiciary and fundamental rights) would continue right up to, and most likely after, accession.

Croatia, according to Gallup's *Balkan Monitor*, now has the lowest percentage in the region (29 per cent) agreeing that membership would be a 'good thing'. There has been no increase in those thinking that membership was a bad thing, rather there has been an increase in scepticism and this is ascribed to the length of the process: 43 per cent (down from 55 per cent in 2006) believed the Commission want Croatia to join. Support tends to be highest among urban groups (35 per cent) and the university educated (51 per cent). although many Croats from all socio-economic groups expect little benefit from the EU, 37 per cent believed that the country's general welfare will decline and 41 per cent that national identity will be undermined by membership. Gallup found 65 per cent of respondents identified very/strongly with Croatia, suggesting that most Croats are still primarily interested in establishing their national identity. In earlier enlargements, when the scale of the transformation required became apparent, public opinion became more critical of the EU, but Croatia is the only Western Balkan country 'where a relative majority are not supportive of EU membership and where a majority do not consider the consequences of EU accession to be beneficial for the country' (Gallup 2009: 10). In a referendum on 22 January 2012, 67 per cent voted in favour of membership.

In July 2009 Sanader stepped down, declaring his intention to leave politics. In early 2010, however, he announced his intention to return but was expelled from the HDZ. His successor as Prime Minister, Jadranka Kosor, initiated an anti-corruption drive, partly in response to pressure from the EU, which led to the arrest of several leading members of the HDZ, including ex-ministers. This provoked major unrest in the HDZ and led to defections from the governing coalition. In October 2010 Sanader took up his parliamentary seat to preserve his immunity (later revoked) from prosecution, but in December he fled to Slovenia and was subsequently arrested in Austria in order to face corruption charges. The parliamentary situation is complicated by, and complicates, relations with the EU as the HDZ argues stability is needed as negotiations increasingly focused on two extremely complex and politically sensitive issues: the reform of the judiciary and the privatisation and/or liquidation of Croatia's shipyards. Slovenia prevented the closure on the chapter dealing with the free movement of capital in a dispute over Slovenian banks' access to the Croatian market and fisheries continue to pose problems. Despite the vicissitudes of the process, Croatia has been subject to Europeanisation and the EU has been, without a doubt, 'the most important international actor in spurring change in the new era' (Fisher 2006: 173). Increased anti-EU sentiment reflected not resurgent nationalism but frustration with the length of the accession process.

Macedonia

Historically, the existence of a Macedonian people, identity and polity has often been questioned (Poulton 2000).[8] For Bulgaria, 'Macedonian people' means a civic identity embracing all groups within the territory as opposed to the Slav majority. Bulgaria was the first state to recognise Macedonia's independence while questioning the notion of separate Macedonian language and nationhood (states recognise other states, not populations), whereas Greece resists both notions of the polity and the national identity. The Republic of Macedonia, the southernmost part of Yugoslavia, became the object of massive EU attention in the early 2000s because of its geopolitical location and recent history of instability that threatened to make it the flashpoint for a further cycle of interethnic conflict (Rae 2002: 271–92). Yet, Pond notes, 'by 2006 it was the improbable third in line among the ex-Yugoslav states for future EU membership, after much richer politically more stable Slovenia and Croatia' (2006: 168). Many inside and outside the region and in the EU contend that Macedonia's rapid progress was due more to the EU's wish to avoid the creation of another protectorate, and this seems to be confirmed by a deceleration in Macedonia's progress reflected in the highly critical 2010 Progress Report (CEC 2010d). Nevertheless, the EU has been enormously influential in constituting Macedonia's post-independent polity and politics.

Ottoman rule generated a number of national liberation movements. In 1903 the Internal Macedonian Revolutionary Organisation (IMRO) staged the Illinden Uprising. The uprising was crushed but nevertheless remains central to the republic's identity. After the Balkan Wars of 1912–13 and the dissolution of the Ottoman Empire in 1918, most of the European Ottoman territories were divided between Greece, Bulgaria and Serbia. The territories of the present Republic of Macedonia were named Southern Serbia and became part of the newly formed Yugoslavia. In 1941, after Yugoslavia was invaded and occupied by Germany and Italy, Southern Serbia was divided between Bulgaria and Italian-occupied Albania, which also included Kosovo. Macedonia suffered comparatively lightly compared to other parts of Yugoslavia (where some 20,000 died, including Jews transported to death camps) and both partisan support and communist party membership were limited. In 1944 the Anti-Fascist Assembly for the National Liberation of Macedonia (ASNOM) was held (about one-third of delegates did not attend) and declared the People's Republic of Macedonia to be a constituent nation and republic within federal Yugoslavia. The People's Republic became one of the Yugoslav federation's six republics; after the establishment of the SFRY in 1963 it became the Socialist Republic of Macedonia. 'Socialist' was dropped in 1991 when Macedonia seceded peacefully. Macedonia's geopolitical situation, landlocked and bordered by Serbia to the north, Bulgaria to the east, Greece to the south and Albania to the west, profoundly influences its history and contemporary politics. This is reflected in the long-running dispute with Greece over the republic's name, which led to it being admitted to the UN in 1993 as the Former Yugoslav Republic of Macedonia (FYROM); in December 2005 it became a candidate for EU membership.

On 8 September 1991 a referendum endorsed independence from Yugoslavia. Over 97 per cent of ethnic Macedonians voted for independence but, ominously, ethnic Albanians (some 25 per cent of the population concentrated in the north-west on the borders of Albania and Kosovo) abstained because, while the new constitution guaranteed minority rights, those of the ethnic Macedonian majority were given precedence. The Arbitration Commission of the Peace Conference on the Former Yugoslavia (the Badinter Commission) recommended EU recognition in January 1992. The new republic remained outside the wars of the 1990s. The major threat to its stability was the Kosovo crisis (1999–2000) when, in response to Serb ethnic cleansing, 360,000 ethnic Albanian refugees took refuge in the Albanian areas in the north-west of the country, placing great strain on Macedonia's slender resources. The refugees returned to Kosovo after the Serb withdrawal and NATO's intervention, but radical Albanians (sometimes indistinguishable from organised criminals) influenced by the example of the Kosovo Liberation Army (KLA) established a Macedonian equivalent, the National Liberation Army (NLA), with the aim of winning autonomy for the Albanian-populated areas. A few advocated the creation of a Greater Albania composed of Albania, Kosovo and the north-west of Macedonia (Rusi 2004: 1–16).

For the first seven years Macedonia was ruled by ex-socialists, the Social Democratic Union of Macedonia (SDSM), who prevented the country from being drawn into any kind of conflict but could not push through a radical reform in a country plagued by corruption and organised crime, exploiting the

UN embargo on Serbia. The SDSM lost the 1998 elections and was replaced by a coalition of the nationalist Internal Macedonian Revolutionary Organization – Democratic Party for Macedonian National Unity (VMRO–DPMNE), the Democratic Alternative (DA) and the Democratic Party of Albanians (DPA). The new government rapidly lost popularity and in November 2000 the DA withdrew and was replaced by the Liberal Party. Scandal, corruption and economic problems weakened the coalition and worsened relations between ethnic groups as Albanians sought greater cultural and educational rights (such as the establishment of a university at Tetovo), and increased representation in the government, armed forces and police. The conflict in Kosovo, the flood of refugees and the conduct of the 1999 presidential elections exacerbated interethnic tensions. Smuggling and corruption were blamed by many Macedonians on Albanian mafias and in the Kosovo crisis stockpiles of weapons (many stolen from Albanian arsenals in 1997) intended for KLA were stored in villages on the border with Kosovo but many found their way into Albanian hands in Macedonia. This combination of ethnic tensions and organised crime was massively destabilising.

In the face of these developments, the central government in Skopje at first did nothing, accepting assurances that all activity was directed towards Kosovo and not against Macedonia. Some critics were bought off and some were intimidated into silence. The appearance of the NLA in January 2001 changed this, although the NLA was not supported by the two main ethnic Albanian political parties (Gournev 2003: 229–40). After several NLA attacks on Macedonian security forces, groups of Macedonians attacked and destroyed Albanian-owned shops, mosques and homes without interference from the security forces. Government forces and ethnic Albanian insurgents clashed sporadically between March and June 2001. The insurgency mercifully cost few lives compared to other conflicts in former Yugoslavia but was, nonetheless, formative (Philips 2004). This resurgence of violence so soon after the Kosovo crisis prompted immediate intervention by the United States, NATO and the EU in order to secure a ceasefire and peace agreement (International Crisis Group 2001). Leading Eurocrats, Javier Solana and Chris Patten, pushed for a negotiated settlement and discussions were held at Lake Ohrid involving Albanian and Macedonian representatives, and participants from the United States and the EU. The US and EU representatives made it clear that in the aftermath of Kosovo and the earlier wars they would not tolerate a further round of violence. The EU emphasised that without a peace agreement there would be no reconstruction aid and progress towards eventual membership would be indefinitely delayed. Confronting this level of external pressure and having looked into the abyss of civil war, the Albanian and Macedonian elites were predisposed to cooperate, not least because they were fully aware of how Tudjman's politics had frozen Croatia's relations with the EU.

The Ohrid Framework Agreement was signed on 13 August 2001. The agreement ended the conflict between the NLA and the security forces, laying out a consociational framework intended to improve the rights of ethnic Albanians. The government agreed to decentralise political power and conceded substantial cultural recognition to the Albanian minority, which agreed to abandon separatist demands and recognise all Macedonian institutions and the legitimacy of the Republic. The NLA were to disarm and hand over their weapons to NATO forces. Ohrid provided for altering the recognition of official languages: any language spoken by over 20 per cent of the population became co-official with the Macedonian language. Only the Albanian language satisfied this criterion (Brunnbauer 2002; Popetrevksi and Latifi 2004).

Implementation of the Ohrid Agreement was not trouble free (Analytica 2006; International Crisis Group 2011). A referendum (7 November 2004), largely organised and financed by the ethnic Macedonian diaspora, produced a low turn-out (26 per cent). A majority rejected the reforms but a turn-out under 50 per cent rendered the result invalid (Marko 2004). Implementation proceeded and despite some low-level violence the agreement held. Decentralisation laws giving greater local autonomy to ethnic Albanians took a long time to negotiate but once passed, and after elections in 2005, many central government functions were decentralised to 78 municipalities. Skopje, the capital, is composed of, and governed as, ten municipalities and boundaries were redrawn (some Macedonian politicians preferred gerrymandered) to ensure Albanian majorities. Politics was, and remains, dominated by ethnically based political parties representing ethnic Macedonians and Albanians. The July 2006 parliamentary elections were marked by a decisive victory of the centre-right party VMRO–DPMNE led by Nikola Gruevski. Gruevski's inclusion of the Albanian DPA in the government, rather than the Democratic Union for Integration-Party for Democratic Prosperity (DUI-PDP) coalition, which won the majority of Albanian votes, triggered protests in the Albanian community. Nevertheless, the spirit of Ohrid, though under strain, was sustained and a dialogue involving the DUI and the ruling VMRO–DMPNE began, inspired by a perceived need to avoid violence and a recognition that Macedonia had no long-term future outside the EU. Macedonia remained a deeply ethnically divided society and Ohrid entrenched these divisions, institutionalising them within a framework of consociational governance in which the EU played a major developmental role. UN Security Council Resolution 1371 sanctioned the EU taking over NATO's peacekeeping role (Operation Concordia) and the EU oversaw the implementation of the decentralisation and redistricting plan, during which the EU made it crystal clear that progress in Macedonia's relations with the EU depended on implementation (Pond 2006: 177–8; Rehn 2007: 1–4).

In terms of economic restructuring, the World Bank, for example, regards Macedonia as a relative success. Benefiting from a close relationship with the EU, an open economy has developed, with trade accounting for more than 90 per cent of gross domestic product (GDP). Economic growth has been steady but unspectacular, although the economic crisis has damaged Macedonia's prospects with unemployment around 37 per cent. Corruption and weaknesses in the legal system are serious and these represent major issues with the potential to derail negotiations with the EU. For instance, a German investigation into bribes paid by Deutsche Telekom (of about €24m) to Macedonian politicians during the 2005 privatisation, when a number of cabinet ministers (including the current prime minister) were employed as consultants by Analitico, which had a contract for SIM card services, resulted in a major political scandal. Moreover, the Macedonian judiciary is accused of passivity and secrecy, refusing to publish details of any ongoing enquiries. The grey (informal) market is estimated at close to 20 per cent of GDP and Macedonia is a major smuggling route into Central and Western Europe, so organised crime retains a significant presence. Moreover, little progress has been made on the issue of 'lustration' (removing from office those who are hostile to democracy and who have violated human rights) despite the unanimous passage in January 2008 of the Law on Lustration, which requires collaborators with the previous regime's secret services to leave office. The process is largely symbolic and the constitutional court limited the process to a time frame from 1944 to the end of 1991. In addition, it also forbad the publication of the names of former collaborators. At the time of our fieldwork, only *one* individual had been confirmed as a suspect under the 2008 law and this accusation was widely assumed to be politically motivated.

The dispute between Greece and Macedonia, dating from 1991, originally focused on the republic's flag, which incorporated the Vergina Sun, associated with the ancient Greek kingdom of Macedon. The flag was eventually changed but, more seriously, the Greek government charged Macedonia with harbouring territorial ambitions over northern Greece (Greece has a province named Macedonia) and is demanding a geographic qualifier (for example, 'northern' or 'upper'), which the Macedonian government rejects. For years Greece obstructed the development of relations between the EU (and NATO) and Macedonia, arguing the name 'Macedonia' belongs exclusively to Greece's history and culture. On the other hand, the Macedonian political elite has been willing to exploit difficulties with Greece for internal political reasons and has sometimes behaved provocatively as when, for example, Skopje airport was renamed 'Alexander the Great' in 2006 (Kavala International Airport in the Greek region of Macedonia is also named 'Alexander the Great') and when the authorities erected a statue of a mounted warrior in the centre of Skopje that bore more than a passing resemblance to Alexander the Great. The danger is that the name issue could turn into a frozen conflict despite pressure from the EU and the US for compromise. The UN has been facilitating talks since 1995 with no result and Macedonian efforts to persuade West European governments to pressure the Greek government to agree to Macedonia joining NATO while the name talks continued, backfired. The Commission's line is that the UN is the best forum for what is a bilateral issue unrelated to the enlargement process and has come around to the view that the Greek government is now keener than its Macedonian counterpart to find a compromise to what is regarded by many as a bizarre, typically 'Balkan' issue. The Slovenian government, one of Macedonia's strongest supporters in the EU appears to have become increasingly annoyed at the Macedonian position and privately Commission officials criticise the Macedonian government for being provocative. What is clear is that until the name issue is resolved further progress towards the EU is not possible. Despite this and many other difficulties, Macedonians themselves still expect to join the EU in 2015.

As with Slovenia and Croatia, Macedonia's accession to the EU enjoyed both popular endorsement and the highest strategic priority (Analytica 2005; CRPM 2007). Macedonia submitted its application for EU membership on 22 March 2004 at the Dublin summit and six months later began answering the European Union's Questionnaire exploring an applicant's capabilities and capacities for membership. The Questionnaire was an essay in member state-building:

> The issues covered ranged from consumer protection to prison management, from agricultural policy to the organisation of the judiciary. Macedonia's Department of European integration . . . was put in charge of mobilizing hundreds of civil servants across all ministries and public agencies to prepare responses that would run to many thousands of pages. Some of the questions had never before been asked in Macedonia. Institutional islands within a highly fragmented administration suddenly found themselves forced to articulate their role and justify their existence. In effect, the EU asked for an X-ray of the Macedonian state.
>
> (International Crisis Group 2006: 6)

By the end of January the government had prepared a 15,000-page response. Radmilla Sekerinska, the Deputy Prime Minister for European Integration, pointedly emphasised that 'answering the questionnaire amid the turmoil provoked by the resignation of the Prime Minister [over divisions in the coalition] . . . the election of a new government and a hotly debated [decentralization] referendum . . . all show that Macedonia's institutions can work – and achieve results – in extraordinary circumstances' (quoted in Pond 2006: 185). The Commission reviewed the answers and recommended candidate status, which the European Council granted on 17 December 2005, noting the progress made in satisfying the Copenhagen Criteria. Recognised as a consolidating democracy, Macedonia received EU aid under the PHARE programme. Macedonia was the first country in SEE to sign a Stabilisation and Association Agreement (SAA) on 9 April 2001, coming into force on 1 April 2004. On 6 September the government adopted its 'National Strategy for European Integration', a document that enjoyed near universal support (Analytica 2005). *The National Programme for the Adoption of the Acquis* (NPAA, April 2007) sets out the commitments and the requirements of both the SAA and the European Partnership and is meant to be tightly coordinated with the government's Annual Work Programme. The NPAA is monitored and regularly updated.

There is, therefore, a very high level of central activity designed to align Macedonia with the *acquis* such as the new methodology to align the budget and the NPAA and the December 2008 manual dealing with transposition of EU law into domestic legislation but serious weaknesses remain. These weaknesses stem from resource shortages, over-politicisation and a willingness to bypass formal procedures. The government's Annual Work Programme and the NPAA appear fairly well coordinated. The General Secretariat provides logistical support, records decisions and monitors implementation; the Legislative Secretariat, an independent technical service, provides legal advice, reviews all draft laws and secondary legislation; and the Secretariat for European Affairs (SEA) has overall responsibility for the process. Founded in June 2005, SEA is an autonomous expert body that monitors and reports on EU integration; it is led by a deputy prime minister. In contrast to the General and Legislative Secretariats, SEA developed slowly because of staff shortages (especially at senior levels), which reduced its political influence and weakens its effectiveness in vertical coordination; because of this, the deputy prime minister is frequently drawn into internal political battles. All ministries have a unit for integration issues but capacity is often weak: thirty-five working groups were created to consider law approximation but have become more concerned with the *acquis* chapters. Capacities are not evenly distributed 'and it seems tasks are performed by a small number of capable but overburdened people' (SIGMA 2009b: 8). Central state coordinating capacities have 'reached the point when they can become the backbone of the reforms that link important processes, such as the budget process, the policy-making process and the EU integration process' (SIGMA 2009b: 11). Ambitious programmes to develop central capacity, and develop the participation of civil society, are threatened by capacity weaknesses but the main problem was implementation which 'casts doubts about the capacity of the public administration and judiciary to ensure the appropriate implementation and enforcement of the EU acquis' (SIGMA 2009b: 6–7).

Progress on enlargement slowed with the French and Dutch rejection of the EU constitution, growing 'enlargement fatigue' and concern over its costs among member states (European Stability Initiative 2005a). Successive annual Progress Reports show that the Commission still entertains doubts about the scope and effectiveness of police and judicial reform, the extent of corruption and organised crime, cooperation with the ICTY and electoral violence. Nonetheless, support for EU membership remains high: 66 per cent (down from 76 per cent in 2006) believe that joining the EU would be a good thing, with 24 per cent being neutral (up from 14 per cent), although there is a sharp distinction between ethnic groups. Gallup found that 57 per cent of ethnic Macedonians support entry; the figure is 84 per cent for Macedonian Albanians. Indeed, joining is such a priority for this group that 67 per cent would be willing to give up the country's name, whereas 95 per cent of Macedonians reject giving up the name (Gallup 2009). Macedonia's progress was, despite the complexities of domestic politics and the process itself, a national goal and was seen by elites as a technocratic process of state formation, but as a result they tended to overlook or underestimate the difficulties involved (International Crisis Group 2006). In November 2005 the Commission estimated that of the 33 *acquis* chapters Macedonia would have no major difficulties with 10, further efforts would be needed on 5, 15 required considerable effort, 3 (free movement of goods, intellectual property rights and competition policy) would prove very hard to adopt, and 1 (environment) was judged totally incompatible with the *acquis*. Chapter 23 (Judiciary and Fundamental Rights) and Chapter 24 (Justice, Freedom and Security) were in the 'required considerable effort' category, and these are precisely the areas where the Commission has serious concerns and these two chapters alone could stifle progress (CEC 2005). Moreover, doubts have been raised about the quality of legislation. A survey found that between July and August 2008 parliament adopted 172 laws, of which 50 were totally new. In one session in August, 52 laws were adopted and the average time for adoption was 35–40 *seconds*. Adopted under an urgent business parliamentary procedure, 140 were proposed by a caretaker government that 'justified the use of this parliamentary procedure with the argument that most of these laws were needed for the EU integration process.' Laws made 'like mass-produced goods in an "assembly-line procedure"' undermine quality, legitimacy and implementation (SIGMA 2009a: 6). Membership by 2015 looks very optimistic indeed.

Europeanising governance?

State weakness (or strength, for that matter) 'is like an elephant: you cannot exactly define it, but you are sure that when you see it, you will recognize it' (Krastev 2002: 9). A familiar description of governance in SEE is of weak states 'struggl[ing] with distrust between ethnic groups, poor governance, corruption and criminality. Political passivity and dependence on external pressure are common characteristics. Political will – the capacity to generate internal drivers of reform – seems to be lacking' (Avery and Batt 2007: 1). Even Greece, a long-established state and EU member, suffers, as events in 2011 demonstrated, from chronic weaknesses in governance. The European Administrative Space (EAS) assumes convergence in governance when 'public administration operates and is managed on the basis of common European principles, rules and regulations uniformly enforced in the relevant territory' (Olsen 2002: 1). Subsequent chapters explore the national consequences of EU policies, but first we consider broad patterns of governance in our four cases.[9]

Measuring governance

The World Bank Governance Indicators (WGI) aggregate subjective views on governance derived from the public and private sectors, NGOs, experts and citizens, and commercial firms (Kaufmann *et al.* 2008). Perception data is used because it is widely available and because it distinguishes between the de facto and *de jure*, between what is supposed to happen and what actually happens, and what citizens believe to be happening. WGI's composite indicators are useful for broad cross-country comparison and the identification of broad trends.[10] The WGI permit both cross-country comparisons and comparisons over time, but should be used with caution because the margins of error of each country estimate remain non-trivial even though the margins of error have declined over time. The WGI suggest governance can change significantly, improving and deteriorating, in quite short periods of time (Kaufmann *et al.* 2008: 3).

The six indicators are: *voice and accountability* ('perceptions of the extent to which a country's citizens are able to participate in selecting their government, as well as freedom of expression, freedom of association, and a free media'); *political stability and the absence of violence* ('perceptions of the likelihood that the government will be destabilized or overthrown by unconstitutional or violent means, including politically motivated violence and terrorism'); *government effectiveness* ('perceptions of the quality of public services, the quality of the civil service and the degree of its independence from political pressures, the quality of policy formulation and implementation, and the credibility of the government's commitment to such policies'); *regulatory quality* ('perceptions of the ability of the government to formulate and implement sound policies and regulations that permit and promote private sector development'); *rule of law* ('perceptions of the extent to which agents have confidence in and abide by the rules of society, and in particular the quality of contract enforcement, property rights, the police, and the courts, as well as the likelihood of crime and violence'); and finally, *control of corruption* ('perceptions of the extent to which public power is exercised for private gain, including both petty and grand forms of corruption, as well as 'capture' of the state by elites and private interests') (Kaufmann *et al.* 2008: 7–8). The WGI project estimates have a mean of zero, with estimates ranging from –2.5 to +2.5.

In *voice and accountability* (Table 3.2a), Greece and Slovenia begin with a higher rating than Croatia and Macedonia, and Slovenia has a consistently higher rating than Greece, which did, however, manage to close the gap. Both are below the EU27 average. While Greece and Slovenia have slipped back on this indicator (as has the EU27) both Croatia and Macedonia have made significant progress over the period, albeit from a low starting point. Greece and Slovenia have high *political stability* (Table 3.2b) ratings, with Slovenia's being above the EU27 average even before it joined the EU, with the gap widening. Croatia has consistently made progress in contrast to Macedonia, which is perceived to have regressed somewhat. Slovenia and Croatia are closest to the EU27 average. In *government effectiveness* (Table 3.2c), Slovenia and Greece began with a comparable rating and although both improve, Slovenia pulls away. Croatia makes progress comparable to that of Slovenia but from a lower starting point; Macedonia's indicator remains negative

Table 3.2 a–f Estimating 'misfit' and 'convergence'

a) Voice and accountability	1996	2003	2009
Greece	0.72	0.99	0.88
Slovenia	1.10	1.16	0.99
Croatia	−0.34	0.61	0.56
Macedonia	−0.04	−0.10	0.13
EU 15/27	71.26	1.39	1.15

b) Political stability	1996	2003	2009
Greece	0.37	0.58	−0.06
Slovenia	1.03	1.14	0.87
Croatia	−0.10	0.35	0.60
Macedonia	0.22	−0.97	−0.22
EU 15/27	0.94	0.97	0.73

c) Government effectiveness	1996	2003	2009
Greece	0.83	0.82	0.61
Slovenia	0.81	1.07	1.16
Croatia	−0.06	0.37	0.64
Macedonia	−0.34	−0.26	−0.14
EU 15/27	1.08	1.72	1.12

d) Regulatory quality	1996	2003	2009
Greece	0.74	1.02	0.80
Slovenia	0.84	0.87	0.89
Croatia	0.16	0.39	0.55
Macedonia	−0.29	−0.26	0.32
EU 15/27	1.25	1.26	1.27

e) Rule of law	1996	2003	2009
Greece	0.94	0.77	0.64
Slovenia	0.87	0.92	1.11
Croatia	−0.56	0.06	0.22
Macedonia	−0.15	−0.57	−0.22
EU 15/27	1.57	1.53	1.17

f) Control of corruption	1996	2003	2009
Greece	0.38	0.57	0.12
Slovenia	1.05	0.84	1.06
Croatia	−0.59	0.06	0.03
Macedonia	−1.06	−0.59	−0.03
EU 15/27	1.69	1.72	1.06

Source: World Bank Governance Indicators.

despite very obvious improvement. The EU27 average rises and falls but, taking the period as a whole, the case closest to the EU27 average is Slovenia. The *regulatory quality* (Table 3.2d) indicators for Greece and Slovenia follow the same broad trajectory, with Croatia and Macedonia making substantial improvements and in Macedonia's case from a negative assessment. All are, however, below the EU27 average, which remains stable. Slovenia has the best indicator for the *rule of law* (Table 3.2e) and comes closest to the EU27 average due largely to the decline in the latter. Croatia has made substantial progress but remains some distance from Greece and the EU27 average. After an initial improvement, the indicator for Macedonia worsened and then recovered but rule of law is still perceived to be a greater problem here than in our other cases. Finally, Slovenia's record in *control of corruption* (Table 3.2f) is closest to that of the EU27 but this is due less to Slovenia's improvement than a worsening on the EU's part. Perceptions of Greece have worsened but not as fast as for the EU27. Croatia's record improved from a negative to positive perception whereas this indicator for Macedonia remains negative despite considerable improvement.

Averaging the governance indicators produces the following overall change between 1996 and 2009: Greece +0.285, Slovenia +0.06, Croatia +1.03 and Macedonia +0.18. It is tempting to ascribe these outcomes, at least in part, to the impact of conditionality. With so few data points it is impossible to draw hard-and-fast conclusions, but it is possible to identify some general trends. First, Slovenia, the latest member of the EU of this group, is closer to the EU average than is Greece, the oldest member; second, both Croatia and Macedonia, in general, have made progress in reducing the 'misfit' with the EU but from a low base. Third, the data, particularly on Greece, points to the continued influence of historical legacies. In Greece's case these historical legacies have been relatively unchallenged by critical junctures comparable in their intensity and pervasiveness to those experienced by Slovenia, Croatia and Macedonia as a result of Yugoslavia's break-up, and mediated by domestic elites under far less pressure to engage in transformative politics. A further factor is the continuation of relatively weak state enforcement capacities in the absence of both conditionality and Commission enforcement.

Perceptions of Europe

The Eurobarometer (EB) standard survey provides a useful snapshot of our four states' relationship with, and attitudes to, the EU and it found that 'the majority trend is for a decline in support for Europeanisation' (Eurobarometer 2008: 9). Perhaps the single most important perception is whether or not citizens believe their country has, or would benefit, from EU membership (Table 3.3).

With the exception of Macedonia, where respondents invariably rate the EU positively, respondents not only doubt the value of membership but are below the EU27 average. On the other hand, apart from Croatia, the others

Table 3.3 Evaluation of EU membership (2009)

	Membership of the EU is/would be a good thing	The country has/would benefit from membership of the EU	Tend to trust the EU	Very/fairly positive image of the EU
EU 27	53	56	47	45
Greece	45	64	55	45
Slovenia	48	64	50	50
Croatia	24	37	31	26
Macedonia	64	75	54	59

Source: Eurobarometer (2010) *Standard Eurobarometer 71*, Brussels: Directorate General for Communication.

(and Macedonia decidedly so) see their country benefiting from EU membership. EB71 shows that respondents, except in Croatia, tend to trust the EU more than the average; also, a near majority of Slovenes and a clear majority of Macedonians have a very/fairly positive image of the EU. Greeks' perceptions are around the average and Croats have a decidedly poor image of the EU.

In terms of trust (Table 3.4) Greeks are remarkably pro-EU, apart from the ECB, while Slovenes are closer to the EU average in the degree of trust they profess in EU institutions. Croats have a uniformly low level of trust and are particularly distrustful of the Commission, having become very distrustful very quickly. Macedonians have more in common with Slovenes and, like Greeks, retain a higher than average trust in the EU. Turning from trust to responsiveness (Table 3.5), Greeks had a generally low evaluation of the EU's responsiveness even before the eurozone crisis but, compared to the EU average, they saw their own government as even less responsive than the EU. Slovenes favourably evaluated their ability to influence domestic and EU institutions but are more confident of their domestic influence. Croats view domestic responsiveness similarly but, given their candidate status and the length of the process, it would be surprising if they (and the Macedonians) did not see the EU as unresponsive. Macedonians are unconvinced about the responsiveness of domestic institutions. Apart from the citizens of Slovenia, all respondents regard the EU as dictatorial, with Greece and Croatia well above the EU average in this regard. Not surprisingly, as in Croatia, a majority of Macedonians see the EU as imposing its views, but in fact 64 per cent seems surprisingly low given Macedonia's candidate status and the EU's highly visible role in Macedonia's recent history.

Eurobarometer 70 found that, generally speaking, enlargement from 15 to 27 members strengthened (48 per cent) rather than weakened the EU (36 per cent). A small majority of Greeks (53 per cent) and a substantial majority

Table 3.4 Degree of trust in EU and domestic institutions

Do you tend to trust the:	European Parliament	European Central Bank	European Commission	European Union
EU27	(52) 48	(50) 44	(47) 44	(50) 47
Greece	(61) 56	(51) 42	(57) 51	(60) 55
Slovenia	(60) 48	(63) 49	(58) 47	(66) 50
Croatia	(40) 38	(38) 37	(36) 14	(34) 31
Macedonia	(54) 45	(45) 42	(49) 43	(64) 54

Source: Eurobarometer (2009) *Standard Eurobarometer 70*, Brussels: Directorate General for Communication and Eurobarometer (2010) *Standard Eurobarometer 71*, Brussels: Directorate General for Communication. 2008 in parenthesis.

Table 3.5 Perceived responsiveness of EU and domestic institutions

My voice counts in:	My country	The EU	The EU imposes its views on our country (2008)
EU27	(48) 46	(31) 30	60
Greece	(28) 21	(34) 26	79
Slovenia	(61) 74	(41) 51	57
Croatia	(61) 63	(–) 32	85
Macedonia	(40) 48	(–) 24	64

Source: Eurobarometer (2009) *Standard Eurobarometer 70*, Brussels: Directorate General for Communication and Eurobarometer (2010) *Standard Eurobarometer 71*, Brussels: Directorate General for Communication. 2008 in parenthesis.

(62 per cent) of Slovenes (perhaps not surprisingly) believed enlargement was good for the EU. In contrast, the climate of opinion is broadly against further enlargement despite the commitments given by the EU: 39 per cent for and 42 per cent opposed in the EU and 40 per cent/57 per cent in Greece. In contrast, Slovenes favour further enlargement by 63 per cent to 31 per cent. Not surprisingly, Croats (by 60 per cent to 29 per cent) and Macedonians (85 per cent to 8 per cent) endorse further enlargement.

Taken in the round and allowing for specific circumstances (notably the case of Greece as this data deals with the situation prior to the eurozone crisis), this data shows that the EU is still regarded positively as something worth becoming part of. This does not, of course, preclude specific complaints, notably in the case of Greece and Croatia, and in all states there is often a perceived distance between the EU and the domestic, although this is not universal. All states do, however, tend to see the EU as to some degree dictatorial and 'anti-national', but what is also clear is that whatever the specific or general gripes about the EU, there is a recognition that the EU is the only game in town and that it is therefore better to be in rather than out. This suggests that domestic populations will bear the costs inherent in the sovereignty bargain.

Conclusions

One of this chapter's broad aims was to provide some conception of the misfit between our cases and the EU prior to embarking on the detailed case studies. We are, however, conscious of the need to avoid simplistic representations of misfit between our cases and the EU; we see our cases as specific instances of a more general process. This is the process whereby sovereignties, boundaries and identities are challenged by European integration while also enhancing state capacities and capabilities in negotiating, implementing and sustaining the necessary changes. This is an essentially national process, hence variation between states and policy sectors.

Transformative events such as the break-up of Yugoslavia or the Greek *metapolitefsi* reinforced movement towards (neo-)liberal capitalist democracy, a movement that becomes self-reinforcing with any reversal unlikely (Pierson 2004: 10). A decision to seek EU membership represents a threshold of great historical significance, but Europeanisation is slow-moving in some respects (the internalisation of values and norms) while fast-moving in others (changing in structures and processes). The critical junctures identified all involved an acceleration of Europeanisation whether or not they entailed an acceleration of MLG is less clear. The analysis of critical junctures often focuses on the immediate aftermath of shocks, rather than the downstream consequences, but the EU's engagement with Croatia and Macedonia in the enlargement process and the consequences of integration for Greece and Slovenia (as well as their attitude to enlargement) means institutions are not unchanged until the next critical juncture. Indeed, our focus on Europeanisation as a dynamic process is explicitly concerned with institutional development, and this forms the core of the policy chapters. The EU's prescription of norms, rules and processes in enlargement and integration, are intended to render alternative development paths unreachable and unthinkable. A decision to pursue membership and the EU's acceptance of this locks a country into a single development trajectory. This is why a juncture is critical. Europeanisation as path dependency aspires to establish a long-term enduring trajectory but 'A variable's effect cannot be predicted without an appreciation for when it appears within a sequence unfolding over time' (Pierson 2004: 67).

To avoid determinism, we analyse not event chains but event sequences, reflecting the historic and contemporary dynamic of European integration as an ongoing process subject to challenge. Institutional development after a critical juncture is not static. Boundary creation and transcendence coincided during the 1990s and are integral to Europeanisation:

> The long struggle to create a nation-state – of which the Yugoslav wars could be seen as the last phase – had taken the entire twentieth century. The irony was just as this struggle ended, economic and political changes at the international level threw the very idea of the nation state into question.
>
> (Mazower 2001: 141)

The EU was central to economic and political changes and the coincidence of boundary creation and transcendence. If we want to see Europeanisation's impact on domestic politics as simple cause and effect, the links in a causal chain must be strong and obvious but our data, while showing that these links exist, also show their variability in scope and intensity. It is therefore safest to abandon causal chains in favour of event sequences.

Enlargement and integration involve the impact of EU policies on a state's governance and attempts by states to influence EU policies. Despite variations, the general direction points towards decentralisation and a more complex polity, the enhancement of strategic steering capacities and,

> Assuming a lack of policy fit . . . domestic actors favouring similar policies will use EU policy requirements as a resource to strengthen their position in the national political conflicts. The EU policy demands may help overcome the resistance of formal and factual domestic veto players that would otherwise have blocked the policy reform because of the adjustment costs they accrue.
>
> (Héritier 2005: 200)

This seems sensible and reasonable as a general observation but does not account for sectoral policy differences in states at different stages of involvement with the EU where external pressures might strengthen reformers or opponents.

Héritier's Europeanisation East is profoundly influenced by the initial conditions (marketisation, democratisation, accession) that expand the scope and type of policies, as well as the processes involved (more top-down, more tightly controlled and monitored). Héritier argues, 'the EU plays an important role by reinforcing and accelerating transition to democracy and market economies. It acts as "a conduit", giving transition a certain shape' (Héritier 2005: 204). This contrasts with Europeanisation West where 'European' institutions were in place (Anderson 2002: 793–822). Europeanisation East is encompassing because of the range of policies and the degree of monitoring. The sanctions available to the EU over existing member states are fewer. Europeanisation East is more one-way, whereas Europeanisation West gives member states a role in formulating and developing the policies they will be required to implement, and policy initiatives frequently come from member states who seek to negotiate a more favourable position. With Europeanisation East, the opposite is the case. Enlargement and integration are separate but connected processes underpinned by a common normative agenda, but

> The Union's conditionality principle, defining the conditions that will make the administration of applicant countries compatible with the EU standards and able to implement the *acquis*, gives the most detailed guide to EU preferences . . . While the convergence criteria have become more

precise over time [particularly so in the case of SEE], the administrative obligations of EU membership are still not well specified.

(Olsen 2002: 8)

It is not a question of imposing a common European model, because none exists, but articulating a normative model coupled with insistence on reforms (greater democracy, transparency and subsidiarity, improving policy impact and legitimacy) constitutive of EU membership. The Commission's concept of good governance stressed openness, participation, accountability, effectiveness and coherence to bring civil society and European institutions closer in a 'transnationalised' policy agenda (CEC 2001a). National governance is a repository for national sentiments. The EU has shown little interest in, and has little capacity for, direct or deep intervention in governance. There are no governance *acquis* and member states jealously guard their autonomy (Scharpf 2001; Sloat 2003; Curtin and Wessel 2005). This is the contrast between the general and the specific, the declaratory and the actual. It is extremely difficult to track a causal relationship between EU incentives and change because of the 'the interaction between multi-level actors, perceptions, interests, different rewards and sanctions, temporal factors, institutions and policy compliance' (Hughes *et al.* 2005: 3).

With respect to an EU governance model there has been no critical juncture, transformative event or implementation crisis to stimulate greater EU or Commission engagement. As suggested, the eurozone crisis may constitute such a juncture, although Olsen argues that

administrative convergence is more likely to follow from attractiveness than from imposition. Convergence is also more likely to be an artefact of substantive policies than the result of a coherent European administrative policy. If so, convergence could be expected to be incremental and putting constraints on national administrative solutions, rather than generating a full-scale exemplary model.

(2002: 6)

This implies that convergence is most likely at the sectoral, not national, level. It is here that pressures for convergence (policy transfer, learning and emulation, and so on) and structural change (as a result of, for example, cohesion policy or cross-border issues) are most likely to be felt. Membership (actual or aspirational) is itself a convergence pressure, but adaptation to Europe remains a national phenomenon and

European-level developments have not dictated convergence on a single form of administration [as opposed to regime]. In the Union there has been no support for imposing a unitary solution. Sector specific policies and court decisions have generated change. They have constrained the structural options available, yet they have created limited convergence.

(Olsen 2002: 7)

This will be explored further in the policy chapters.

Isomorphism restricts cross-country comparison, a restriction amplified by the countries' different relationships with the EU but macro-patterns of adjustment are influenced by the micro-politics of implementation, which are themselves influenced by history. Variation flows from the nature of the state's relationship with the EU and the conditions prevailing at the start of that relationship. This is why the sectoral case studies are so important: they permit variation to be explored at the meso- and micro-levels. There are differences between Greece, which joined the EU in 1981 and was subject to no formal conditionality, Slovenia, subject to the regime that governed the fifth enlargement, and Croatia and Macedonia, which were (and are) subject to far more intensive and intrusive conditionality over a longer period of time. The conditionality applied to Croatia and Macedonia differs markedly in intensity and intrusiveness from that applied to Slovenia, which in turn was far more extensive and intensive than Greece's. Each subsequent conditionality regime was a response to the preceding one, differing country conditions, and different political imperatives operating in the EU and its member states. Europeanisation has macro-effects on governance and national policy-making, but pressures to converge are filtered by national differences bringing variation in impact. We now turn to the sectoral manifestations of this.

4   Cohesion

Introduction

This chapter examines adaptation to the cohesion and regional policy *acquis* in Greece, Slovenia, Croatia and Macedonia. Cohesion policy is quintessentially multi-level and is the foundational case for MLG theorising, which is now routinely applied to other policies (Piattoni 2010). The chapter addresses three key issues. The first is the effect of engagement with the EU on both domestic political structures and modes of governance, together with the transfer of 'European' norms (for example, the encouraging of participation) into centralised polities. This is done via the capacity bargain, which represents a specific sectoral adaptation as part of the wider process of engagement with the EU. Second, it examines the transfer of the cohesion and regional policy template into different national contexts to explore the modalities of adaptation and the similarities and differences generated. Of particular importance is the degree to which power is (or is not) redistributed within the policy sector in each country and especially the degree to which civil society becomes an active participant and counterweight to the core executive. Finally, it considers the extent of convergence on a common 'European' model of governance that emphasises, *inter alia*, regionalisation, partnership and programming. The main focus is, therefore, on the internal politics of the policy network generated by the capacity bargain and the possibilities of movement towards EU governance preferences where these are challenged by the polity's history and traditional modes of governance.

Cohesion policy's purpose is to reduce socio-economic disparities between and within countries. Danuta Hübner, the Commissioner for Regional Policy, told a conference in Zagreb that cohesion 'is perhaps the most concrete manifestation of the solidarity which underpins the process of European integration' (CEC 2007b: 3). As a *redistributive* policy it addresses relations between broad categories of actors and, although it impacts at a higher level than the individual, cohesion is concerned with 'haves and have nots'. Resources are transferred from the wider Community for use in clearly specified situations; much of the politics generated is concerned with these specificities. Winners tend to be concentrated; losers are more diffuse, with

Instrument	Governance requirements	Application
Integrated Mediterranean Programme	partnership programming	Greece 1985-1992
ERDF ESF EAGGF	partnership programming regionalization	Greece 1989 → Slovenia 2004 →
Cohesion Fund	partnership	Greece 1994 → Slovenia 2004 →
PHARE OBNOVA SAPARD ISPA	decentralization	Slovenia 1992-2003 Croatia 2004-2006 Macedonia 1996-2006
EDIS	decentralization	Slovenia 2004-2006 Croatia 2005 → Macedonia2005 →
IPA	decentralization partnership programming	Croatia 2007 → Macedonia2007 →

Figure 4.1 Pre- and post-accession cohesion policy instruments

the distribution often being justified by a normative appeal to an ethic such as social justice or solidarity (Lowi 1964: 690–1). Policy instruments (Figure 4.1) include the European Regional Development Fund (ERDF), which applies to member states and the IPA for candidate states, which is intended to mimic cohesion policy, and is designed to help accession countries prepare for managing policy after accession. Programme development and implementation are national competencies conditioned by EU-mandated governance principles and requirements. Cohesion is a redistributive policy with territorial implications; Hooghe (1996) found substantial variation in MLG *specifics* within states. There is a vast literature on cohesion and its effects on governance and implications for the organisation of territory and the state (for example, Bache 2008; Bruszt 2008; Baum 2002; Brusis 2002, 2005; Glenn 2004; Hughes *et al*. 2005; Jacoby 2004; Kettunen and Kungla 2005; Marek and Baun 2002; O'Dwyer 2006; Sturm and Dieringer 2005), and Piattoni provides a broad survey of this literature and its political consequences (2010: 102–32).[1]

National variation can be explained by the prior pattern of territoriality, the government's role in controlling centrally the flow of EU (and non-EU) resources, and the resilience of historical patterns governance (Hughes *et al*. 2004, 2005). Chapter 22 *acquis* are framework and implementing regulations. They define rules for drawing up, approving and implementing structural and cohesion funds within each country. Programmes are negotiated with the Commission but implementation is the member state's responsibility. This requires a legislative framework to permit multi-annual programming at national and regional level, an institutional framework designating and establishing institutions at national and regional levels, plus an implementation system with a clear definition of tasks and responsibilities. The institutional framework requires interministerial coordination, and the engagement and consultation of a broad range of actors in partnerships preparing and implementing programmes. This all depends on the appropriate administrative capacity. Programming requires the preparation of a National Strategic Reference Framework and Operational Programmes, including *ex-ante* evaluations. This constitutes a substantial governance load and a capacity bargain of considerable significance.

The Single European Act (1986) gave cohesion policy a treaty base and in 1989 reform of the structural funds placed the European Regional Development Fund (ERDF), the European Social Fund (ESF) and parts of the European Agricultural Guarantee and Guidance Fund (EAGGF) into a single policy framework. This had a significant regional component and, reflecting this, the EU developed the NUTS classifications for subnational territory. The *Nomenclature des Unités Territoriales Statistques* classification system was adopted in 1988, becoming a Regulation (1059/2003) in 2003. NUTS 1 were groupings of regions; NUTS 2 were regions; NUTS 3 and 4 were subdivisions of regions; in 2004 NUTS 4 became Local Administrative Units 1 (LAU 1) and NUTS 5 became LAU 2. Table 4. 1 gives the NUTS divisions for our cases.

The *acquis* does not specify structures, but a country must agree a NUTS classification with the Commission; these constitute a major tool for the standardisation of policy. NUTS 2 is particularly important because these are defined (using common criteria) by member states for regional policy purposes and are often existing territorial-governmental divisions. Despite the Commission's aim of ensuring regions of comparable size at the same NUTS

Table 4.1 Multi-level governance and territoriality: NUTS

	NUTS level:				
Population (000s)	(3–7m)	(0.8–3m)	(0.15–0.8)		
	Country	Macro-regions	Statistical regions	Local administrative unit	
NUTS Level	1	2	3	LAU 1	LAU 2
Greece	4	13	51	1034	6130
Slovenia	1	2	12	58	210
Croatia	1	3	21	–	546
Macedonia	1	1	8	84	1776

Source: http://ec.europa.eu/eurostat/ramon/nuts/home_regions.en.html (accessed 19 November 2009).

level, regions exist that differ in population, reflecting national conditions. In 1991 the Cohesion Fund was established to aid member states with a GDP of less than 90 per cent of the Community average; this was not subject to the principles underpinning cohesion policy until 2007. Cohesion policy therefore classifies territory, defines access to resources and reconstitutes internal boundaries.

Increased funding was accompanied by governance changes: three principles introduced in 1989 – *regionalisation, partnership* and *programming* (hereafter, RPP) – have major implications for governance. *Regionalisation* (entails the vertical organisation of territory with funds administered regionally, usually NUTS 2), *partnership* (requires funds be administered by actors from different organisations and different territorial levels) and *programming* (requires actors to work cooperatively in partnerships for three to seven years); these principles regulate relations and stimulate new ways of working. The result was a uniform regulatory regime, grounded on the partnership principle and was intended to improve coordination (and create networks) involving central and subnational government and civil society (Hooghe 1996: 1–27; Thieleman 2000: 181–97). In 1999 hitherto permissive regulations dealing with the coordination of actors were tightened when the involvement of subnational governments (in programming, as part of the managing authority, and in programme approval) became mandatory.

Partnership did not eliminate hierarchy in central-local relations but the challenge it posed made the 'steepness' of the hierarchy critical (Long 2003). Engagement does not necessarily constitute empowerment but multi-level networks, in which actors confront the preferences of other actors, requires the exchange of resources. The result, as Ansell *et al.* demonstrate, is a very complex and demanding political process (1997: 347–75). These changes did not prescribe a legal-constitutional framework but implied, to put it no stronger, a normative dimension to the exercise of governance articulated via comparable institutions for management and implementation.

Enlargement triggered further changes. In 1999 new instruments were introduced. PHARE (Poland and Hungary: Aid for Economic Restructuring) and the Special Accession Programme for Agricultural and Rural Development (SAPARD) focused on economic and social cohesion, and developing the institutional and administrative capacities and capabilities necessary to access and absorb the structural funds. The Instrument for Structural Policy for Pre-Accession (ISPA) funded environmental and infrastructural investment as a precursor to the cohesion funds. In January 2007 PHARE, SAPARD and ISPA were replaced by the Instrument for Pre-Accession Assistance (IPA). IPA had four components: transitional assistance and institution building (Component 1), cross-border cooperation (Component 2), regional development (Component 3), human resource development (Component 4) and rural development (Component 5). An important feature of IPA is the Decentralised Implementation System (DIS), under which (once accreditation has been secured from the Commission), planning, management and evaluation becomes the responsibility of national authorities, with the Commission exercising *ex ante* evaluation. *Ex ante* evaluation involves the Commission identifying and appraising disparities and gaps, the potential for development, and future goals and results. DIS is a key driver of Europeanisation and also stimulates network governance and regionalisation. DIS is a key indicator of Europeanisation because, prior to DIS, funds were centrally managed and the Commission was closely involved. Accreditation signals the Commission's belief that a state is on the path of creating the capabilities and capacities to sustain the duties and obligations of membership and is therefore of great significance.

Prior to IPA, the RPP principles were not part of the pre-accession instruments but the demands of the enlargement process encouraged their de facto adoption. IPA was designed to mimic cohesion policy so that candidates could develop the institutions and processes they would need after accession. This change reflects the failure of some of the 2004 enlargement countries to be fully prepared, and the change had implications for the scope and scale of Europeanisation and multi-level governance. Under IPA, DG Regio is responsible for the scope of Components 3 and 4, which aimed at developing the management systems necessary for post-accession funds. Component 1 is obviously linked to Components 3 and 4 and the horizontal aspects of MLG. DG Enlargement is, overall, responsible for pre-accession aid.

The literature identifies the prior pattern of territorial organisation as a critical influence on MLG. Particularly relevant is the finding that governments in centralised states could serve as 'gatekeepers', neutralising the development of multi-level structures and more pluralistic power structures. The 2004 enlargement (which included Slovenia) enabled close attention to be paid to whether or not the Commission was willing (or able) to push the development of MLG. The principle of subsidiarity, when coupled with regionalisation, enhances the role of subnational authorities, and Chapter 22 requires states to implement NUTS and create regional administrations. Initially, the Commission preferred democratically elected governments with financial and administrative autonomy, but under the pressures of enlargement opted instead for the reinforcement of central capacity (Bailey and De Propris 2002; Hughes *et al.* 2004, 2005). Regionalisation is intimately influenced by a country's history and extant power structure, as well as by engagement with the EU, so there will be a substantial variation between states and, while the Commission might want a significant regional tier, it has no power to impose one. Where they existed, regions seldom enjoyed autonomy, so paradoxically decentralisation was reliant on action by the centre (Grabbe 2001; Brusis 2002; Mark and Baun 2002).

Although suggestive, the experience of CEE is not directly transferable as these were more capable and effective states. Other important influences were the recognition of the weakness of subnational government in SEE and the concern of member states about the cost of further enlargement, which encouraged a concentration on the centre (interview, DG Enlargement, 31 March 2009). Cohesion policy is central to Europeanisation and there is an uneven but ever-present trend towards MLG, which, while not entirely due to the EU, in the cases considered here the EU's role is critical. Major differences between our cases' exposure to, and experience of, cohesion policy, as well as the policy's evolution, renders comparison difficult, a difficulty compounded further by historical legacies and administrative traditions. However, all have in common the lack of a regional governance tradition and a tradition of national-sectoral development policy that indicates considerable misfit and downward pressure to change. Policy contours are set by the EU but implemented by national governments, so leaving considerable room for variation.

Greece

Centralisation is deeply embedded in the Greek polity. Despite long exposure and considerable pressure to change the polity has proved resilient in resisting the 'good' governance effects of cohesion (Featherstone 2005: 223–41). A significant difference between Greece and our other cases is the longevity of Greece's engagement with structural and cohesion policy. It is necessary to provide some background to this.

The Integrated Mediterranean Programmes (IMPs) created in 1985 introduced regionalisation, programming and partnership. Territorially, they led to the creation of six regions (whose functions largely were confined to monitoring the IMPs). Thirteen peripheries (NUTS 2 regions) were created in 1986, which took over management and planning at the regional level in 1989. Greek IMPs were extensions of the centre under the then Ministry of National Economy (MNE) and their emphasis was on the speedy absorption of funds. They lacked resources and expertise, these being controlled by the ministries. The IMPs set the pattern that persists today: elements of decentralisation stimulated by the EU but dominated by the centre (Bianchi 1992: 47–70; Papageorgiou and Verney 1992: 139–61; Verney 1994: 166–80; Ioakimidis 1996: 342–66).

Weaknesses, revealed in part by the Greek handling of the IMPs, prompted the Commission to tighten up procedures. The 1988 reform of the structural funds involved major changes in programming and improving the quality of inputs from subnational actors. The 1st Community Support Framework (1989–93, 1st CSF) was highly complex, with 25 centrally managed programmes with implementation left to subnational bodies who managed the 12 sectoral and 13 regional Operating Plans (OPs). Again, the focus was on the centre and the rapid absorption of funds. In the 2nd CSF (1994–99), the Commission advocated the creation of structures independent of the existing public administration, allied to the creation of transparent procedures and the provision of adequate resources to develop the necessary capacity. The 2nd CSF coincided with the implementation of the Kapodistria Plan. Law 2539 (1997) created 13 regions (peripheries) containing 54 prefectures divided into municipalities and communes. The 441 municipalities and 5382 communities were merged into 900 municipalities and 133 communes. Law 2647 (1998) transferred a number of responsibilities from central to local government. The prior managing and monitoring structures were unchanged but were coupled to (variable) improvements in the quality of policy-making. The key relationship was between the Commission and the Greek government, which excluded subnational structures and actors. Non-state actors were coopted by their patron ministries and the regional OPs were largely devoid of civil society engagement (Paraskevopoulos 2005: 445–70). Change, therefore, favoured centralism. Under the 3rd CSF (2000–06) the Commission and the (now) Ministry of Economy and Finance (MEF) favoured a depoliticised and technocratic process to minimise 'external' (i.e. party-political and patron-client) influences.

Institutions

The Greek government was keen to bring programme-managing authorities into the public administration. This was agreed by the Commission which, however, insisted on approving the new management authorities, and improving monitoring and coordination. Change was contained within the ambit of MEF. The 3rd CSF managing authority was the same MEF unit responsible for the two previous CSFs, albeit augmented in resources and personnel. The OP managing authorities were organised along identical lines, invariably dominated by reallocated civil servants, but civil society (and especially private sector) involvement did increase.

While the EU determines both policy content and instruments it plays no direct role in the domestic politics of cohesion (interview, West Macedonia Development Company, 2 April 2008). Generally, interviewees were favourably disposed to the EU; some felt the Commission could be too intrusive but relations with the EU were more positive than a decade earlier (interview, Ministry of the Economy and Finance, 11 January 2008). After 2000 the Commission disengaged from the domestic policy process but remained important ('this is where the money comes from') but 'is no longer involved in implementation . . . it monitors and watches things' (interview, Federation of Greek Industries, 15 January 2008). Policy content was shaped by domestic actors but this caused some difficulties as Greek planners 'are not encouraged to think strategically' (interview, Ministry of the Economy and Finance, 16 January 2008).

Interviewees stressed centralisation. There had been, one suggested, *no* significant shift to 'bottom-up' operation because at this level 'organisations lack both the information and competence' and so were seldom influential no matter the degree of participation (interview, Institute of Labour, 12 February 2008). Ministries and, to a lesser degree, regions were the most influential, with MEF the most significant institution but 'the social and economic and local partners influence their decisions . . . They are involved planning . . . monitoring the implementation of the programmes and, in some cases, they are themselves the final beneficiaries of the programmes' (interview, Ministry of the Economy and Finance, 11 January 2008). MEF retained its gate-keeping and coordination role throughout the changes of the 1990s, many of which (for example, programming) *strengthened* its position. An interviewee involved with the ROP for Western Macedonia argued 'The essence of central programming is the creation of the overall programming architecture. MEF monopolised this . . . line ministries [and] the regions are able to influence only the allocation of funding' (interview, 21 March 2008). Regions were isolated from the Commission by MEF; municipalities were important because they were elected and were closest to the policy problems 'but operate according to different [i.e. party political] criteria' which meant that they were often 'granted projects without having the necessary resources and capacity for managing and monitoring (interview, Ministry of Economy and Finance, 13 February 2008). A Ministry of Development civil servant, closely involved with the Commission and the regions, agreed there was 'extensive central coordination'. This was not, however, a conspiracy but reflected the regions' capabilities and despite their increasing proficiency 'the management framework is much more complicated and the result is a substantial learning lag' (interview, Ministry of Development, 17 January 2008). An interviewee at the regional level complained that in order to justify their role 'domestic policy-makers often add too many processes and restrictions on the policy delivery system, which becomes too complicated' (interview, Development Company of Western Macedonia, 22 May 2008).

Successive iterations increased policy complexity and reinforced the centre. We were told that at regional level there was little partnership: 'What is actually happening is that there is a state institution – the region – which collects demands coming from the social [partners] and subnational actors' transmitting them to the centre. This, 'Generally speaking this is the standard pattern of partnership in Greece' (interview, Institute of Labour, 12 February 2008). Moreover,

> The allocation of competences is not always clear, there are also overlapping responsibilities. The procedures are complex [and] complexity permits the participation of more actors [but] complexity is not solely the outcome of EU regulations . . . national legislation . . . adds a second layer of complexity.
>
> (Interview, Ministry of Economy and Finance, 13 February 2008)

Policy change and pluralisation has created complexity, which necessitated greater central coordination that limited the influence of subnational and civil society actors despite their being brought into participation. The net result was 'that the main sectoral and regional actors were given the opportunity to 'fill in the details' in a centrally defined framework and as a result 'A more centralised and complicated system is being built' (interview, Regional Operating Programme, Central Macedonia, 21 March 2008).

As a consequence, 'the social partners are presented with faits accomplis'. This was a distributive policy and conflict, and mutual suspicion were, and remain, rife; 'it is very hard to find common ground among the social partners, many of which see themselves as representative of mutually antagonistic interests' (interview, Institute of Labour, 12 February 2008). The inclusion of social partners and civil society in managing authorities 'does not automatically lead to more cooperation. All the same, there was more opportunity to "learn from each other" and to find common ground' (interview, Federation of Greek Industries, 15 January 2008). Consensus was achieved easily nationally but below this level 'there is no genuine consensus between the social partners regarding development priorities and the ensuing actions' (interview, Institute of Labour, 12 February 2008).

MEF was the prime mover in the development of *The National Strategic Reference Framework 2007–2013* (NRSF) and in the coordination of OPs. This involved relevant line ministries and subnational entities, and promoted enhanced multi-level partnership working. The NSRF was developed 'within the framework of a partnership stronger than the previous period':

> The principle of partnership was fully applied in the NSRF elaboration process and was based on the principle of transparency. Partners' participation . . . was based on national and regional representation of policy fields and of social groups, full coverage of policies and special horizontal issues developed in the NSRF, according to the requirements of the General Regulation.
>
> (Ministry of Economy and Finance 2007: 3)

Planning began in June 2004. The Inter-ministerial Coordination and Policy-setting Committee for Development Programming was chaired by the MEF and was 'the key mechanism for setting the main NSRF policy framework'. The NRSF Task Force Programme Planning Groups (PPGs) liaised between ministries and regions in drafting proposals and supported the ministries and regions in NSRF and Operational Programme planning (Ministry of Economy and Finance 2007, 3–4). PPGs were staffed by personnel from managing authorities, ministries, regions and experts. Between 2004 and 2006 the NSRF evolved by 'constructive cooperation [. . .] wide consensus [and] broad participation in all the phases of the strategic planning' (Ministry of Economy and Finance 2007: 5). This was also extended to monitoring and imple-mentation.

The network

Greece has enjoyed considerable exposure to, and engagement with, cohesion policy and the evidence indicates two long-term developments: improvement in the quality of programming and a broadening of participation. However, has power been redistributed? Our evidence is that the central ministry retained a major gate-keeping and coordinating role. Line ministries were engaged in the planning process on issues specifically and directly related to their remit while regions have influenced the distribution of funding between OPs. OP budgets were decided through a process of interministerial bargaining with the prime minister acting as arbiter. The centre established the framework in which regional and sectoral actors operated, essentially confining them to the details of the policy. Ministerial (i.e. non-MEF) and regional planning agencies lacked the resources, technical capacities and political support to challenge MEF and play a strategic role and, in effect, regional planning was 'devolved' to the managing authorities, which were controlled by MEF. This system might be described as 'arm's length but hands on'; the 2007–13 system does not differ substantially from its predecessors and change *strengthened* centralisation in an increasingly complicated and complex process, characterised by opaque responsibility and bureaucratic decision-making.

Policy remains centralised and dominated by MEF (Figure 4.2). Centralisation means regions are weak, a weakness compounded by a long-standing lack of capacity and capability; the situation worsened after 2007 as they no longer plan and administer OPs and because managing authorities are controlled by the ministry. Moreover, there is no evidence of a coherent dialogue between social partners and civil society; rather the state arbitrates between competing subnational and societal actors.

Greece has a very complex network reflecting the longevity of engagement with the EU and the pressures of domestic politics. The core of the network, however, is composed of relatively few organisations engaged in a permanent relationship focusing on strategic issues. Core actors come from three groups: peak organisations, bodies responsible for monitoring and managing OPs, and central ministries, of which the Ministry of Economy and Finance is the most significant. Some non-governmental bodies have become central actors in the network, notably the Federation of Greek Industries. The partnership principle, so significant in the 2nd CSF, generated the monitoring committees that played a not insignificant consultative role but the government-Commission relationship was most significant. Over time, participation has increased and under the 3rd CSF managing authorities did have a decision-making role but this had limits. These changes indicate 'The system is opening up in response to Commission pressure and the complexity of policy' (interview, Federation of Greek Industries, 15 January 2008). Despite its central coordinating role, or perhaps precisely because of that role, the MEF sees itself as a participant in a network that could not function under central direction; the path to success was via synergies and cooperation (interview, 16 January 2008). Nevertheless, pluralisation has limits. Two in particular were cited: weakness in the regions and municipalities (discussed later); the second was the 'Greek' way of doing policy:

> There is a tradition of 'radial cooperation' with the state: each individual actor advances his own demands, and there is no coherent articulation

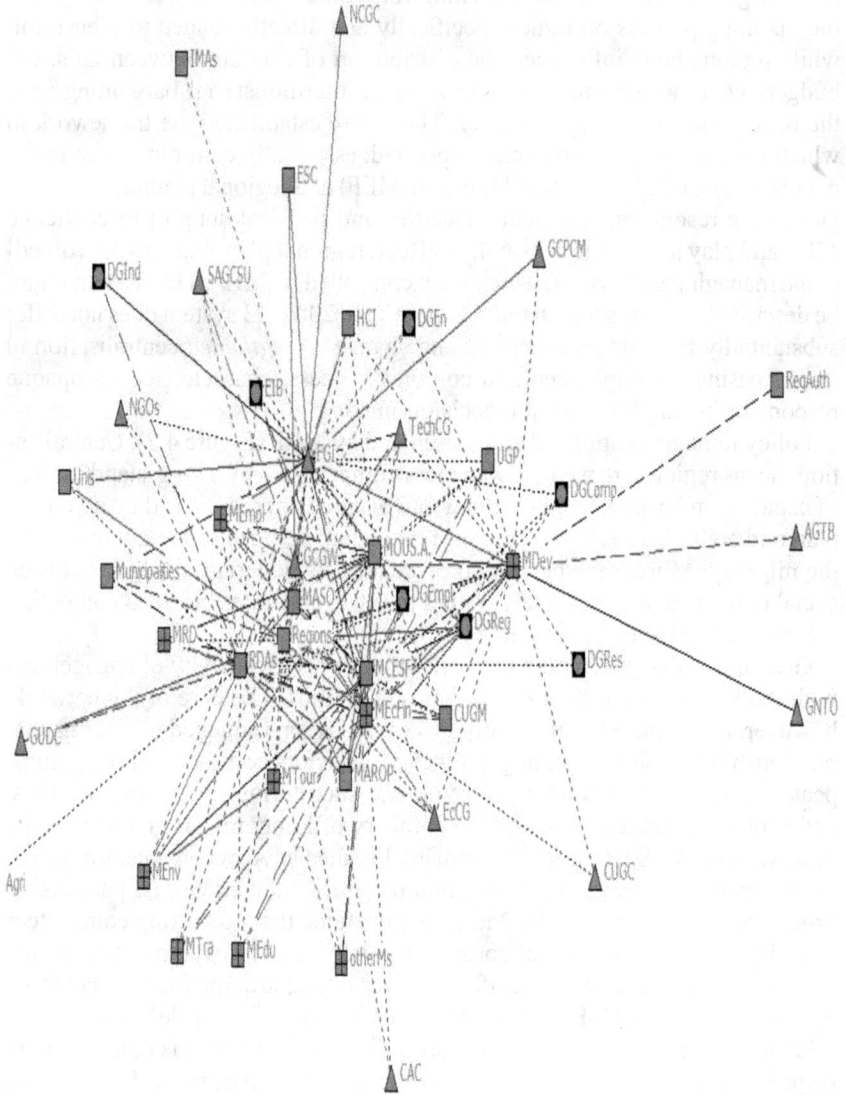

Figure 4.2 The cohesion network: Greece

Organisation	SNA abbreviation
Association of Greek Tourist Business	AGTB
Pan-Hellenic Confederation of Unions of Agricultural Cooperatives	CAC
European Commission	CEC
Central Union of Greek Chambers of Commerce	CUGC
Central Union of Greek Municipalities	CUGM
DG Competition	DGComp
DG Employment	DGEmpl
DG Energy	DGEn
DG Industry	DGInd
DG Regional Policy	DGReg
DG Research	DGRes
Economic Chamber of Greece	EcCG
European Investment Bank	EIB
Economic and Social Committee	ESC
Federation of Greek Industry	FGI
General Confederation of Greek Workers	GCGW
General Confederation of Professionals, Craftsmen and Merchants	GCPCM
Greek National Tourism Organisation	GNTO
Greek Union of Development Companies	GUDC
Hellenic Centre for Investment	HCI
Intermediate Management Agencies	IMAs
Managing Authorities Regional Operational Programme	MAROP
Managing Authorities Sectoral Operations	MASO
Special Service for the Coordination and Monitoring of ESF actions	MCESF
Ministry of Development	MDev
Ministry of Economy and Finance	MEcFin
Ministry of Education	MEdu
Ministry of Employment	MEmpl
Ministry of Environment, Physical Planning and Public Works	MEnv
Management Organisation Unit S.A.	MOUS.A.
Ministry of Rural Development	MRD
Ministry of Tourism	MTour
Ministry of Transport	MTra
National Confederation of Greek Commerce	NCGC
Non-Governmental Organisations	NGOs
Other Ministries	otherMs
Regional Development Agencies	RDAs
Regulatory authorities	RegAuth
Regions	Regions
Supreme Administration of Greek Civil Servants' Unions	SAGCSU
Technical Chamber of Greece	TechCG
Union of Greek Prefectures	UGP
Universities	Unis

> of collective interests. Moreover, existing collective organisations are
> captured by political and/or particular interests [and] many participants do
> not possess the necessary economic, organisational, human resources . . .
> (Interview, Institute of Labour, 12 February 2008)

Competition, capture and capability weaknesses tend to shift influence towards network actors possessing an agenda, autonomy and resources, which almost inevitably means the centre and its clients. Participation was described as a 'travesty' in terms of its effects on planning, although there were beneficial effects for implementation (interview, Regional Operating Programme, Central Macedonia, 21 March 2008). Network activity is profoundly influenced by control of information. Management committees, for instance, convene rarely and OPs are amended not by discussion but by the president circulating a draft decisions on which members are asked to comment within twenty days or less. Once a majority of voting members had expressed a view, this was construed as a decision, hence the judgement that 'participation is all but a fiction' (interview, Institute of Labour, 12 February 2008).

One of our interviewees, an academic expert on regional policy, a former OP head and member of an ROP secretariat now working in the private sector, stressed the relative unimportance of the regions. Their *existence* reflected EU demands but their *form* was a national adaptation reflecting increased complexity (interview, Egnatia SA, 4 April 2008). The post-1996, and especially post-2000, rules, norms and management structures were an important contribution to this as they were intended to weaken political interference. As a result, 'a two-tier system is emerging. Some have responded . . . some have not and are lagging behind' (interview, Ministry of Economy and Finance, 16 January 2008). A participant with wide experience of OPs felt that underlying power relationships were unchanged despite increased participation. Newer actors were, however, learning (some rapidly) but lacked the resources and capabilities to fully engage with the network (interview, Federation of Industries of Northern Greece, 4 May 2008). A senior Ministry of Economy and Finance civil servant believed the network's culture was cooperative, not conflictual, but implementation remained problematic. This, along with the persistence of bureaucratic sloth, was mitigated to some degree by the influence of technocrats (interview, 16 January 2008). Network dynamics put technocrats in a difficult position, in danger of becoming an 'interest', forgetting that their role is to 'receive and translate the messages coming from society' (interview, Ministry of Economy and Finance, 11 January 2008).

The overall impression is that the subnational consumed policy but lacks the ability to significantly shape programmes but is sufficiently influential to secure projects and the conseqence of EU requirements meshing with the party-clientilism of Greek politics meant projects went to institutions lacking the necessary capacity. Again, the centre is reinforced. Public–private partnership under the 2nd CSF did improve management techniques, increased professionalism and reduced political interference at the margin. However, because MEF domination did not change significantly, neither did power relations: 'Some actors are more amenable to EU guidelines than others. *The higher the level of authority, the greater is the understanding between the actors involved*' (interview, Ministry of Economy and Finance, 17 January 2008; emphasis added). Party and patron–client politics are important but more significant (and irrespective of the party in government) is the dominance of the centre and the different rates of adaptation by different components of the network (interviews, ROP Central Macedonia, 21 March and Ministry of Development, 17 January 2008).

Sources of change

Greece's long involvement with cohesion policy has stimulated change; it would be nonsense to suggest otherwise. Successive iterations of the policy compelled actors – public, private and civil society – to 'up their game'. So, 'compared to ten years ago, there is a clearer framework of cooperation and also better cooperation. The most important players – ministries and regions – have started speaking the same language' (interviews, Ministry of Economy and Finance, 11 and 16 January 2008). Others identified 'a tendency for more cooperation . . . local politicians have accepted there are rules and procedures to be followed' (interview, Development Company of West Macedonia, 2 May 2008). Change is a combination of social learning and strategic calculation, Commission criticism, threats to funding, and redistributive politics and the EU has stimulated organisational learning: 'The transfer of know-how has been more important than the transfer of funds . . . What matters is [EU] conditionality . . .' (interview, Ministry of Development, 17 January 2008). The EU is a major stimulus for change but the response conformed to domestic imperatives, the effect of which was to sustain centralisation.

'The rise of the regions' can be exaggerated as they are an extension of a long-established centrally dominated power structure, not a challenge to it (Featherstone and Yannopoulos 1995: 249–66). During the 1990s pressure from a Commission concerned about the efficiency and effectiveness of Greek policy led the Simitis government to promote extensive *managerial* reform in a way that did not weaken centralisation by multiplying the number of task-based/task-specific bodies (Type II MLG) operating at different territorial levels and which overlapped. The winner is the centre, setting operational parameters (albeit within EU guidelines) and coordinating.

MEF's centrality to the capacity bargain can be seen in the description of the NSRF as promoting the 'strategic supervision of development program-ming and policy implementation, capacity building in programming, man-agement, control and implementation authorities . . . and the strengthening of partnership and co-responsibility of regional and local authorities' (Ministry of Economy and Finance 2007: 123). Other key institutions are the Inter-ministerial Committee, chaired by the Minister of Economy and Finance, which 'monitors the progress of development programmes and makes policy decisions at strategic, management and operational levels' and the Central Coordinating Authority, also under MEF, which 'ensured rational programming of actions and funds and conformity with Community regulations' (Ministry of Economy and Finance 2007: 123). This panoply of central coordination is the product of complexity and actors exploiting the interaction of EU rules and guidelines with national legislation and regulations. This enables MEF to create (and defend) its gate-keeper role. Our evidence is that 'thick' learning has occurred but this is largely confined to the ministries, employers' organisations and technical experts. EU influence has been most visible in management, evaluation and control; these have been gradually incorporated into domestic processes and have spilled over into the managing authorities, but there has been no system-wide horizontal or vertical dissemination. After the 2nd CSF the Greek state strongly favoured the creation of territorial task-specific bodies that lacked autonomy. The core of the policy process remained unchanged as changes were incremental and served to augment rather than challenge the status quo. Thus, managing authorities were not incorporated into the regional administration but were conduits for central control (Getimis and Demetropolou 2004: 355–78). The 2001 management system was a response to criticisms of a failure to satisfy the principles of cohesion (transparency, accountability and effectiveness) but despite its emphasis on promoting these principles the NSRF has as its primary objective 'full absorption' of available funds (Ministry of Economy and Finance 2007: 123).

Undoubtedly the scale and scope of cooperation has increased but so has conflict (often described as 'competition') which is inevitable with a distributive policy. Some interviewees downplayed the significance of conflict, emphasising its containment in a rule- and norm-based network; others, with an eye on the volatility of Greek politics, doubted the network's ability to contain the stresses of 'competition' as funding decreased (interviews, Ministry of Economy and Finance, 13 March; Federation of Greek Industries, 15 January 2008). Broader participation, however, offers social partners, civil society organisations and municipalities 'freedom to shape policy content. These bottom-up interventions will increase' (interview, Ministry of Economy and Finance, 11 January 2008). Even so, it is incontrovertible that the most noticeable changes have been an improvement in the quality of *national* planning and programme evaluation. In principle, an 'EU logic', as it were, permeates the network, albeit with variations, but smaller subnational actors in particular tend to embody 'traditional attitudes but these will be transformed over time by engagement and learning and this diffusion is an irreversible process' (interview, Ministry of Economy and Finance, 16 January 2008).

Slovenia

Slovenia is a unitary state with two tiers of administration: central government and 210 municipalities. The 1993 reform of local government created 58 administrative units to perform public administration tasks with a territorial dimension that covered more than one municipality. The Law on Balanced Regional Development (LBRD, 1999, 2005) added twelve development regions, but these are associations of municipalities for statistical and planning purposes and 'Regional policy remains strongly centralised because of the lack of an intermediate regional tier with strong operational powers' (European Policies Research Centre 2008: 1; see also Lajh 2003: 89–111). Subnational authority is, since 1994, vested in the municipalities and in accordance with the *European Charter on Local Self-Government*, competences were devolved but no regional tier was created. Under the constitution municipalities were empowered, if they so wished, to unite voluntarily but none did so. Two aspects of Slovenia's engagement with cohesion are significant: first, the resilience of centralisation; and second, the difficulty of organising subnational government. Central coordination and a regional structure stimulated a (contentious) process that generated multi-levelled-ness while EU pressure stimulated changes favouring consultative and participatory politics within nationally determined institutions (Lajh 2004: 11).

Institutions

Accession forced Slovenia to think about cohesion policy and regional development, rather than a sectoral approach (interview, Ministry of Environment and Spatial Planning, 30 January 2008). The LBRD is the legal framework for *acquis* implementation, but prior to 2000 planning and management were divided between the Ministry of Economy (policy design), the Council for Structural Policy (national coordination, implementation and EU assistance) and the National Agency for Regional Development (NARD, day-to-day management and coordination). Not surprisingly, this proved complex and unwieldy, and in December 2002 policy design and coordination was transferred to the Government Office for Structural Policies and Regional Development (GOSP) under a Minister without Portfolio.

Between 2003 and 2005 GOSP worked closely with NARD and the Council for Structural Policy to improve interministerial cooperation. This ceased to function after 2003, its tasks being transferred to the Council for Sustainable Development (a weekly meeting of ministers involved with implementation) that worked closely with GOSP and NARD on the National Development Plan and the Single Programming Document. The *Strategy of Economic Development of the Republic of Slovenia 2001–2006* and the *National Development Programme* provided the basis for the *Single Programming Document* (SPD). The SPD involved social partners, professional organisations, NGOs, the municipalities, experts and so on. Coordination worked at two levels: GOSP managed the relevant line ministries (Labour, Family and Social Affairs for the ESF; Agriculture, Fisheries and Food for the EAGGF; and Economy for the ERDF) and promoted cooperation with partners, especially in the case of cross-cutting issues. The draft was sent to the European Commission in

December 2003 and approved in June 2004. Programme Councils, inter-ministerial institutions headed by the ministry designated as the Intermediate Body, coordinated strategic and operational work but 'vertical communication and horizontal coordination [entailed] lengthy procedures and implementation delays also led to the transfer of the Intermediate Bodies . . . to the Managing Authority' (European Policies Research Centre 2008: 6). In March 2006 Intermediate Body functions for ERDF and ESF were transferred to the Government Office for Local Self-Government and Regional Policy (GORP). Despite efforts at simplification, complexity remained a problem.

In 2004 a change of government led to further change. The Slovenian Democratic Party led a coalition focused on improved interministerial coordination and improved cooperation between actors. In effect, it created a new system. In 2005 GORP was created by merging GOSP and the Directorate for Local Self-Government (Ministry of the Interior) and under the LBRD (2005) NARD was folded into GORP (January 2006) and GORP became the central policy coordinator. A former GOSP official now working for the Government Office for Development stressed GORP's 'gatekeeper' role in the cohesion policy network (interview, 6 June 2008). GORP relies on policy inputs from line ministries and negotiates directly with the Commission, so is present at European, national and subnational levels and is the managing authority for all national operational programmes. A GORP civil servant emphasised GORP's 'active involvement in the whole process or preparation and implementation . . . at all levels . . . Their most important role . . . was the preparation of strategic documents' (interview, 31 January 2008). Despite institutional change, there is significant continuity flowing from 'the experience acquired during the implementation of pre-accession instruments, Slovenia decided to maintain centralised institutional arrangements for the management of Structural and Cohesion Funds' (European Policies Research Centre 2008: 4).

In 1999 the LBRD sanctioned the creation of Regional Development Agencies (RDAs) which mapped on to the twelve NUTS 3 regions. These regions were established in 2001 to implement the structural and cohesion programmes and are overseen by a council composed of mayors. RDAs coordinate, implement and monitor regional development programmes but there is considerable variation in their performance. In the pre-accession period (1998–2004) funding was agreed annually with the Commission followed by the submission of strategic planning documents; projects were implemented at the national level by a ministry or agency. This raised the issue of territorial organisation. Slovenia's implementation of NUTS proved controversial for Slovenia–EU relations and the government-municipality relationship. During the pre-accession negotiations Slovenia and the Commission reversed their positions. Slovenia sought three regions – Eastern, Western and Capital – whereas the Commission argued Slovenia's population warranted no more than one region. The municipalities objected to both proposals, arguing there were significant interregional disparities and the Commission's proposals would overcentralise power. The issue was not resolved at accession and a decision was postponed until 2006. At dispute was funding. As a single NUTS 2 region Slovenia's GDP would fall below the threshold to qualify for structural and cohesion funds and make Slovenia a net EU budget contributor; two or three regions would make areas outside Ljubljana eligible for Objective 2 funding, but NUTS 2 regions generally have a population of 1.5–2.0m; Slovenia has a population of 2.06m (Faro 2004: 6; Lindstrom 2005: 7). The relative success of some of the RDAs and the growth of lobbying in Brussels by involving RDAs in cross-border projects led to the Commission agreeing to more than one region.

The network

Slovenia has a less 'dense' capacity bargain network than Greece (Figure 4.3). This reflects the Slovenian authorities' decision to manage the capacity bargain through a centralised network, albeit one capable of drawing on the knowledge and expertise of key societal interests. The network's evolution reflected the shift from accession to member state and, despite the change, the actors remained the same. The core strategic network is dominated by GORP, the Zagreb Chamber of Commerce, the RDAs, and the municipalities, which are regarded by some interviewees as more significant than the RDAs. Accompanying this strategic core are functional implementation networks. This reflects Slovenia's tradition of social partnership and centralisation. The EU is not perceived as engaged with the network (a contrast with Greece) but, as the interview (and other) data shows, the Commission profoundly influences the network.

GORP's dominance has been reinforced in both the pre- and post- accession periods to the extent that new actors (such as the Government Office for Development) find it difficult to gain access to the network. To some degree this also applies to the RDAs and municipalities, but other influences are at work here. GORP's influence flows from its central coordination role, whereas implementation is more pluralistic (interview, Government Office for Development, 6 June 2008). GORP interviewees did not deny their centrality but disputed its consequences. The abolition of two intermediate bodies and the centralisation of coordination boosted GORP's influence, but this was neutralised by a much higher level of participation than previously at the regional and local levels and, despite on-going difficulties with municipalities, their influence could only increase in time. It is the case that the number of ministries involved in implementation had increased, reflecting the much more demanding nature of cohesion policy after accession. GORP's position bred resentment in ministries who particularly disliked its power to move funds between ministries. GORP's response was that it was merely implementing EU policies, the classic response to domestic criticism (interview, GORP, 6 June 2008).

A civil servant at the Ministry of the Economy considered cooperation with GORP to be variable in quality but the general trend was of improvement;

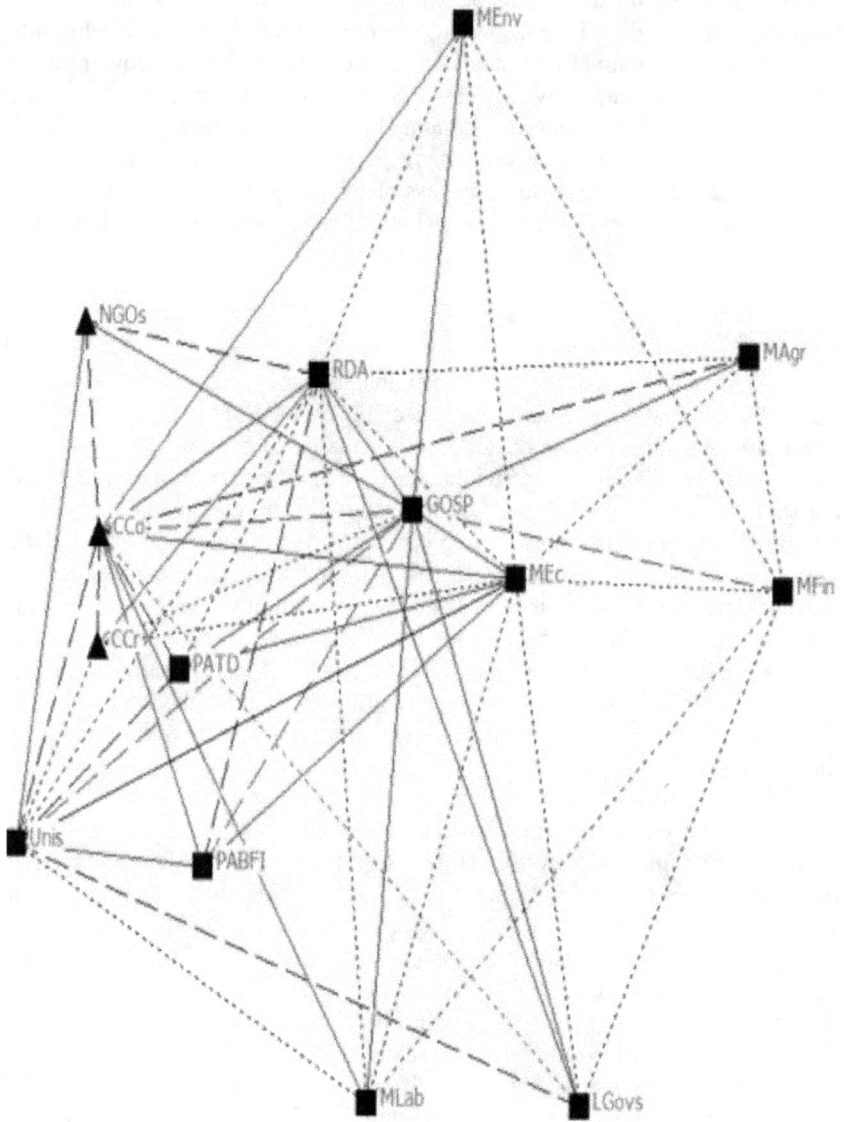

Figure 4.3 The cohesion network: Slovenia

Organisation	SNA abbreviation
Chamber of Commerce	CCo
Chamber of Crafts	CCr
Delegation of the European Commission	DelCEC
European Agency for Reconstruction	EAR
Government Office for Local Self Government and Regional Policy	GOSP (after 2006 GORP)
Local Governments	LGovs
Ministry of Agriculture	MAgr
Ministry of Economy	MEc
Ministry of Environment and Spatial Planning	MEnv
Ministry of Finance	MFin
Ministry of Labour	MLab
NGOs	NGOs
Public Agency for Business and Foreign Investments	PABFI
Public Agency for Technologic Development	PATD
Regional Development Agencies	RDA
Secretariat for European Affairs	SEA
Universities	Unis

a major source of change was the recognition that Slovenia's experience with IPA was not a good guide. Accession created a far more complex system that required more effective central coordination, which was not necessarily incompatible with wider engagement and participation (interview, 30 January 2008). GORP-trained personnel are scattered throughout the bureaucracy and both the organisation and these individuals are active in trying to push ministries towards a more strategic, cross-cutting approach and away from the traditional sectoral approach. This naturally causes tensions as it threatens established 'vertical' networks but GORP does have real power, for example, with regard to the allocation of funds, where it has blocked ministerial proposals (interview, GORP 31 January 2008). The general tenor of interviews at GORP was that it was slowly developing greater interministerial cooperation but that this was taking far longer than was anticipated or thought desirable.

Away from the centre, the picture is less clear. An interviewee from the Pomurje Business Incubator, for instance, argued there were relatively few conflicts over principles or goals in the network. The real conflicts were over implementation and distribution of funds, in particular over whether regional disparities were best addressed by 'bottom-up' programmes or by focusing on 'top-down' national development goals at the regional and local level. Although the bias was towards the former, the effect of centralisation and what was considered GORP's insistence on the 'rigid' interpretation of EU rules, was slow implementation that bred conflict (interview, 14 January 2008).

Despite variations in activism and performance among the RDAs, there was a widespread recognition that their role was to support the municipalities in what was invariably described as 'a very centralised system'. Despite the emphasis on encouraging 'bottom-up' initiatives and efforts to decentralise, the state GORP revealed itself reluctant (so far) to weaken its control of decision-making (interview, Lower Podravje RDA, 11 January 2008). A second RDA – Maribor – echoed this, expressing concern that the abolition of intermediaries had reduced the number of access points in the network and the regions lacked sufficient resources and capabilities to wield effective influence. NGOs were thought to be effective only during the implementation phase (interview, 12 February 2008). There was a view that regions were *less* influential in developing the 2007–13 programmes because power had been pulled upwards to GORP and pushed downwards to the municipalities, many of which were incapable of meeting the demands placed on them and were, moreover, subject to party-political influence (interview, Pomurje Business Incubator, 14 January 2008).

Civil society organisations tended to be the most pessimistic about their participation and influence. Participation *had* increased, albeit from a low level, and there *were* more opportunities for engagement but the perception remained that this was because it was expected and was formulaic (interview, Ministry of Environment and Spatial Planning, 30 January 2008). An interviewee at the Ljubljana Chamber of Commerce described the Chamber's role as 'Just official, but no important role' in a system characterised by slow decision-making and relatively weak cooperation within the network. Change was largely confined to the top of the hierarchy and had not yet filtered down and this had stimulated competition, not cooperation, between actors (interview, 18 December 2007). This was echoed by an interviewee at an NGO active in trying to promote the influence of the municipalities. The situation was described thus: 'in Slovenia there is a problem of competition between development organisations. Instead of being partners, they are in many cases competitors ... In this situation, all can lose' (interview, Lower Podravje Region, 11 January 2008). Competition can reinforce the role of the centre because of the inability of subnational actors to meet the demands being placed on them. This interpretation was disputed by GORP. While conceding centralisation, GORP civil servants stressed the confusion caused by the Commission. DG Enlargement initially favoured some regionalisation but pulled back as accession neared, choosing instead to emphasise absorptive capacity; Slovenia prepared for regionalisation only to have its proposal rejected by the Commission. After accession, DG Regio was keen to promote regionalisation but the process became mired in domestic political concerns. Despite this, great efforts were being, and had been, made to involve civil society and NGOs in preparing the most recent programming and planning documents (interview, 6 June 2008).

Complex procedures and institutions proved difficult to operate in accordance with EU governance principles and this was complicated further by coalition politics that reach down to the municipal level to influence policy and programmes. Slovenia is a centralised polity but regionalisation created opportunities for subnational mobilisation but responses varied according to resources and leadership. Institutionally, the network can be described as 'thin', reflecting Slovenia's history of strong regional cultural and geographic identities but no corresponding political structures. Simplifying the network (abolishing the Intermediate Bodies, for instance) was part of attempts to improve responsiveness, efficacy and transparency that reflected

> An approach based on learning-by-doing . . . at the beginning, too many organisations were involved . . . the system was not transparent, and decision-making responsibilities were not always clear . . . High levels of staff turnover contributed to this situation. Implementation problems were also caused by the relatively late start made to implementation and inadequate preparation of the administrative bodies (with too much reliance placed on the positive experiences under pre-accession assistance).
> (European Policies Research Centre 2008: 14)

Permeating the network is a common understanding of the problems to be addressed, an understanding that reinforces centralisation. Subnational entities have opportunities to engage but municipalities, lacking political clout and resources, are competitive not solidaristic in the face of the centre. Kajnč and Svetličič comment that the expertise developed under IPA and during accession was top-down 'characterised by a slow flow of information and information being kept at too high a level . . . decision-making is also centralised . . .' (2009: 11). Accession required a radical reorientation to address the consequences of centralisation for vertical and horizontal governance manifested as a push for central coordination.

Sources of change

The 2007 *National Strategic Reference Framework* (NSRF), Slovenia's strategy for promoting convergence with the EU, was accompanied by a *National Development Plan* covering the RDAs and NUTS 3 regions. *Regional Development Programmes* (RDPs) are indicative framework documents used to plan and finance projects and the RDAs prepare, monitor and implement the RDPs. RDAs have no autonomous political existence but have developing representational and lobbying functions. If, however, the RDAs became 'regional bases of a meso administrative level financed by the state budget, they will no longer be eligible to apply for project financing from the Structural Funds themselves; new development authorities would be needed' (Faro 2004: 7). The Association of Municipalities is suspicious of the RDAs as a regional tier that threatens municipal autonomy. Municipalities have grown rapidly; in 1995 there were 62, in 2004 there were 193 and there are now 210; around half have fewer than 5,000 inhabitants. Municipalities are pulled between conflict and cooperation: securing their position vis-á-vis other municipalities but cooperating within the RDAs. The LBRD, NUTS and the RDAs encouraged some municipalities to take an increased interest in regional policy. Ministries were the most active but the regional dimension and inclusion of subnational actors sustained the influence of political parties, particularly at the county level (interview, Ministry of Environment and Spatial Planning, 30 January 2008).

The complexity of MLG in Slovenia was demonstrated in the long-running saga over the creation of provinces. In October 2009 the then Minister for Local Self-Government and Regional Policy, Zlata Ploštakner, resigned and was replaced by Henrik Gjerkeš who identified cohesion policy and the introduction of provinces with elected governments as key aims. By January 2010 the governing coalition had agreed in principle to create 6 provinces but needed the support of the opposition for the necessary two-thirds majority in parliament. The opposition SDS had already submitted a bill calling for 14 provinces; a similar proposal had been defeated in 2008. Faced by growing concern over cost and opposition from, for example, mayors (some of whom wanted 25 provinces), the Strategic Council for Decentralisation offered a third proposal (3 to 5 big provinces). Gjerkeš backpedalled, implying this was no longer a major government priority and that provinces should not been seen as political entities but development bodies. In March 2010 Gjerkeš bowed to the inevitable and dropped legislation on provinces because there was no agreement, opting instead to 'tweak' the existing system. It was more important, he argued, to create networks of regional development institutions with links to the state and other regions, giving the government the ability to intervene quickly to address regional problems. On 28 October 2010 the government adopted a bill on balanced regional development. Gjerkeš contended that the bill represented a new departure because hitherto Slovenia lacked a regional policy: 'institutions of regional policy are weak, non-transparent and unstable . . . there has been no focus on key problems and key regional projects'. A 'systematic' (for which one can read 'centralised') approach was needed to pull together competing interests and respond to immediate problems caused by recession as well deep-seated structural problems. The bill proposed no new institutions or funding but rather sought to strengthen the existing system by networking RDAs and business incubators (Republic of Slovenia 2010).

A theme permeating Slovenia's engagement with cohesion policy is the continuation of centralisation. Centralisation characterised the management of pre-accession aid and carried over into the management of the structural and cohesion funds. There is one coordinating body (GOSP/GORP) and one paying authority (Ministry of Finance); other ministries involved with ERDF, ESF and EAGGF were gradually drawn into this centralised web and after 2006 only the Ministry of Agriculture, Forestry and Food acted as an intermediate body. Intermediate functions under ESF and ERDF were transferred to GORP with the intention of improving responsiveness, effectiveness and transparency.

The preparation of the NRSF, the *National Development Programme* (NDP) and *Slovenia's Development Strategy* (SDS) built upon previous experience and the government's response was 'to completely amend [the] institutional and development framework that Slovenia became part of after accession to the EU' (Republic of Slovenia 2007: 5). In preparing the NRSF close attention was paid to developing consultation and ensuring extensive participation by 'competent regional, local and other public bodies, economic and social partners and [others] representing civil society, environmental partners, non-governmental organisations and bodies responsible for the promotion of gender equality . . .' (Republic of Slovenia 2007: 5). This approach embraced preparation as well as implementation, monitoring and evaluation, and was justified by an explicit reference to the principles articulated in *European Governance* (CEC 2001a). The objective was 'a more focused implementation of the partnership principle' (Republic of Slovenia 2007: 6). The government assessed partnership between government levels as effective, 'cooperation with [NGOs] was considered good if compared with the practice of previous preparation of development documents but *still insufficient and not in line with expectations*' (Republic of Slovenia 2007: 9; emphasis added). The engagement of the RDAs and municipal government was variable but critical as development was to be 'bottom-up', reflecting local needs and priorities.

The NSRF's SWOT analysis concluded incomplete local government reform and the absence of a regional tier meant 'too many competences are centralised at the national level'. The question mark over the ability of existing regional development institutions was 'low participation' by civil society and the tendency of municipalities to engage in wasteful competition (Republic of Slovenia 2007: 46). Implementation had experienced some difficulties because 'the cohesion policy system is rather complex and this inevitably requires [a] learning period' but the national focus was judged correct (Republic of Slovenia 2007: 54). The main lesson was to focus on implementation by improving initial planning and by GORP being more active and making greater use of technical experts to neutralise political interference. The changes would promote the SDS's vision 'of the social market economy that will encompass a more liberal market economy with a more economically effective and flexible but social state' (Republic of Slovenia 2007: 59). Despite a tradition of interest group engagement, there were doubts that interest groups would be able to meet the expectations of this new and far more intensive approach to governance (Fink-Hafner 1998: 285–302). The NRSF noted:

> the potential of the non-governmental sector has not been utilised. To improve this situation [programme] will endeavour to support social partnership and [the] non-governmental sector aiming to improve their qualifications so that they can get involved in the preparation, monitoring and implementation of policies, programmes and projects *particularly*

in those fields where the non-governmental sector can play a key mobilisational and developmental role.

(Republic of Slovenia 2007: 101; emphasis added)

In this evolving system 'EU *imposed* regional policy measures, although still largely centrally coordinated, have spurred different degree and kinds of regional policy networks . . . *EU conditions* did lead to the creation of [NUTS] regions . . . and RDAs, it has not led to further political decentralisation' (Lindstrom 2005: 16; emphasis added). The national authorities' preference for central direction was maintained within the parameters set by the EU. The aim was

> to avoid the establishment of new bodies and the emphasis will rather be put on the content and coordination role of the management authority. The central role will be played by the ministries . . . because they represent the main initiators and implementers of development priorities in line with the programming documents and at the same time they are competent for individual development areas in compliance with Slovene legislation.
>
> (Republic of Slovenia 2007: 116–17)

GORP, as the management authority, remains *the* central institution in the capacity bargain network and we see substantial institutional change *and* continuity.

A major stimulus for change was Slovenia's 2008 Presidency of the European Council. We have already noted how Europeanisation is a process not a destination, and Slovenia found a successful pre-accession to be of limited value after accession. Membership exerts adaptive pressure requiring further adjustment. Kajnč and Svetličič contend that only on assuming the Presidency did Slovenia gain real familiarity with the nature of the EU's policy process and the skills needed to exploit that process (2009: 6, 10). Europeanisation has so far tended to reinforce the status quo. The extent to which exposure to the EU as a member state will move Slovenia away from this is unclear. Some RDAs have demonstrated a capacity to exploit the system, but what we see overall is accommodation not transformation. Centralisation was reinforced by pre-accession instruments but the RDAs (a creation of these same instruments) grew steadily in importance producing (at the time of our research) a mixed 'top-down, bottom-up' approach where subnational actors combined to develop proposals with the centre as gatekeeper.

Croatia

As might be expected of a candidate state, implementing pre-accession EU aid in Croatia was centralised but with definite indications of developing multi-level governance. Whether this represents a challenge to centralisation is a different question. Until 1993 Croatia had no intermediate tier of local government and some HDZ politicians feared that regional policy would promote centrifugal tendencies. While Croatia was establishing its identity as a state, regionalisation had few attractions, but this changed as the country moved away from immediate post-war reconstruction (interview, Institute for International Relations, 10 December 2007).

Institutions

The Law on Local and Regional Self-Government (2001) created twenty-one counties responsible for health, education, spatial planning and economic development but with resources provided by the centre. The Regional Operating Programmes (ROPs) date from 2001 and operated at county level. The original six were developed with United Nations Development Programme (UNDP) support and mark the shift from post-war reconstruction to regional policy – a new concept in post-conflict Croatia (Committee of the Regions 2008a: 3). In 2004 Croatia became a candidate country and eligible for PHARE, ISPA and SAPARD, and subsequently for IPA funds. In 2006 Croatia received DIS accreditation. Notwithstanding this assistance, Croatia found 'the management system for pre-accession programmes to be a time-consuming and complex process' because of the gap between EU requirements and national capabilities. Croatia expected to join the EU shortly after the 2007–13 financial perspective, which meant that 'it cannot afford a lengthy compliance assessment procedure [so] the number of new institutions involved in [management] will be kept at a reasonably low level, and new institutions will be introduced only if needed' (Republic of Croatia 2010a: 47–8).

The core institution is the Central Office for Development Strategy and Coordination of EU Funds (CODEF). CODEF was responsible for technical and administrative tasks, monitoring the implementation of the Strategy and the coordination of EU funds in cooperation with state bodies, NGOs and the Commission. CODEF was headed by a state secretary, who was also IPA coordinator, appointed on the proposal of the prime minister, to whom the state secretary is accountable. Two deputies were appointed after proposal by the state secretary, to whom they are accountable. The state secretary participates in the weekly meetings on progress with the EU, can propose priorities for funding to Cabinet members and arbitrates in disputes over priorities. The state secretary was deputy chief negotiator for EU accession, the sectoral coordinator for Components III and IV, and is a member of the working group on Chapter 22.

CODEF coordinated the preparation of the *Strategic Development Framework 2006–2013* (SDF) and the *Strategic Coherence Framework 2007–2013* (SCF) and prepared the *National Strategic Reference Framework*. The Ministry of Finance was responsible for budgets. This was strongly vertical and centralised, but the Commission expected the 'IPA institutional structure will evolve into the Structural Funds management structure', the governance of which required horizontal interministerial coordination extending into partnership working with civil society (CEC 2007e: 5). Regional policy's contribution to developing European-style governance 'will require a significant effort on the part of government to strengthen the institutional base for the management of the Funds from the centre . . .'. IPA was designed to 'make it possible for administrations in the accession states to simulate the management and programming conditions for EU Structural Funds' (Fröhlich 2006: 2, 6) and this inevitably had consequences for Croatia's politics, policy and polity. Much was learned from IPA, as an interviewee in the Ministry of Foreign Affairs and European Integration make clear: 'we learned the skills, on the national as well as on the local level and the regional, how to prepare projects, use funds' (interview, 15 May 2008). However, IPA's focus was on central institutions and strengthening capacity in an already centralised state.

The difficulties involved and the scale of learning required were revealed by the *National Strategy for Regional Development* (NSRD) (Fröhlich 2006: 7), which addressed national priorities 'in line with EU principles and priorities' (ECORYS 2003: 1). The problems demanding a response were a lack of capacity nationally and subnationally; poor interinstitutional coordination and greater consultation with social partners. Sectoral development strategies were 'stand-alone' technocratic documents and inappropriate as EU policy required a national strategic policy framework and partnership working. What existed was simply not up to EU standards (ECORYS 2003: 12; Fröhlich 2006: 11). Experience in Croatia and elsewhere showed that 'fundamental requirement for regional development is the emergence of social capital (shared vision and values, new collaborative working methods and basis of trust and confidence among diverse stakeholders)' (ECORYS 2003: 13). To achieve these new ways of working Croatia could draw on the experience of others, but this could not be mechanistically applied. Croatia's approach would be 'constructed on the bedrock of good experience' but grounded in Croatian conditions, which would necessitate great change in governance at all levels, and the engagement of civil society would be critical (ECORYS 2003: 25). Substantial misfit meant substantial downward adaptational pressure: 'the most important factor is EU pressure . . . more is expected of policy-makers . . . The EU policy framework has been [the] guiding framework for policy change and also the source of learning' (interview, EPOR, 15 May 2008).

Adopted in August 2006 after extensive consultation with business, unions, NGOs and the public, the SDF is the umbrella strategic development document. Identifying ten strategic development concerns, the SDF called for the restructuring of the state and governance to create an enabling state promoting a competitive market economy and modern welfare state grounded on engagement with, and the involvement of, society. The change envisaged is dramatic, 'the state and governance . . . become instruments of "social mediation" rather than instruments of "social intervention". Social mediation means the involvement of government in the pursuit of common elements that motivate citizens and key social actors' (Republic of Croatia 2006b: 12). Given the SDF's centrality to regional development and social cohesion, consultations were held with civil society organisations, the Economic and Social Council and the National Competitiveness Council. The state was responsible for *acquis* transposition which required an efficient, not a centralised, state. The state would be 'stronger' as all levels would be endowed with significant responsibilities and bound together in policy networks producing a harmonised multi-level system of joint decision-making under a single development framework (Republic of Croatia 2006b: 15, 68–9, 77). CODEF developed the strategy via the partnership principle but recognised 'different institutions . . . have different or even competing interests' and played a critical role in conflict resolution (interview, CODEF 14 December 2007).

The *Strategic Coherence Framework* (SCF) is sometimes referred to as the 'mini-NRSF'. Approved by government on 25 May and by the Commission on 18 June 2007, its preparation relied on extensive consultation (Republic of Croatia 2006a: 9–11). SCF was a critical indicator of Croatia's adaptation to EU membership by clearly distributing responsibilities, strengthening institutional capacity and involving all relevant actors. This latter consideration was particularly significant because 'Since the end of the 1990s great attention has been given to the development of partnership between national/local authorities and civil society organisations' (Republic of Croatia 2006a, 27). One of IPA's guiding principles in capacity building is partnership. Operational Programmes would, for example, use 'a partnership of appropriate public authorities at the national, regional and local levels with economic, social and environmental partners, and representatives of civil society, non-governmental organisations and bodies responsible for promoting equality between men and women' (Republic of Croatia 2006a: 52).

The *National Strategic Reference Framework 2007–2013* (NSRF) sets out the strategy for closing Chapter 22 and presages the post-accession Structural and Cohesion funds. NSRF thematic priorities (the development of transport; environment and energy infrastructure; competitiveness and balanced regional development; developing employment and human resources; and administrative capacity) are covered by operational programmes. Built upon the SCF, which 'completely adhered to the principles of the structural funds', made the NSRF 'a useful "learning by doing" exercise' and was 'a continuation of the efforts and lessons learned' (Republic of Croatia 2010: 5, 8). A Coordinating Body, created in November 2008 to draft the NSRF, consisted of representatives of line ministries and other state bodies; NSRF Working Groups provided analytical and sectoral information while CODEF staff coordinated the process. CODEF provided the Coordinating Body's chair (CODEF's state secretary) and its deputy chair and CODEF's 'responsibility for coordination, implementation and control [means it] retains its central role' a (Republic of Croatia 2010: 96). Programming (combining strategic vision, long-term national policies and budgetary planning with EU requirements) 'requires attention from the highest level of government . . . and involvement of partners from [the] non-governmental sphere'. Experience showed the value of 'early communication with stakeholders that do not formally belong to the programme management structures – notably the local level authorities and representatives of civil society organisations' to minimise opposition after approval has been given to an OP (Republic of Croatia 2010: 47). Post-accession institutions would rest on those developed pre-accession; transition will be smoothed by CODEF and the Ministry of Finance continuing their central roles, while Managing Authorities will be required to develop horizontal links 'to develop genuine and effective partnership working to achieve real socio-economic impact' (Republic of Croatia 2010: 95).

In March 2007, three NUTS 2 regions (Northwest: six counties including Zagreb; Central and Eastern: eight counties; and Adriatic: seven counties) were agreed with the Commission and constituted both a significant development and issue of concern (interview, Virovitica-Podravina County, 19 May 2008). It was clear that the central government needed to enter a new development and partnership relationship at county and intercounty level, requiring a new relationship with civil society, between the counties, and between counties and government. However, 'Such an outcome is more than solely the product of administrative reform, or the creation of formal partnerships for rubber stamping approval. It will require a sustained effort to create the shared norms, common values and mutual trust which underlie effective performance' (Fröhlich 2006: 13).

The counties lack resources and their vitality often depends on the professional interest and personal commitment of mayors and officials. One estimate was that some 310 individuals were engaged in preparing and implementing EU-funded projects at county level (an average of 15). This was a 40 per cent increase on 2007, but five counties employed over half of all staff and three fewer than five. Four counties were responsible for 71 per cent of the total value of approved projects (Maleković *et al.* 2010: 10–11, 13). Intercounty cooperation is underdeveloped because of conservatism, weak capacities and party-political competition, and progress depended on forging links between counties and the RDAs (interview, Virovitica-Podravina County, 19 May 2008). A member of Croatia's Chapter 22 negotiating team stressed, however, that neither regional development nor subnational governance was a priority and was seen as threatening the interests of the war-affected regions that had done well out of the existing distribution of resources. Change would therefore be very difficult (interview, Institute of Economics, 15 May 2008). Some 50 per cent of counties reported cooperation with an international partner on more than three projects in the previous three years. A total of 60 per cent reported no such projects compared to 70 per cent who reported partnerships with another county or actors outside the county; five reported not a single project with partners from their own or another county. Some 65 per cent reported at least one project involving an NGO but 35 per cent had no such experience (Maleković *et al.* 2010: 14–15).

The Strategy for Local Regional Development (2005) led to the Law on Regional Development (2009) which reflected the demands of accession and the weaknesses of IPA. Partnership councils at NUTS 2 were a significant development in defining development priorities and reflect similar institutions in other EU states, drawing together county development strategies as the main strategic programming documents. Members were to be drawn *inter alia* from the local and regional tiers, economic interest groups and NGOs to influence policy. Although a significant institutional innovation, their impact would depend on their capabilities, which were, as we have seen, poorly developed. Historically, policy has lacked resources and coherence, political will and effective governance, both horizontal and vertical, which tended to boost the influence of powerful local notables, not institutions (Maleković *et al.* 2010: 7).

The network

Visually, the network is closer to Greece's than Slovenia's (Figure 4.4). Its complex architecture reflects, in part, the scale of the demands placed on Croatia during its long accession and the government's determination to satisfy EU requirements. In Croatia's case it is difficult to separate the core strategic and functional implementation networks because of the dense pattern of interactions, which raises serious issues of coordination and coherence. Another distinguishing feature when compared to Greece or Slovenia is the involvement of international institutions (for example, UNDP, World Bank, USAID) other than the EU. This is a historical legacy, reflecting Croatia's status as a post-war, post-conflict society, and the EU is the dominant 'external' body and is an active, not proximate, actor. As Croatia was a candidate state we would expect this. Central government and the EU are identified, not surprisingly, as the most influential actors (with CODEF as the single most influential central institution), reflecting the historic pattern of centralisation. Other ministries lack capacity and policy coordination needed to be improved as regional policy is, by definition, multi-sectoral and depends on extensive consultative and participatory frameworks. Regional institutions are accorded a more influential role than in Greece or Slovenia. By far the weakest components are the civil society actors (interview, Ministry of Economy, Labour and Entrepreneurship, 15 June 2008).

One interviewee believed that only greater conflict between central and subnational actors would challenge the distribution of power in the capacity bargain network because, despite organisational change, the network displayed considerable inertia. The EU had been critical in stimulating change but it had also stimulated complexity, which served to buttress the centre (interview, Virovitica-Podravina County, 19 May 2008). Conversely, a Ministry of Foreign Affairs and European Integration interviewee was adamant that while government retained the initiative because of the nature of the accession process, there was greater (and increasing) plurality in the network. In particular, counties were beginning to press for greater involvement and develop joint lobbying (interview, 15 May 2008).

It is not surprising, therefore, that 'with respect to the highly centralised state and state budget, I am afraid that the ministries decide on all issues and it is

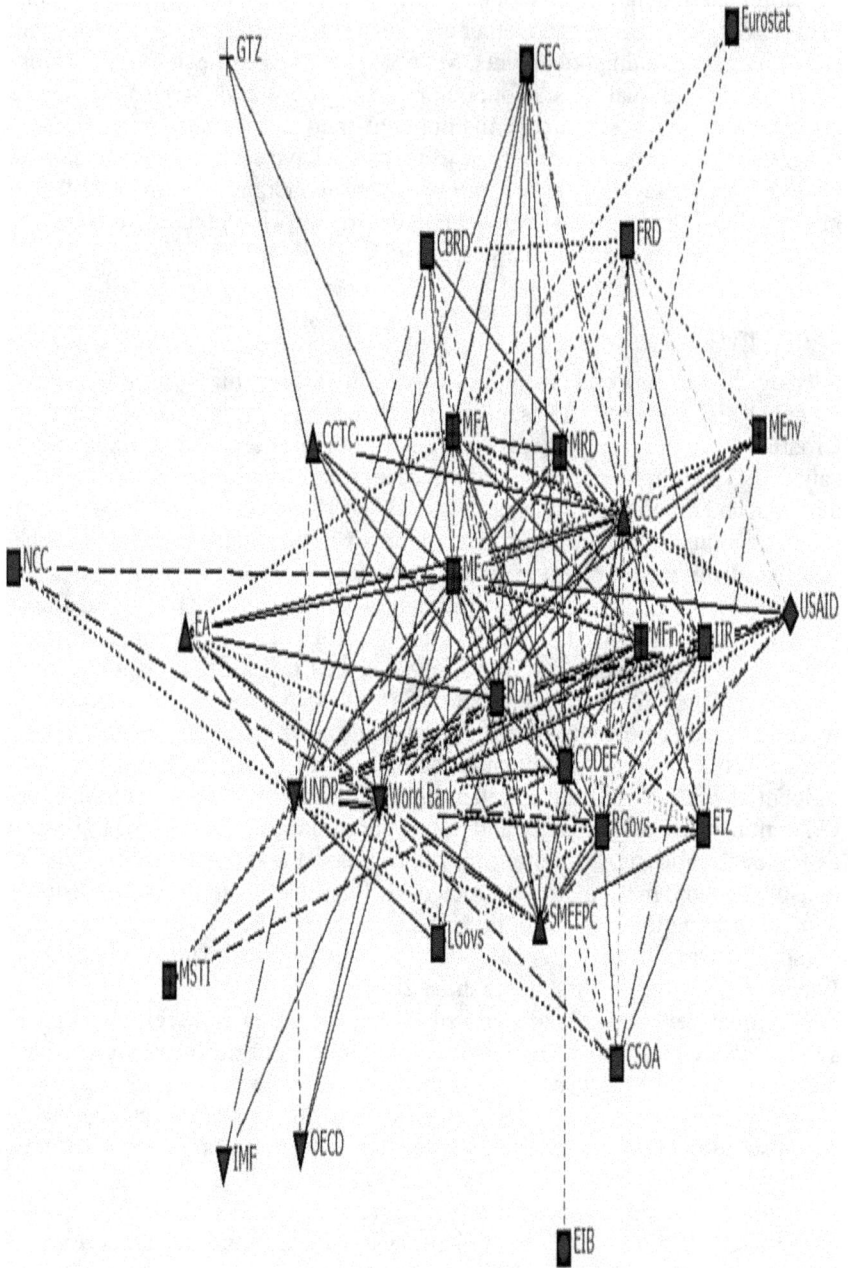

Figure 4.4 The cohesion network: Croatia

Organisation	SNA abbreviation
Croatian Bank for Reconstruction and Development	CBRD
Croatian Chamber of Commerce	CCC
Croatian Chamber of Trades and Crafts	CCTC
European Commission	CEC
Central State Office for Administration	CSOA
Central Office for Development Strategy and Coordination of EU Funds	CODEF
Employers Association	EA
European Investment Bank	EIB
Economic Institute Zagreb	EIZ
European Union Statistical Agency	Eurostat
Fund for Regional Development	FRD
Agency for Technical Cooperation, Germany	GTZ
Institute for International Relations	IIR
International Monetary Fund	IMF
Local Governments	LGovs
Ministry of Agriculture	MAgr
Ministry of the Economy	MEc
Ministry of the Environment	MEnv
Ministry of Finance	MF
Ministry of foreign affairs	MFA
Ministry of Regional Development	MRD
Ministry for Sea, Transport, and Infrastructure	MSTI
National Competitiveness Council	NCC
Organisation for Economic Cooperation and Development	OECD
Regional Development Agencies	RDA
Regional Governments	RGovs
SME and Entrepreneurship Policy Centre	SMEEPC
United Nations Development Programme	UNDP
United States Agency for International Development	USAID
World Bank	Worldbank

within their domain whether they will listen to any advice' (interview, Istrian RDA, 22 February 2008). Coming from one of the most effective RDAs, this was a telling judgement. The preparation of the regional development strategy document as part of the Chapter 22 negotiations was 'a team exercise . . . the same applies to the financing of projects. However, on the regional and local level, there is almost no self-initiative' (interview, Fund for Regional Development, 14 January 2008). When process and power are combined, centralisation is reinforced, especially with respect to NGOs and civil society as 'policy is primarily influenced by the government, the parliament and the ministries' (interview, Varazdin RDA, 12 February 2008) and even when consultation had occurred interviewees felt this had little effect: 'they consult us and ask for our opinion but ideas and criticisms . . . [are] not found in the final drafts' (interview, Virovitica-Podravina RDA, 19 May 2008).

Networks are dynamic and the RDAs have a common interest in promoting decentralisation (but not necessarily *regionalisation*) and some have been active not only in their own interests but in encouraging others to raise their game and increase their influence at the centre. A good example is the RDA covering Istria, which has participated in consultations jointly with counties on issues that relate to regional development. At the national level, however, the government retains its role as gatekeeper. The Adriatic Development Agency operating at NUTS 2 organises all development agencies to lobby at the centre and will, it is expected, become active in Brussels. The Istrian Development Agency does not meet ministers regularly but does meet regularly with local and regional bodies (interview, 22 February 2008). Familiarity with strategic planning at subnational level is growing but 'it is still very unclear at the state level how the NUTS region will work, how the Regional Plan will be implemented and who will be in charge of management, planning and implementation' (interview, Varazdin RDA, 12 February 2008). The IPA experience and the wider demands of accession point to an increase in complexity *and* participation but central actors must understand 'that the local level are not some stupid people who don't know what they want, but [that] they are treated as equal partners' (interview, Institute for Economics, 10 December 2007). A similar point was made at the Zagreb Chamber of Commerce: 'the bottom-up approach will have to be accepted as the [RDAs] are best in defining the problems that will have to be targeted . . . There should be a synergy between the national and regional level' (interview, 22 May 2008).

In the preparation of strategic documents, especially early ones, actor engagement was undermined by a weak consultative culture that made a shift to partnership working difficult. An uncertain institutional structure was a particular problem. The Commission summed up the situation thus:

> Croatia involves socio-economic partners and NGOs in policy-making initiatives and coordination groups. NGOs are also involved in programming and monitoring . . . The involvement of local and regional authorities . . . will need to be increased . . . Croatia should avoid a

multiplication of complex structures below the NUTS 2 level in order to achieve appropriate synergies.

(CEC 2007e: 10)

At the Committee of the Regions, Iva Frkić (CODEF) noted that operating IPA had proved difficult, requiring constant dialogue with the Commission; representatives from RELEX and DELARG conceded this but contended (Frkić agreed) that this stimulated extensive and rapid learning, and the creation of appropriate forms of governance (Committee of the Regions 2008a: 4–5). Nevertheless, while network governance was stimulated by engagement with the EU, the pre-accession experience was not necessarily a good indicator of future developments (Maleković *et al.* 2010: 13).

Sources of change

Our interviewees were in no doubt about EU influence: 'Croatia is currently doing everything in order to fit to the EU's requirements. Learning happens everyday' and that as policy complexity increased 'it is not possible to steer everything from the centre' (interviews, CODEF, 14 December 2007; Virovitica-Podravina County, 19 May 2008). A senior civil servant at the Ministry of Economy, Labour and Entrepreneurship (MELE) emphasised that 'Earlier, more or less everything was centralised and projects came explicitly from government, from the ministry [but] counties are starting to develop self-initiative [and] capability'; a civil servant at the Ministry of Foreign Affairs, on the other hand, described some subnational elements as being sceptical and even uninterested due to a lack of confidence, knowledge and resources but agreed the counties were of increasing significance (interviews, 5 June and 15 May 2008).

The most visible change over time is increasing decentralisation, but is this the result of EU engagement? Ministries, such as MELE, have promoted close relationships with counties and municipalities, leading to what interviewees described as 'networks' based on partnership not participation. Decentralisation and partnership are realities: 'compared to ten years ago there is a big difference [but] this goes slowly because the state is hardly giving away control . . . the counties have gained responsibility . . . without receiving the corresponding resources' (interview, Virovitica-Podravina County, 19 May 2008). This combination of pursuing EU membership with post-1991 domestic political developments promoted the 'over-institutionalisation' reflected in Figure 4.4. Both reinforce the centre but downward pressure stimulated by the EU over an extended period of time cannot but modify this via 'trickle-down' effects (interview, EPOR, 15 May 2008). No interviewees saw a major redistribution of power taking place (as yet), but agreed that 'pluralisation' had occurred, improving responsiveness, engagement and the quality of policy, and this was taken as evidence of learning from engagement with the EU despite shortcomings at the regional level and poor horizontal coordination between ministries (interview, Varazdin County, 12 February 2008).

Change takes time and resources, and the variations between regions require capacity building (Maleković *et al.* 2010: 6). Croatia aspires to 'joined-up' government linking 'central government ministries and institutions with socio-economic actors and institutions across the country in a concerted "top-down – bottom-up" approach . . . to achieve more balanced development' (Fröhlich 2006: 5). Centralisation was often accounted for by interviewees by reference to resource deficiencies subnationally and a failure by subnational actors and institutions to challenge the extant distribution of power. This and the primacy of EU membership encouraged inertia: 'Maybe it would have been better if there had been more conflict' (interview, Virovitica-Podravina County, 19 May 2008). Engagement with the EU has stimulated MLG but it has also stimulated complexity, which tends to reinforce the centre even though central actors recognise the unsustainability of centralisation and its incompatibility with EU notions of 'good governance'. Paradoxically, powerful central institutions are necessary for the development of subnational engagement and intercounty cooperation (interview, Zagreb Chamber of Commerce, 22 May 2008). Despite over-institutionalisation and complexity 'we [have] a participatory procedure of policy development, which includes discussions between all stakeholders' and 'for the first time you [are] seeing stakeholders coming together from very different areas . . . Of course it sometimes disappears after the purpose of the partnership goes, but there are so many initiatives nowadays that are partnership based' (interview, EPOR, 15 May 2008). The Commission's Screening Report on Chapter 22 noted:

> Croatia has produced a wide range of programming documents notably at national but also at regional levels and amassed considerable experience in doing so. However, besides being of diverging quality, the operational value of these programming documents . . . is limited. Some, notably, the National Strategy for Regional Development, have been produced essentially in view of gaining experience in the process of programming.
>
> (CEC 2007c: 11)

This is a 'three steps forward, two steps back' learning process and interviewees were in no doubt that for partnership working, bilateral cooperation and twinning were crucial in promoting Europeanisation subnationally. The EU's downward pressure to resolve misfit is 'immensely important' because 'politicians want to accede to the EU and they have been given the rules of the game, which they have to follow' (interview, EPOR, 15 May 2008). How they follow these requirements is, of course, profoundly influenced by domestic politics.

Despite ample evidence of their involvement in preparing strategic documents, subnational governments are critical of what they perceive as excessive centralisation and party-political considerations influencing decisions. This tends to encourage the conclusion that there has been no transfer of power in the vertical dimension; such a conclusion is erroneous. An important theme in our interviews (and supported by other evidence) is the scale and ambition of the changes and the centrality of EU pressure in these changes. Decentralisation and partnership are integral to arriving at the common destination of EU membership, so it is hardly surprising 'there has been some progress towards more cooperation, especially when we take into account the creation of the county development agencies [which] are now providing services . . . in relation to the preparation of projects' (interview, Fund for Regional Development, 14 January 2008). A senior figure in CODEF emphasised the primacy of satisfying the Commission, which meant that the system was in constant flux with the regional level being the most problematic, but that it was only a matter of time before the regions became key actors (interview, 14 December 2007). At the time of our fieldwork, some counties had already developed horizontal and vertical connections, building up considerable experience in winning funding and creating networks. Istria, for example, tended to have quite difficult political relations with the centre but had demonstrated considerable skill in exploiting opportunities created by engagement with the EU (interviews, UNDP, 12 February and 4 June 2008). Others would follow.

What we see is a combination of pressure from the EU and a wider modernisation agenda creating opportunities for subnational and societal mobilisation, and engagement with an institutional framework explicitly designed in accordance with EU principles and preferences. There are weaknesses, but regional institutions have a clear remit and potentially are more important than counties in preparation and implementation. Danuta Hübner declared that the EU's and Croatia's 'joint objective is to ensure that Croatia will have the institutional, administrative and budgetary capacity in place in due time to participate in EU cohesion policy. This is a crucial issue' (CEC 2007b: 6). Issues requiring attention included a strong central coordinating body, efficient interministerial coordination, capacity building and appropriate regional management structures.

The Commission has expressed concern that such weaknesses would limit progress. Effective governance needed a strong civil society but the reforms have

> not led to significant changes as [civil society organisations] tend to remain excluded from the policy-making process. Their participation in the legislative process is mostly non-obligatory and the new system for including the public remains vague. With a few notable exceptions, the analytical and financial capacities of [civil society organisations] for monitoring political developments and government decisions remain weak.
>
> (CEC 2010b: 11)

On Chapter 22, 'full implementation of the legislative framework *at all levels* needs to be ensured by further building up administrative capacity'.

The institutional framework was well developed 'but the track record of implementation under IPA so far is mixed, notably due to limited administrative capacity' (CEC 2010b: 45 and 46; emphasis added). Several interviewees doubted that IPA could resolve the misfit. Negotiations on Chapter 22 were, however, declared closed on 19 April 2011.

Macedonia

Macedonia experienced a complex transition after the fall of Yugoslavia and has been exposed to a decade of pressure to modernise and strengthen its institutions, much of which was stimulated by engagement with the EU (interview, United Nations Development Programme, 18 January 2008). When completing the Commission's questionnaire in 2005 the sections dealing with regional indicators were left blank as the data did not exist, even though statistical regions had been created in 2001. Regional development was never a priority and Macedonia had no tradition or experience of regional development politics but the EU forced change. The process was, however, extremely politically sensitive and Macedonia's capacity bargain has implications far wider than in the other cases.

In the aftermath of the 2001 crisis there were fears 'that any form of regionalization would inevitably have to consider regional identities, such as a region inhabited by ethnic Albanians, which in turn would incite talk of territorial autonomy that could lead to secession' (Karajkov 2007: 13). Regional policy's MLG effects were bound up with the Ohrid Framework Agreement (OFA), a wider process of decentralisation generating substantial MLG effects by mandating functional decentralisation to the municipalities. Cohesion is an element of a decentralisation process that created fewer but bigger municipalities with increased responsibilities and which reflected Macedonia's ethnic composition. IPA and DIS stimulate network governance and regionalisation and IPA supports OFA by strengthening Macedonia's ability to assume the obligations of membership, central to which is transferring the management of IPA funds under the DIS, which also encourages the development of civil society organisational capacities and participation (CEC 2010d: 6). The government received accreditation for the national management of Components 3, 4 and 5 in 2009 and accreditation for Component I was granted in December 2010.

Macedonia has a history of centralisation but is subject to powerful external and internal pressures to decentralise, producing a complex process involving the balancing and reconciling of forces tending to reinforce the centre (interview, European Agency for Reconstruction, 15 January 2008). The EU insisted that there could be no territorial solution to ethnic issues even though the OFA created ethnically defined municipalities, so regionalisation had a troubled history. Politicians, fretting over national unity, 'were reluctant to devolve power to the regional level and were more inclined to devolve power to the local [municipal] level' (Karajkov 2007: 13). Notwithstanding, Musa

Xhaferi (Minister for Local Self-Government) noted that decentralisation was well underway and would continue because it was an explicit recognition of 'European standards' (Committee of the Regions 2008b: 3).

Institutions

The Secretariat for European Affairs is the central coordinator and gatekeeper. Its influence flows from accession and the IPA requirement that a single body should be responsible for coordination and monitoring. Its gatekeeper role and technical expertise ensure a leading role but as decentralisation proceeded and accession came closer, it believed that its influence would decline (interview, SEA, 30 January 2008). Strategy documents were generated by SEA but considerable efforts were made to ground these on extensive consultation. SEA found that as policy developed it increased in complexity and, despite actors' growing familiarity with the policy, management of it did not become easier (interview, Secretariat for European Affairs, 30 January 2008).

The Commission Delegation observed and advised but was not an 'active' participant. The Delegation was sanguine about the degree of centralisation, regarding this as necessary for accession and therefore temporary. At the time of our fieldwork, IPA was at a critical point with respect to DIS as accreditation would change the pattern of Commission engagement. The Commission and Delegation's role was to smooth, not guide, Macedonia's transition by ensuring that it created the necessary capabilities and capacities, hence the significance of DIS accreditation. The Delegation did not regard conflict resolution as part of its responsibilities ('we are not referees') (interview, EC Delegation, 19 and 28 May 2008). DG Enlargement, for example, acknowledged the ambitious scale of the reform but criticised 'a persistent lack of constructive dialogue between . . . the different political groups' as a threat to the programme's success (Committee of the Regions 2009: 5). The Commission Delegation regarded cohesion/regional policy as a component of a deeper and broader decentralisation that was fundamental to Macedonia's modernisation and Europeanisation. An important element in this was encouraging subnational actors and the Delegation (for example) worked closely with ZELS (Community of Local Self-Government Units) (interview, EC Delegation, 19 May 2008; Committee of the Regions 2009: 6).

IPA is implemented via multi-annual programmes aligned to the Commission's triennial Multi-Annual Indicative Planning process, promotes familiarity with cohesion processes and encourages institutional development. IPA and DIS are of enormous significance for the capacity bargain, enabling Macedonia to undertake programming, programme management, financial control, monitoring, and programme evaluation and address the legal, administrative and institutional misfit with the EU. Those elements of the state with the closest involvement with IPA tend to be the most Europeanised and 'spillover' was happening because 'IPA assistance is focused on capacity building, particularly those capacities which are necessary for becoming a member state' (interview, Ministry of Finance, 28 May 2008). The SEA State Secretary, Dusica Perisic, argued that Macedonia's use of IPA funds 'demonstrate initiative, participation, ownership' and most important of all reveal an 'understand[ing] of how the process worked' (Committee of the Regions 2009: 5). DIS accreditation would establish 'that the country will be able to implement and use [structural] funds on its own.' DIS is a key indicator of Europeanisation because prior to DIS, funds were managed 'through a centralised system where the Commission was in charge of the implementation of the projects and the use of funds.' DIS was 'a major step forward . . . without accreditation we will not be able to use the funds available to support regional development' and signals the achievement of EU governance goals (interviews, Ministry of Finance, 28 May and Secretariat for European Affairs, 18 April 2008).

By 2008, 57 of 84 municipalities had completed the transfer of functions and were about to begin fiscal decentralisation, an essential precursor to regional development. Five of the eight regional planning centres (each composed of around nine municipalities) had been established to 'prepare and implement the development strategy of the region'. After adoption by the Council for Regional Development and the government, an action plan would be developed but 'the administrative and financial capabilities of municipalities were still limited. Furthermore, the exchange of experience and sharing of know-how with other European countries was needed' (Committee of the Regions 2008b: 5–6). Addressing regional inequalities and variations in public service delivery meant that 'Significant additional efforts at central and local level are needed to strengthen the administrative capacities of some municipalities'. Further action was required to end partisan appointments and dismissals (CEC 2010d: 9–10).

In April 2001 eight NUTS 3 regions were created but 'Macedonia has a consistent history of one-tier local self-government with the municipality as the basic unit' (Karajkov 2007: 15). The Law on Balanced Regional Development (2007) represented a major policy shift as previously there was no regional policy and it created eight planning regions and related institutions. Regional capacity was politically controversial as it appeared to threaten both the municipalities and the centre, so change was minimal: regions were not part of the local self-government system but were under the central government (Karajkov 2007: 15). Implementation proved difficult (for several months there was no local government minister because of problems in the governing coalition) but the broad policy was clear and a range of institutions (such as the National Council for Regional Development, the Bureau for Development and regional Centres for Development) were authorised. This was 'a major change of direction [requiring a] shift from thinking in largely sectoral terms to thinking in territorial terms' (Karajkov 2007: 16) and 'we are for the first time putting in place a mechanism and a system with a bottom-up approach, through engaging with the municipalities [now] joined in planning regions' (interview, Ministry of Local Self-Government, 25 May 2008).

The Council for Balanced Regional Development was composed of representatives of the line ministries, the Regional Councils, which coordinate sectoral policies and regional development plans, and representatives of the municipalities (who prepare and implement projects) in each region. The Bureau for Balanced Regional Development was the operational body under the Ministry of Local Self-Government (MLSG) (which coordinates policy development and liaises with the line ministries which prepare projects) and coordinates the work of the Regional Planning Centres, which supported the Regional Councils. The Council was intended to interact with municipalities, civil society organisations and business, the purpose being to establish a 'meeting point between the two, the top and the bottom priorities, in order to come up with joint national priorities for the planning regions' (interview, Ministry of Local Self-Government, 25 May 2008). However, central government remained dominant and the new system was slow to come into operation. Issues of compliance and capacity, particularly financial and technical, were rife; problems exacerbated by shifting political alliances and the demands of ethnic politics, but the direction of change was towards the subnational. The EC Delegation saw the LBRD as a significant milestone, forming the basis for a 'new policy for regional development and constituted a partial precursor to EU regional policy'. Centralisation was admitted and capacity problems at regional and local level were serious, but this was to be expected given the newness of the policy (interview, EC Delegation, 19 May 2008).

In Slovenia and Croatia we noted the emphasis placed on developing *national* capacity in the accession process. IPA focused on the development of robust interministerial cooperation in drafting plans and programming, whereas the OFA pushed functions down to the municipalities. Emmanuelle Guienheuf of the Commission Delegation argued that IPA's added-value flowed from implementation: 'local and regional authorities were managing the programmes themselves and could thereby acquire valuable knowledge' (Committee of the Regions 2009: 5). Engagement with the EU, therefore, has been central to the evolution of Macedonia's governance since 2001. IPA intersects with the OFA decentralisation process as both depend on the appropriate state capacities and capabilities. Horizontally, consultation not partnership dominated because central ministries controlled the drafting of documentation and granting of access, and although there was engagement with civil society, the latter's influence was limited. There was, naturally, conflict over the distribution of resources and this had greater political sensitivity because of the potentially divisive impact of ethnicity.

The network

Compared to the other cases, Macedonia's network is very simple and centralised (Figure 4.5), reflecting both its newness as a state and candidate status, both of which necessitate extensive state-building. In common with

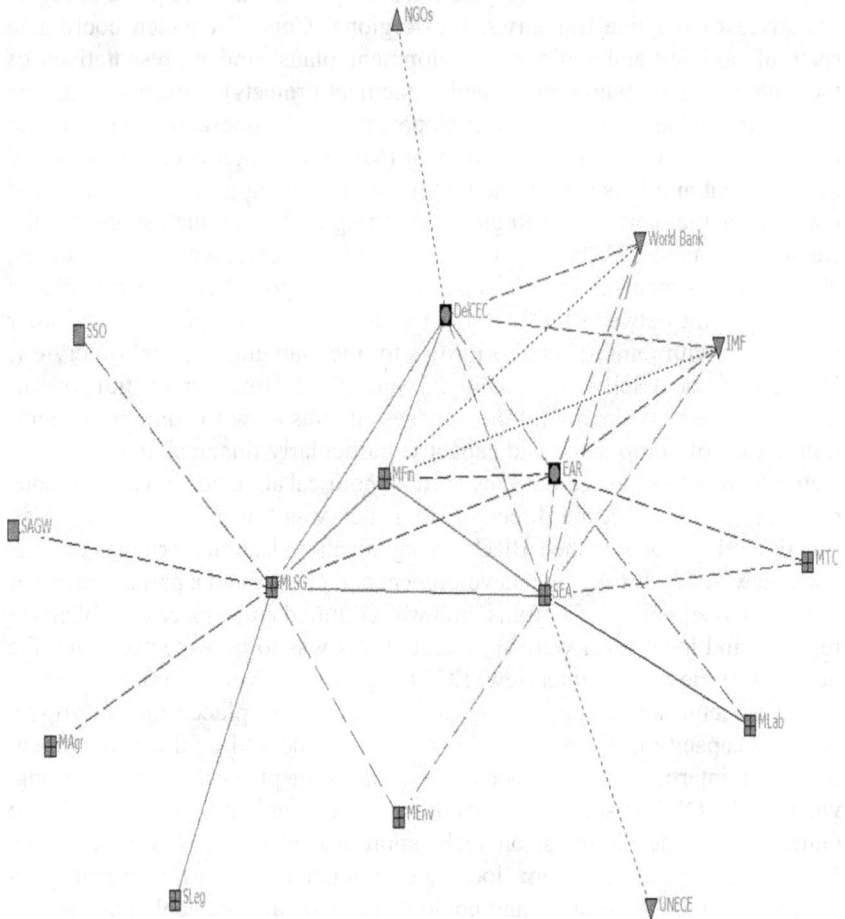

Figure 4.5 The cohesion network: Macedonia

Croatia, international bodies other than the EU (for example, World Bank, IMF, United Nations Commission for Europe) are in the network but are of declining importance. The Delegation of the European Commission is a direct participant as, of course, is the EU via enlargement policy and its sponsorship of the OFA, both of which condition the operation of the Macedonian polity. The network's focus on a few central institutions – the SEA, Ministry of Local Self-Government and the Ministry of Finance – reflects the preferences of elites concerned about centrifugal forces jeopardising membership by undermining stability, and a Commission anxious to see the development of an effective and legitimate state. Both are constrained by past commitments and rhetoric concerning participation and decentralisation. The problem is how to enhance central effectiveness while decentralising power and responsibility.

Organisation	SNA abbreviation
Delegation of the European Commission	DelCEC
European Agency for Reconstruction	EAR
International Monetary Fund	IMF
Ministry of Agriculture	MAgr
Ministry of Environment	MEnv
Ministry of Finance	MFin
Ministry of Labour	MLab
Ministry of Local Self-Government	MLSG
Ministry of Transport and Communication	MTC
Non-Governmental Organisations	NGOs
State Authority for Geodetic Works	SAGW
Secretariat for European Affairs	SEA
Secretariat for Legislature	SLeg
State Statistical Office	SSO
United Nations Economic Commission for Europe	UNECE
World Bank	World Bank

Rhetorically, the Commission and government see the two as so intertwined as to be indistinguishable but in reality the network has two core actors – MSLG and SEA – that manage decentralisation and accession respectively as interconnected processes and which provide access to the centre for subnational and civil society interests in their capacity as gatekeepers. This ensures access to the centre and central control; the Commission accepts this because central capacity is essential for accession and political stability. The Secretariat for the Legislature is part of this core network because of the need to ensure speedy legislation and to ensure parliamentarians are locked into the twin processes of accession and decentralisation. However, as we saw in Chapter 2, legislation can be passed too quickly to be absorbed.

A SEA civil servant described the network as under EU 'guidance' but that 'there is more consultation and cooperation, openness and participation' than hitherto (interview, SEA, 18 April 2008). The *National Programme for the Adoption of the Acquis* discussed the problem of network governance, arguing for a multi-level process characterised vertical and horizontal 'cooperation, connection and active participation' by national, regional and local actors (Republic of Macedonia 2007: 214). Despite rapid institutional development, network relationships remained problematic. Preparing strategic documents did bring actors together, something central to the EU's preferred mode of governance, the specific requirements of cohesion policy and the wider decentralisation process. SEA pushed strongly for a shift from participation to partnership and was sometimes criticised by subnational actors (and by central ministries and party politicians) for so doing.

The *National Development Plan*, for example, was prepared 'with the active participation of state bodies, local self-government units and other institutions coordinated by the Ministerial Committee on the political level and the Secretariat at an operational level' (Republic of Macedonia 2007: 215). Interviewees at SEA were resigned to the accusation of subnational actors – governmental and non-governmental – that they were excluded, a charge often made (it was argued) to disguise their own inadequacies. SEA interviewees emphasised the system's newness and it needed time to settle down; establishing the regional policy system had been technically and politically difficult (interview, SEA, 18 April 2008, for example). The eight planning regions are more or less equal in terms of resources and potential but there are substantial disparities in economic development. The least developed tend to be ethnic-Albanian areas. The most developed wish to retain their position; the least developed to close the gap by redistribution, raising the prospect of serious conflict (Arsova n.d.: 2). Observing the operation of this system the Commission Delegation concluded that it was both participatory and conflictual, a combination deemed positive. As this was redistributive politics involving limited resources, 'every side would like to get as much as they can [but] all sides cannot be satisfied'. This reflected the growth of 'normal' politics with conflict contained within institutions and subject to the 'rules of the game' (interview, EC Delegation, 19 May 2008).

The relationship between DIS and the growth of network governance is obvious. DIS signals an ability to manage increasingly complex policy in a process that requires the aggregation of a wide range of competing interests into a consensus over policy lasting an extended period of time. This means that domestic political institutions must achieve levels of capability, effectiveness and legitimacy broadly comparable to those found in the EU (interview, Ministry of Finance, 27 May 2008). A common complaint made of this emerging network is that resources and capabilities weaken with distance from the centre, so reinforcing centralisation. However, a network's purpose is to *combine* actors and their resources so that the exchange of resources achieves common goals. A civil servant at the Ministry of Local Self-Government commented: 'we had a Slovenian delegation visiting a couple of years ago when we started discussing how to use EU funds. They informed us that the office responsible for the management of [their] funds comprised six people' (interview, Ministry of Local Self-Government, 25 May 2008). Influence in network governance depended, in other words, not on bureaucratic resources controlled but on the coherence of the network. The transfer of competences from the national is central to OFA, IPA and EU accession and to be effective decentralisation must be accompanied by adequate resources and expertise. This will take time to negotiate and complete (interview, United Nations Development Programme, 18 January 2008).

Decentralisation focused on the vertical, regionalisation on horizontal connections, but both are interconnected because regions depend on the engagement of the municipalities, as well as on engagement between regions and between regions and the centre. To be effective, all actors will need to surrender some autonomy (interview, EC Delegation, 19 May 2008). A Danish adviser commented that 'IPA funds represented a promising opportunity for cooperation between municipalities. However, certain barriers prevented local authorities from participating fully [for example] the lack of capacity to prepare and implement projects' (Committee of the Regions 2009: 7). Under the National Strategy, the 'bottom-up' principle and the alignment of party, municipal and ethnic interests will pull actors into networks, the Ministry of Self-Government expects, to undertake planning and programming, as well as implementation, thereby promoting a more plural power distribution (interview, 25 May 2008). The visibility of the municipalities has increased and the regions will increase in visibility, albeit from a low base. Hitherto 'central government has been reluctant to transfer resources' to the regions and municipalities, hence their frequent complaints about 'how much they receive in relation to the transferred competencies' but interviewees at SEA insisted this would change (interview, SEA, 16 April 2008).

Fostering partnership working and network governance was essential for regional development and 'A multi-level approach was therefore being applied since capacity at all levels was paramount' to extend vertical and horizontal working (Committee of the Regions 2009: 8). Decentralisation increases complexity but also reinforces incentives to develop networks. Civil society organisations remain the weakest component. The Commission recognised that the 'Involvement of civil society in the policy development process and in legislative drafting is growing. Nonetheless, a consistent approach to encouraging all-inclusive public participation ... needs to be developed' (CEC 2010d: 17). It is not that civil society bodies do not exist, there are many, nor are they ignorant of the process or reluctant to engage with it; the difficulty is that many are at an early stage of development and there are few authoritative peak organisations (like ZELS). Consequently, civil society organisations often spend more time competing against each other rather than trying to influence the policy process (interview, EC Delegation, 19 May 2008).

Sources of change

Macedonia is the most complex of the polities considered; its institutions are dealing with thorny political issues, as well as the legacy of corruption and poor governance. Engagement with the EU permeates this complexity. When asked to explain change, a member of SEA responded, 'It is something that we want and it is required by the regulations of the EU' (interview, 16 April

2008). The EU has been important in resolving domestic tensions, being described as a 'trigger effect' stimulating change but 'This does not mean that there is no local ownership' (interview, SEA, 18 April 2008). From the EU's perspective, IPA and DIS were vital in stimulating change, the latter being invested with huge practical and symbolic significance (interview, EC Delegation, 19 May 2008). While the Commission has in no sense 'disengaged', the relationship has evolved, reflecting progress on (for example) decentralisation, political stability and improved capabilities, as well an increased domestic participation consequent on Macedonia's engagement with the EU (interview, EC Delegation, 30 January 2008).

Our evidence suggests that combining the accession and OFA decentralisation dynamics will generate horizontal links and task-specific groups at the regional level. This will not happen quickly because 'government seeks to build capacity at a regional level, not least to conform to the requirements of the accession process [but] It is difficult to expect anything more than an "institutional regionalization"' (Krajkov 2007: 20). Regional policy development is complex, lengthy, politically sensitive and inherently multi-level. It is also a component of a ten-year strategy utilising EU governance principles – partnership, coordination, co-financing, transparency, subsidiarity and sustainability – and constitutes an extremely complex governance agenda. A primary aim is intermunicipal cooperation at all levels of the polity (Arsova n.d.: 1). The unanswerable question at this stage is the likelihood of these embryonic-Type II MLG developments breaking out of ethnic political silos. Taking both the OFA and IPA, the net EU effect has been to stimulate MLG via the strengthening of territorial governance and strengthening the capacities of subnational and non-state actors with an emphasis on cross-institutional cooperation and coordination.

Interviewees could point to a substantial accumulation of knowledge and experience through learning-by-doing, reinforced by the OFA decentralisation process (interview, EAR, 15 January 2008). IPA was characterised as the 'primary school' and to progress further Macedonia needed external help and a willingness by domestic elites to push radical change (interview, MLSG, 25 May 2008). Cumulatively, the pressure from, and engagement with, the EU improved the government's ability to steer and not row; as a result, the EU would become less directive but much of this remains in the realm of the potential (interview, SEA, 18 April 2008). Learning and building is slow and obstacles remain ('lack of information, rigidity of central government, sometimes the negligence of local government . . . lack of communication') and resources, especially at the subregional level, remain in short supply (interview, SEA, 16 April 2008). Reviewing Chapter 22, the Commission concluded that 'No relevant progress has been made in the legislative framework', the implementation of the regional operational programme was 'significantly delayed' and 'The administrative capacity of the national structures dealing with IPA Component III, and in particular of the relevant line ministries needs further strengthening.' The Commission concluded that 'preparations in the area of regional policy and coordination of structural instruments need further effort and improvements' (CEC 2010d: 35, 56).

Decentralisation 'improved the possibilities for citizens to take part in the decision-making process' and in the case of regionalisation, 'EU support in the form of funds for technical assistance, administrative reform and infrastructure' was very important. IPA had been instrumental 'in support-ing the candidate and potential candidate countries' efforts to comply with the accession criteria' (Committee of the Regions 2009: 3). Nevertheless, 'the impression is that government is doing things just to have the necessary paperwork done to demonstrate it to the European Commission. The concept of regional development is completely new . . . and it will take considerable restructuring of competences' (Karajkov 2007: 20). Evidence of partnership working is, because of ethnic politics and the OFA process, of greater significance in Macedonia than in the other three cases. This significance has implications for both types of MLG reflecting 'a clear EU requirement for wider partnership, the involvement of all stakeholders . . . no programme will be applied without a wider participatory approach'. In the preceding decade 'there has been growing cooperation between the government and NGOs as civil society became increasingly significant' (interview, SEA, 18 April 2008). This is undeniable. Nevertheless, a theme in the interviews was the divergence between what is *supposed* to happen and what *does* happen. Considerable misfit persists and neither the IPA nor DIS appears sufficiently powerful to span this gap and the danger is that change will be confined to the centre. This is reflected in the network architecture where central actors have a dual role of gatekeeper and proxy for subnational actors. From the perspective of OFA this could stimulate tensions that might be difficult to control. Such tension might be mitigated by the widespread agreement on the value of EU membership and what needs to be done to secure that goal. The main problem is one of MLG, the complex and highly political relationship between the centre and the municipalities.

Conclusions

The number and scope of the policy instruments and their governance implications outlined at the start of this chapter means that the cohesion capacity bargain is highly visible and of broad impact. Candidate and member states must conform to secure EU funds so that we can identify extensive Europeanisation and MLG effects in all our cases. Europeanisation and MLG are fundamental to the capacity bargain and explain changes in governance but MLG lacks explanatory power. This is because all states – even the most unitary – are multi-level, so what is of consequence is how multi-levelled-ness works and what this tells us about power. In all our cases we see centralisation contrary to core tenets of the policy, but the source of that convergence is not just the policy per se but also the filtering and processing of that policy by national authorities.

There is a substantial EU impact on policy and governance but the capacity bargain network has a limited effect on territorial organisation. In Greece, regions were created for the absorption of funds and were a modification of existing institutions. After 1993, EU pressure on the pro-EU Simitis government (committed to a domestic reform agenda) saw a series of changes that promoted accommodation with EU policy without weakening centralisation by expanding task-specific bodies at various territorial levels. Further layers of complexity were added after 2000. What we see in Greece, therefore, is the incremental adjustment of the status quo (primarily Type II MLG but with weak Type I elements, notably the thirteen regions created in 1989) that, despite the spill-over of EU principles and practices, served to reinforce centralisation.

In Slovenia 'traditional' governance is modified by the capacity bargain network as part of accession. Prior to accession, Slovenia's government was keener than the Commission to promote regionalisation; though small, Slovenia has clearly defined geographic and socio-economic regions but the Commission favoured central capacity. This, given the subsequent controversy over regions/provinces after accession, was probably the correct choice. During accession the Slovenian authorities opted for a simple network dominated by the centre and this continued after accession, albeit with an opening to non-central and civil society organisations. Slovenia has not moved beyond Type II MLG; RDAs and the NUTS regions are off-shoots of the centre.

In Croatia Europeanisation is obvious. Substantial change has been generated as the capacity bargain with the EU develops and is reflected in the complex architecture of the network, but this is a network with a relatively simple distribution of power. There is considerable subnational/subregional activity and participation encased within this framework. Horizontal activity is developing but takes the form of interministerial coordination. Some actors (e.g. RDAs) are starting to develop autonomy and horizontal cooperation, exploiting the opportunities offered by programming and partnership, but the dominant mode of governance is via Type II MLG.

Macedonia is the most complex case. The capacity bargain is a complicated decentralisation driven by both the demands of accession and the OFA. For this reason Type II MLG predominates. This is reflected in the network's architecture, which is centralised with few actors so as to promote coherence and coordination. Its main participants seek to manage access by subnational and societal actors, and the flows are largely vertical. Horizontal developments have more to do with developing central capacity to coordinate than with developing Type I MLG. The regional planning councils are, in any case, too recent to have any substantive effect as yet.

The SNA indicates the existence of two subnetworks comprising the cohesion policy network. The first is the *strategic* subnetwork. This is composed of few central actors (in some cases including regional actors as extensions of the centre) responsible for interpreting EU policies and preferences and applying these to the national context via the preparation of key documents and determining institutions and processes. In Slovenia municipalities were identified by SNA as core actors but interviews confirmed participation rarely equalled influence. Participation by actors from outside the core is common, but these are essentially auxiliary and reactive; the initiative remains with the core, whose membership remains stable over time and which sets the operational parameters. The second subnetwork is primarily concerned with *implementation*, including the development of proposals, subject to centrally determined strategy. This subnetwork (or, more accurately, cluster of subnetworks) is composed of multiple actors and its operation is more pluralist than that of the strategic subnetwork. Individual actors may have considerable longevity and experience but they are subject to a centrally originated strategy which reduces their autonomy and influence. The subnetworks are, therefore, function- and task-driven, when the function or task ends the subnetwork either dissolves and its components recombine or it mutates to reflect new tasks and functions. In all cases central actors operate as gatekeepers and representatives for non-core actor interests.

Cohesion is presented by the EU as a major example of the Community working for its citizens. The capacity bargain, potentially, helps counter-perceptions of a distant and autocratic Commission and our evidence is that, without the EU, regional policy in this form, perhaps in any form, would not exist. The potential political benefits are that the provision of resources to address embedded inequalities and to enable a country to benefit from the opportunities offered by EU membership can ease the domestic costs of adaptation caused by addressing misfit. Administratively, the capacity bargain contributes to this by broadening involvement by civil society organisations and locating some distributional conflicts in a rules and norm-based framework. The key word is 'potentially'; whether or not the potential is realised is a different matter.

The cohesion capacity bargain trades externally mandated organisation and policy for additional resources not available to non-candidates and non-members, but states are left to implement policy in accord with domestic needs and traditions. This produces a pattern of domestic redistributive politics contained within an externally determined framework. The capacity bargain requires states to demonstrate their ability to implement policy and the *acquis*, and to conform to EU governance preferences. The policy not only offers the prospect of building a more effective state but also a more legitimate one by encouraging solidarity and economic growth, as well as broader societal participation in making and implementing policy.

The capacity bargain network encourages the growth of infrastructural power, challenging historic patterns of bureaucratic power, with the state having power *through* society rather than power *over* a society. The former, represented by RPP, challenges the historical centralisation of power which is reflected in the associated policy network (or 'crystallisation') dominated by the state. Our cases illustrate, however, the difficulty of establishing infrastructural power in polities with a tradition of bureaucratic power.

The consequences are policy networks, albeit with national variations, showing signs of increasingly diverse participation and growing complexity but where power remains dominated by the centre. The capacity bargain means that the state remains central to the specific network(s) generated. Its role is to mobilise and coordinate interests, ensure programme development and ensure implementation; while there is evidence of pluralisation (civil society being the biggest winner) it is also apparent that states can capture policy (Slovenia) and resist it (Greece) to reinforce the status quo. Candidate states have less room for manoeuvre but certain structural features (particularly that implementation is a national task) enable national governments (sometimes with the connivance and tacit consent of the Commission) to elevate aspects of the policy (e.g. absorptive capacity) over others (e.g. partnership). The effect is to reinforce the centre. In the cases examined here, Europeanisation and MLG have altered how policy is done, often very significantly: new actors have been empowered and new structures created, but the fundamental distribution of power remains unchanged.

5 Migration and border security

Introduction

This chapter analyses adaptation in Greece, Slovenia, Croatia and Macedonia to the EU *acquis* in the areas of migration and border security, and the capacity bargain networks generated by this engagement. Migration and border security are not typically included in analyses of MLG because they tend to be seen as tightly hierarchical policy fields with little scope for MLG dynamics. Our rationale for exploring developments in the area of migration and border security are, first, that it is clearly a transboundary issue that does involve an extensive role for the EU in policy development; the ordering of capacity across governance scales to include both a supranational and a subnational dimension; and a role for international organisations other than the EU. Second, by analysing migration and border security it is possible to explore variation by policy type in the dynamics of MLG and Europeanisation. Compared to distributive policies, regulatory policies such as migration and border security are specific and focused. They target the behaviour of individuals defined by policy-makers as a group requiring regulation and seek to limit the discretion of those implementing policy by specifying who is to be subject to regulation. Individual regulatory decisions are based on the application of general rules and the costs are borne by those subject to regulation, while benefits accrue to the wider group. Normatively, regulatory policies stigmatise those being regulated as a 'threat' to the wider community.

The chapter addresses three key issues that are central to this book's analysis. First, it shows how political engagement with the EU has changed domestic modes of governance of migration and border security in our four case countries as an outcome of processes of Europeanisation. This is done through application of our 'bottom-up-down' design (Graziano and Vink 2007: 10) that captures key components of policy development in all four case countries, as well as the interplay between the EU and national levels. The specification of the functional, political and administrative dimensions of the 'capacity bargain' in the area of migration and border security also facilitates assessment of the *types* of adaptation and *forms* of policy approach. This is shown to be particularly relevant given the EU's self-declared 'fight against illegal immigration' with its strong focus on external frontier controls.

Second, the chapter reveals the important role played by other EU member states in providing policy templates, advice and guidance, and also by international migration organisations (IMOs) as service providers in 'migration management'. There is thus a distinct multi-level scaling of policy, but rather than prompting the development of new modes of participation or the empowerment of NGOs, emphasis has been placed on the inclusion of domestic officials (usually from interior ministries) within transgovernmental networks with a security focus. This is hardly surprising given the nature of policy-making on migration and border security in other EU member states, but does, of course, provide a contrast with cohesion policy.

Finally, the chapter explores policy convergence and, more specifically, asks whether the EU induces convergence. It will be shown that there is substantial pressure for adaptation to the EU migration and border security *acquis* and that this does induce pressure for policy convergence. The main focus is on external frontier control with far less attention paid to the internal dynamics of migration. This is particularly the case in Greece, where there is shown to be an important role for local governments and private actors, such as employers.

Borders and migration policy

International migration encompasses those forms of population movement that involve the crossing of state borders for a given period of time, usually exceeding a year (thus excluding tourism and short-term business travel). The location and meaning of state borders is central to the analysis of international migration, as too are shifts in location and shifts in their meaning (Zolberg 1989). State borders make international migration 'visible' as a process distinct from mobility within state borders. The EU, through the creation of a free movement framework between its member states, obviously changes the relationship between member states because it facilitates mobility for EU citizens. This chapter's main focus is on movement by non-EU or 'third country nationals' (TCNs) into EU member states, although, as we shall see, visa liberalisation for Croatian and Macedonian nationals allowing them to move more freely into EU member states is an important part of their move towards the EU and of policy conditionality (Schimmelfennig and Sedelmeier 2004; Trauner 2009).

Broad definitions of international migration mask issue complexity. People may move from one country to another to work, to join with family members, to study or to seek refuge. Each of these categories can then be broken down into further subcategories. For example, labour migration may be into higher or lower skilled employment and may be for shorter or longer time periods. It may also be that labour migrants have a regular or irregular status. In Greece, for example, the absence of an immigration policy until the late 1990s meant that most migrants moved into the 'twilight zone' of the informal economy where 'free markets reigned' and where their irregular status left many migrants vulnerable to exploitation (Baldwin-Edwards 1999). The three former Yugoslavian cases all had to deal with the population effects of Yugoslavia's break-up while, in the context of EU policy, they have been defined as 'transit countries' for 'irregular migrants' seeking to move into other EU member states. Terms such as 'transit migration' and the 'fight against illegal immigration' are commonplace in EU discourse about the causes, drivers and effects of international migration by TCNs and the location of the policy challenges.

There is a further important dimension to this point as the EU's role in developing border controls and systems of migration management has been an important component of state-building in new member states. As Thomson puts it: 'the harmonisation of Slovenia's migration policies in line with EU standards has provided a structure for this process [of state-building], and has partly shaped the contours of its fledgling nation-state' (2006: 10). The same insight with different temporal sequencing can be applied to Croatia and Macedonia. In Greece, there is an association with state 'modernisation' rather than state-building.

Given the centrality of borders, it is useful to reflect on their meaning within the EU's Area of Freedom, Security and Justice (AFSJ). The official EU viewpoint expressed by the European Commission (CEC 2007d: 14) is that efficient and effective border management will enable citizens to live in an area of security and freedom where they can travel more freely and where cross–border trade will be facilitated, all of which are key prerequisites for economic growth and poverty reduction. Enhanced cross-border flows will also support the development of more open societies with a better understanding and tolerance of their neighbours and their cultural, religious and linguistic differences. At the same time, threats related to the abuse of malfunctioning border management systems, such as smuggling of goods and trafficking in human beings, drugs and arms, can be more effectively addressed if the authorities responsible for the management of state borders improve their communication, exchange of information and overall cooperation. This essentially positive vision of border management in an AFSJ contrasts with a range of more critical perspectives on EU migration policy (Bigo 2001; Huysmans 2006; Neal 2009).

The tension at the heart of the relationship between mobility and immigration control becomes evident if we consider the issue of what has been called 'boundary build-up'. Work on the US–Mexico border is apposite in this respect because there too we see how

> complex interchanges between state actors and groups of citizens produced a deep set of concerns about the ethno-cultural, socio-economic and bio-physical security of the nation, all of which are inherently geographical given their inextricable relationship to a particular territory. Boundary build-up was thus a territorial strategy to achieve the security and assuage those concerns.
>
> (Purcell and Nevins 2005: 213)

The EU seeks liberalisation in the movement of goods, capital and services, but has a far more ambivalent relationship to population mobility (Geddes 2011). At the same time, regional integration between economically developed countries can produce migration pressures driven by international income inequalities. Andreas argues that there is

> a more complex and paradoxical dynamic: the expansion of cross-border economic activity and the decline of geopolitical tensions are paralleled by a rapid expansion of border policing and rising tensions over prohibited cross-border flows. This is evident, most strikingly, along the United States–Mexico border and along the EU external borders of the European Union. These borders are increasingly protected and monitored, not to deter armies or impose tariffs on trade, but to confront a perceived invasion of 'undesirables', particularly illegal immigrants, drug traffickers, and other clandestine transnational actors.
>
> (1998: 591)

A key point about all four of our case countries is that they are seen as located on Europe's frontline in the 'fight' against 'unwanted' and 'undesirable' forms of migration.

Migration in SEE

Tables 5.1, 5.2 and 5.3 provide some illustrative data on migration flows. Table 5.1 shows Greece to be the major immigration country in SEE with much of the movement from neighbouring Albania. Slovenia has a smaller migrant population than Greece and experienced a relatively smooth process of central state adaptation to the EU migration and border security *acquis*. There is a growing immigrant population in Slovenia (Table 5.1), but flows are often specifically channelled to sectors such as tourism and agriculture because of the growth in these sectors, coupled with the preference of employers for 'flexible' migrant workers deployed for shorter term, seasonal or temporary work. Slovenia, Croatia and Macedonia all experienced refugee flows after the break-up of Yugoslavia. International organisations such as the International Organization for Migration (IOM) have sought to assist with programmes of voluntary return. In the relative absence of immigration, Croatia has undertaken a rapid development of its framework for migration policy that is directly related to the requirements of EU membership. This is consistent with the strong emphasis in domestic politics on adaptation to the EU *acquis*. The policy focus in Croatia has been on border management in a regional context plus attempts to develop a regulatory framework for admissions and labour migration. Data and information on Macedonian flows are sparse, not least because Macedonians may have been categorised as Macedonians, Bulgarians, Greeks, Serbs or Yugoslavs. Following NATO's intervention in 1999, hundreds of thousands of Kosovar Albanians moved

Table 5.1 Population of foreign citizens in Greece and Slovenia (2009)

	Total population (000s)	Non-nationals Total		Citizens of other EU states		TCNs	
		000s	%	000s	%	000s	%
Greece	11260.4	929.5	8.3	161.6	1.4	767.9	6.8
Slovenia	2032.4	70.6	3.5	4.2	0.2	66.4	3.3

Source: Eurostat 2009.

Table 5.2 Immigration and citizenship in Croatia and Macedonia (2008)

	Total immigration	Nationals		Non-nationals Total		Citizens of other EU member states		TCNs	
	000s	000s	%	000s	%	000s	%	000s	%
Croatia	14.5	12.5	86.1	2.0	13.9	0.5	3.7	1.5	10.2
Macedonia	1.1	0.2	20.8	0.8	79.1	0.1	12.0	0.7	67.1

Source: Eurostat 2009.

Table 5.3 Most numerous non-nationals by country of citizenship in Greece and Slovenia (2008)

Greece			Slovenia		
Citizens of	Number	%	Citizens of	Number	%
Albania	577500	63.7	Bosnia-Herzegovina	32500	47.3
Ukraine	22300	2.5	Serbia	13800	20.1
Georgia	17200	1.9	Macedonia	7400	10.9
Pakistan	16200	1.8	Croatia	7000	10.2
Egypt	13900	1.5	Ukraine	1100	1.5

Source: Eurostat 2009.

across the border into Macedonia. High levels of unemployment have led to many Macedonians seeing working abroad as an escape from poverty or reliance on remittances from family members abroad. A policy concern has been trafficking for sexual and labour exploitation to and through Macedonia of people from Ukraine, Moldova, Russia, Belarus, Romania, Albania and Serbia (Surtees 2005).

Of central importance is the EU focus on border security and external frontiers. Greece has land borders of 1,170km, around 16,000km of sea borders and more than 3,000 islands. There are 79 legal points of entry (29 airports, 4 train stations, 12 land and 34 sea crossings). Greece has a key EU role too because it is a point of entry to the Schengen area. This means that Greek officials use the Schengen Information System (SIS) database to alert other member states to those who may have been refused permission to enter Greece. The FRONTEX annual report 2010 estimated that 75 per cent of total illegal border crossings in the EU took place through Greece, an increase from 50 per cent in the previous year, which was seen to indicate the effects of intensified action in Italy and Spain.

This focus on external frontiers does neglect the fact that the majority of irregular migrants enter an EU member state via regular channels and then 'overstay'. The EU policy frame has, however, been strongly focused on the management of external frontiers and 'the fight against illegal immigration' (CEC 2006a). This 'fight' has an external dimension too because of the ways in which the EU's 'global approach' to migration has also focused on coopting neighbouring states and regions (CEC 2006b; CEC 2007e; CEC 2008a).

SEE has been identified by Marenin (2010) as a 'territorial hole' within the EU, by which is meant that EU enlargements in 2004 and 2007 leapfrogged the seven countries (including Kosovo) that emerged after the collapse of Yugoslavia (with the exception of Slovenia) plus Albania and created an external border within the EU. As Marenin notes, 'this poses a starkly different policy problem for IBM (Integrated Border Management) in the Balkans, as the new states lack political stability and much of the transnational illegal movement of people and goods follows the so-called Balkan route which runs right through the territorial hole' (2010: 13). This creates the potential for perverse or unintended effects of policy, as the imposition of Schengen visa standards means that people who could cross freely from non-EU states now need visas with the effect that the Western Balkans faces the prospect of being driven back into an inner ghetto space. This applies, of course, only to law-abiding citizens, since criminals can walk or bribe their way across these frontiers with little difficulty. The introduction of visa requirements is a stimulus for corruption and criminality, since the borders are unenforceable, and the attempts to install them create incentives for illegal activity, including the trafficking of goods and people (Marenin 2010: 37).

This 'territorial hole' can be related to issues of functional, political and administrative capacity for new (or in the Greek case, relatively new) countries of immigration. As an employee of a Greek migration policy research institute linked to the Interior Ministry put it to us,

> It is difficult for other [EU] states to comprehend the weight of the migration problem for the southern states and by this I don't only mean the financial burden, but also the problem of how to prevent these people from moving further into Europe. But this creates a problem for the states

that lie on the south-east border of Europe . . . other EU states should share this problem and the burden that stems from it. And the cost.

(Interview, 20 February 2008)

The language used by this interviewee relates very directly to our understanding of the resource base of the capacity bargains struck by member states and by aspiring member states. There is little sense in any of our case countries that this is an issue that they could deal with alone. It is a transboundary concern and one that is seen to require a common European response and the sharing of the burden or responsibility. That said, there is also an underlying dilemma. While ideas about solidarity have to some extent been accepted in policy fields such as cohesion, they are more contested in migration policy. There is some agreement on financial solidarity to develop policy and capacity in SEE, but much less support for forms of solidarity that might involve the redistribution of migrants themselves within the EU.

EU measures

Cooperation on migration and border security over almost thirty years has led to the development of what Wallace (2004) calls networks of 'intensive transgovernmentalism'. These are seen as distinct from intergovernmental (state cooperation) or supranational (EU-driven) policy types because there is intensive cooperation on a regular basis between groups of ministers and officials with responsibility for migration and asylum. This intensive interaction is sectoral, i.e. focused on a particular area of policy with associated specialisms and expertise. This complements the 'political' aspect of the capacity bargain, as officials from each of our four case countries have been included within transgovernmental networks, often comprising officials drawn from interior ministries and associated internal security agencies.

The main EU legal document dealing with migration and border security is Regulation 562/2006, which establishes a Community code on the rules governing the movement of persons across borders (the Schengen Borders Code). This brings into the EU framework the Schengen Convention of 1990, which implemented the Schengen Agreement of June 1985. The Schengen Convention came into effect with nine participating states in 1995 that abolished checks at internal borders and created a single external border where entry checks for access to the Schengen area are carried out. These checks are based on a common set of rules, such as a common visa policy, police and judicial cooperation, and the SIS to pool and share data. Greece and Slovenia are Schengen members and apply the Schengen *acquis*. Croatia and Macedonia are required to adapt to the requirements of the Schengen border code as a fundamental component of the measures specified in Chapter 24 (Freedom, Justice and Security) of the accession framework. Council regulation 2007/2004 created a European Agency for the Management of Operational Cooperation at the External Borders (FRONTEX). There is also

EU involvement in the expulsion of irregular migrants through the 'Return' directive 2008/115 of June 2008 that seeks standardised procedures for 'voluntary return' or expulsion of irregular migrants.

We can now try to link these various measures and specify what they mean in practice in states applying the *acquis* (Greece and Slovenia) and those adapting to its requirements (Croatia and Macedonia). Article 36 of the Return Directive defines illegal stay as the presence on the territory of a member state of a TCN who does not fulfil or no longer fulfils the conditions of entry as set out in Article 5 of the Schengen Borders Code or other conditions for entry, stay or residence in that member state. If we turn to Article 5 of the Schengen Borders Code (EC Regulation no. 562/2006) we can see that these conditions include: possession of a valid travel document; possession of a valid visa, if required; justification of the purpose of stay and means of subsistence for stay, return or onward travel; no alert on the SIS; and no threat to public policy, internal security, public health or the international relations of any member state.

Any person of whatever nationality can cross the EU's internal borders at any point without checks. Border guards in those states on the external frontiers of the EU (the EU itself is not a state and does not have it own borders) are then required to: control the borders and determine the status of persons crossing borders; check and control the lawfulness of entry by checking visas and passports; and be able to distinguish between illegal migrants and persons who fled from the country in order to seek international protection. Border security agencies are also required to adapt to the requirements of IBM. According to the Commission: 'IBM covers coordination and cooperation among all the relevant authorities and agencies involved in border security and trade facilitation to establish effective, efficient and integrated border management systems, in order to reach the common goal of open, but controlled and secure borders' (CEC 2007d: 2). IBM has three pillars: first, intraservice cooperation and coordination of the different levels of hierarchy within an agency or ministry; second, interagency cooperation and coordination between different ministries and agencies; and third, international cooperation and coordination between agencies and ministries of other states or international organisations. The main agencies are thus: border guards, customs, phytosanitary inspection services and veterinary inspection services. IBM seeks 'interoperability', which means the ability of diverse systems and organisations to work together. At the very least, IBM in an EU context corrects any notion of simple and hierarchical relationships between the centre (interior ministries) and border guards.

The EU borders agency, FRONTEX, has resource constraints but is developing a role in the pursuit of interoperability, which requires cooperation on technology, doctrine, organisation, trust-building and language. The basis for these is constant cooperation and the clear specification of standards. For example, FRONTEX has used its delegated authority to sign a working agreement with Macedonia covering activities such as information exchange, risk analysis, training, research and joint operations. FRONTEX also led the development of a Western Balkans Risk Analysis Network that provides technical training on data exchange to 'risk analysis units' in Albania, Bosnia-Herzegovina, Croatia, Macedonia, Montenegro and Serbia. It has also established Rapid Border Intervention Teams (RABITs) which conducted an exercise at the Slovenian–Croatian border in early 2008. The hypothetical scenario was a sudden massive influx of illegal immigrants along the Balkan route which had to be stopped. Border guards from 20 member states participated in this exercise, which was designed to test 'possibilities of reinforcement of a Member State authority's response capacity in exceptional circumstances' (House of Lords 2008; Vaughan-Williams 2008; FRONTEX 2009; Neal 2009; Euractiv 2010).

This kind of intraservice, interagency and international cooperation in pursuit of interoperability is central to the framing of migration and border security in SEE but has its complexities. The third annual ministerial review conference of security in the Western Balkans held in Sarajevo in 2006 included ministers of interior/security and the chiefs of security services from all the Western Balkan countries; minister and officials from donor countries (Estonia, Finland, Germany, Hungary, Slovenia, Switzerland, Greece, Poland and Romania); representatives of the EU, NATO, OSCE, International Centre for Migration Policy Development (ICMPD), EU Police Mission in Bosnia-Herzegovina, FRONTEX, the Danish Centre for Human Rights, the Peace Support Operations Training Centre (PSOTC) in Bosnia-Herzegovina, Police Assistance Mission of the European Community to Albania, the Stability Pact, and Austrian, Swiss and US Embassy staff. As Marenin puts it, 'In short, a veritable avalanche of advice has flowed into the Balkan states, seemingly without much of an attempt to coordinate and harmonise that advice' (2010: 74).

The Croatian and Macedonian cases are distinct from Greece and Slovenia because they are candidate countries with a very different relationship to the EU. Membership conditionality is, of course, a key component of work on EU enlargement (Grabbe 2002: 93) but the other side of this is credibility. The prospective members need to believe that there is a serious membership prospect that makes it worthwhile doing all this work (Schimmelfennig and Sedelmeier 2004). To this we could add policy conditionality. Particularly important in this respect was visa liberalisation for Croatia and Macedonia as a tangible benefit for their citizens and an indicator of their movement towards membership (Trauner 2009).

Stabilisation and Association Agreements have specific border security provisions. Article 11 provides for supporting projects that have regional or cross border dimensions. Article 74 seeks reinforcement of institutions in the area of law enforcement. Article 75 is on cooperation in the area of border control. Article 78 covers the fight against and prevention of criminal and illegal activities. Article 88 seeks the development of cross-border infrastructure. Article 101 covers cross-border, transnational and interregional cooperation.

Accession Partnerships underline the importance of continuation with the implementation of IBM strategy and require upgrading the equipment of border police and fostering cooperation with neighbouring countries on border management, which we see through the MARRI project (see below). National Programmes for Adoption of the Acquis include setting up information and technological IBM structures and preparing an information system for IBM. This requires additional resources for state border surveillance and equipment for border crossing points, as well as improving the infrastructure, constructing and reconstructing border crossing points and for training of border police. A key issue has been the installation of communications between border points and interior ministries (CEC 2008b).

A vital role in the development of policy capacity is played by the MARRI project, set up in 2004 with six participating states: Serbia, Bosnia-Herzegovina, Macedonia, Albania, Montenegro, Croatia and a secretariat based in Skopje. MARRI aims to create a coalition for the management of migration issues in the Western Balkans. This use of the word 'coalition' is interesting because it takes us back to the definitions of IBM introduced earlier in the chapter. IBM requires intraservice, interagency and international cooperation. It is thus a multi-level reconceptualisation of border security to involve a range of public, private and non-state actors organised across various governance levels. This can be seen as a response to a transboundary issue where there are functional, political and administrative deficits that can best be resolved by interstate cooperation designed to enhance capacity. In the next section we move on to discuss the country networks, beginning with Greece.

Greece

Greece has experienced significant immigration since the end of the 1980s, with acceleration during the 1990s. Movement from Albania was and still is a particularly prominent component of in-flows. Other source countries include Bulgaria, Romania, Georgia and the Russian Federation. Table 5.1 showed that in 2009, 8.3 per cent of the legally resident Greek population were foreign nationals. Much of this migration is centred on Athens and other important urban centres. It is also sectorally focused on particular kinds of economic activity that migrants are more likely to undertake (for example, men into construction and agriculture, and women into domestic work and health/social care). Migrants thus tend to move from particular places in sending countries to particular places in destination countries. Upon arrival, they often live in major urban areas and undertake particular forms of economic activity.

Institutions

The onset of migration in the late 1980s and early 1990s and the development of migration and border security policy in Greece was closely associated with EU membership, but not entirely driven by it. It is essential to factor in to the analysis the relevance and impact of domestic factors that have played a key role in structuring the politics of immigration in Greece. Of particular importance in migration to Greece (and southern Europe generally) was the presence of a large informal sector within which migrant workers, both regular and irregular, have been and are strongly present (Baganha 1997; Arango 2000; Baldwin-Edwards 2009; Finotelli and Sciortino 2009; Sciortino 2010). The informal economy was estimated to account for 28.2 per cent of the Greek GDP in 2004 (Scheider 2004). The informal economy can, and did, constitute a 'pull' factor that draws migrants into the Greek economy. In response to irregular flows, Greece undertook five regularisations in 1997, 1998, 2001, 2005 and 2007, albeit with significant institutional stresses and strains that are indicative of implementation problems generally in relation to the EU *acquis* and specifically in relation to migration and border security (Baldwin-Edwards 2009).

A key factor was Greece's proximity to major sending countries. Much migration to Greece in the 1990s came from Albania. Until 2007, Greece did not have a border with another EU member state. This changed with Bulgarian accession, but Greece still faces major challenges linked to its location and the challenges of securing its external frontiers. A good deal of EU discussion has centred on the challenges of policing Greece's external frontiers. There are more than 3,000 islands that present significant logistical challenges and, as we shall see, led to specific aspects of the Greek case that officials and policy-makers are keen to emphasise. The practical challenges of border control and policing were specified to us by an IOM official, when he used as an example the case of a small boat arriving at a Greek island:

> A small boat arrives at Greek islands where there are no police officers. In the same boat you might have asylum cases, trafficking cases and legal cases. So, if the receivers are not trained, they put everybody in the same room and they have the same treatment and reception.
> (Interview, 20 February 2008)

This is a pressing problem, which has important implications for the rights of migrants. The FRONTEX annual report 2009 shows the pressures on Greece. Data on detections of illegal entry shows fewer detections in Italy and Spain, and an increase in detections of illegal border crossings in Greece from 50 per cent to 75 per cent of the EU total. In 2009, the Greek land-border sections with Albania and FYROM represented the largest share (34 per cent of the EU total), followed by the Aegean Sea (21 per cent) (FRONTEX 2009).

There has been a rapid development of the Greek legal framework regulating immigration. Until 2001, there was a powerful policing and security frame that developed in the wake of large-scale Albanian migration during the 1990s and focused on exclusion. Greece lacked an immigration policy, which meant that most immigrants in Greece were ushered into the 'twilight world' of the informal economy (Baldwin-Edwards 1999). Two presidential decrees in 1997 sought to deal with some of the regulatory problems caused by large-scale immigration by introducing a so-called 'Green Card' which gave temporary settlements rights to the large irregular population. This was then to be followed by the issuance of a 'White Card', but as an interviewee from the Greek Ombudsman's office put it to us, this was 'altogether a terribly confusing administrative mechanism [but] in the end quite beneficial because it brought the administration into contact with the whole mass of migrants in Greece' (interview, 21 February 2008). Baldwin-Edwards argues that the 1997 and 1998 regularisations were 'not the result of popular movement or planned policy, but represented an emergency measure or admission of policy failure' (2009: 298).

New laws introduced in 2001 and 2005 sought to modernise the Greek legal framework (Skordas 2002). At the time during which this research was undertaken, the primary legislative instrument governing immigration was Act 3386 of August 2005 on 'Entry, residence and social integration of third country nationals into the Greek territory'. The legislation was amended by Act 3536 of 22 February 2007 on 'Determining matters in migration policy and other issues falling into the competence of the Ministry of the Interiors, Public Administration and Decentralisation', which relates to our later discussion of the role of local government in immigration policy.

The 2005 law had seven main aims: to plan migration flows in relation to Greek social and economic life; to ensure greater administrative consistency; to protect the employment rights of migrant workers; to introduce an immi-grant integration policy; to apply the law effectively in order to avoid the uncontrolled entry and exit of foreigners; to incentivise the attracting of foreign investment in Greece; and to allow TCNs to exercise rights. The 2005 law also incorporated into Greek law Council Directive 2003/86/EC on the right to family reunification; Council Directive 2003/109/EC on the rights of long-term residents; and Council Directive 2004/38/EC on freedom of movement of third country nationals who are family members of an EU citizen. There was also a clear EU influence on immigrant integration policy through the incorporation of the eleven principles of the EU's 'Common Basic Principles on Integration' established at the Groningen meeting of JHA ministers in 2004, which were then specified in the 2005 'Common Agenda for Integration' (CEC 2005). As Adam and Devillard note, 'Even though the current legislative regime does represent a marked improvement compared to the previous regime, one still feels that 15 years after Greece became a (proportionally speaking) major host country, it continues to experiment with a workable regulatory framework' (2008: 272). This ongoing experimentation had obvious organisational and institutional implications that induced elements of MLG, although with a stronger role allocated for local government than for international organisations.

The network

Our research showed the key actor in Greek migration and border security policy to be the Ministry of the Interior. In 2007 the General Directorate for Migration Policy and Social Integration within the Ministry of the Interior was created, which incorporated units of the Ministry of Public Order that previously dealt with migration. Within the Ministry of Employment there existed a unit whose original purpose was to monitor Greeks working abroad through the gathering of statistical data, whose remit was extended to deal with immigrant workers in Greece.

Figure 5.1 shows policy to be centralised and dominated by the Interior Ministry, which plays a key role in relationships both with other departments of state and in managing relations with the EU. We are, of course, primarily interested in the dynamics of policy change at domestic level rather than the development of EU law. That said, there are important connections between Greek officials and EU decision-making processes. Within Greece, we found only limited evidence of dialogue between the central state and other policy 'stakeholders' such as NGOs. There was a presence for IMOs, but they tended to provide support and migration management services and were not central to the policy- and decision-making process. Present, too, were local authorities, which, as we will see, picked up via processes of delegated authority a great deal of the administrative pressure arising from the need to register and process migrants in Greece, with significant capacity issues.

An interview with a senior official in the Ministry of the Interior at the centre of the policy network provided us with the official view of the Greek government:

> The framework and principles are set out by the EU and from that point onwards we adapt them to the particularities of each state . . . Greece prides itself on being a source of inspiration for the common policy on migration and border control . . . Our European friends are quite confident about the degree of security of our borders . . . On the other hand, they are under constant pressure because of our geographical position.
>
> (Interview, 20 February 2008)

The EU's role was identified as very important in policy development, as the same official noted:

> The role of the EU is very important and several areas related to migration are monitored on the European level. At the same time, the existence of programmes co-funded by the EU gives us the opportunity to participate in the effective handling of the migration phenomenon in the wider EU region.
>
> (Interview, 20 February 2008)

EU funding programmes such as AENEAS have also facilitated partnership work, including with IOM and with the government of Albania for a return programme.

The Interior Ministry cooperated with a range of European and international organisations including Europol, Interpol, IOM, United Nations High

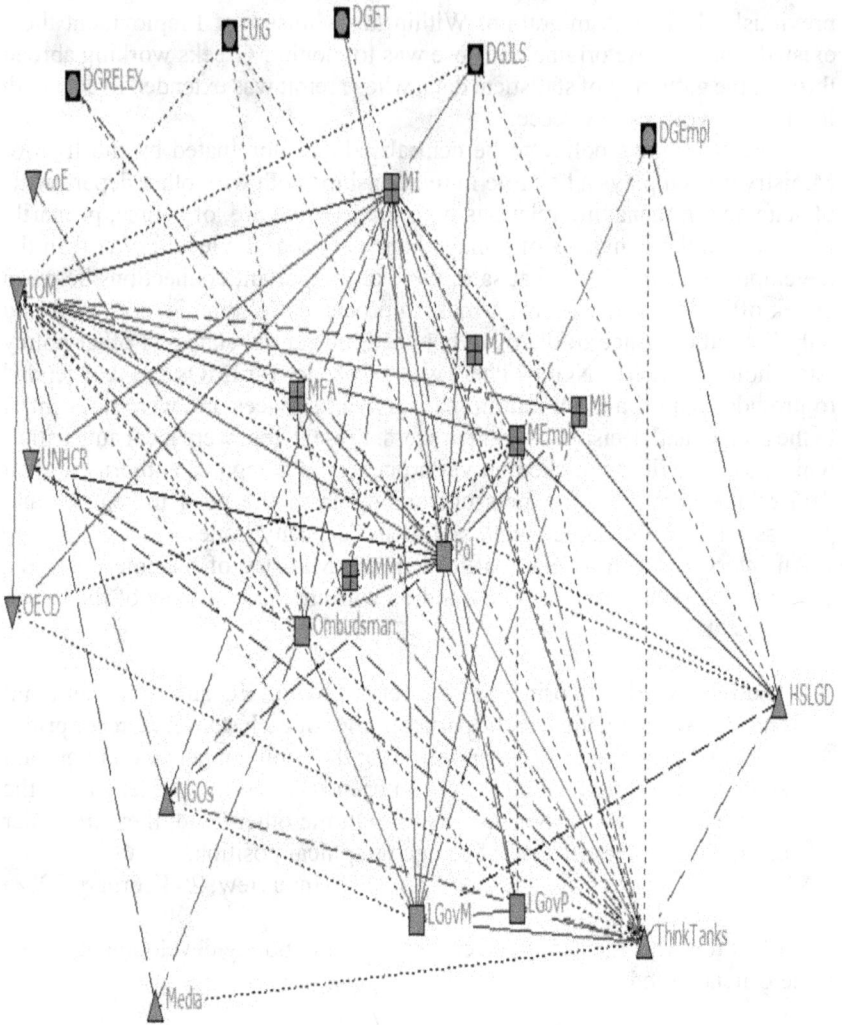

Figure 5.1 The migration and border security network: Greece

Commissioner for Refugees (UNHCR), Red Cross and Amnesty International. The relationship was particularly strong with Europol and Interpol, with continuous flows of information. There was also some caution about the role of international organisations and sensitivity to criticism from outside organisations. The same Interior Ministry official remarked that: 'I consider the role of IOs constructive, but sometimes too judgemental and criticising' (interview, 20 February 2008). An interviewee from the Ombudsman's Office noted that 'the political culture was very defensive against others knowing what

Organisation	SNA abbreviation
DG Justice, Freedom and Security	DGJLS
DE Employment, Social Affairs and Equal Opportunities	DGEmpl
DG Energy and Transport	DGET
DG External Relations	DGRELEX
Ministry of Interior	MI
Ministry of Foreign Affairs	MFA
Ministry for Employment and Social Protection	MEmpl
Ministry of Justice	MJ
Ministry of Mercantile Marine, the Aegean and Island Policy	MMM
Ministry of Health	MH
Hellenic Police	Pol
Local Government: Municipalities (Departments for Aliens)	LGovM
Local Government: Peripheries	LGovP
Hellenic Society for Local Government and Development	HSLGD
NGOs (Antigone, Hellenic Migrant Forum)	NGOs
International Organization for Migration	IOM
UNHCR	UNHCR
Council of Europe	CoE
Representation of the EU in Greece	EUiG
OECD	OECD
Think Tanks (IMEPO, EKKE)	ThinkTanks
Mass Media	Media

was wrong in domestic policy' (interview, 21 February 2008). An IOM official noted that 'it takes time for the Greeks to understand that international organisations serve them and not some other interest. This mentality still exists' (interview, 20 February 2008).

The Greek Ombudsman's Office was created in 1997 to deal with administrative malpractice, but is now dealing with many immigration issues, particularly those linked to residence status and permits. Other institutions have also been created to support policy development and seek engagement with civil society. The Institute for Migration Policy (IMEPO), for example, was created in 2002. Funded by the Ministry of the Interior it links with other ministries, such as MFA, Labour, Education and Economics. As an IMEPO official put it: 'IMEPO has tried to promote the idea that any effort for change must be based on scientific research' (interview, 18 February 2008). We thus see some pressure for engagement with civil society and scientific researchers, which has tended to be weaker in Greece than in other member states. There are, however, limits on these particular dimensions of Greek adaptation to EU migration policy.

Other actors did not share the view expressed from the Interior Ministry and drew attention to some of the tensions evident in Greek migration policy that mediated the effects of European integration. An interviewee from the Ombudsman's Office noted that 'The EU funds a number of programmes but these do not correspond to the Greek reality. Domestic actors view the EU as a source of funding, a cow to be milked, but also as a source of sticks and carrots' (interview, 21 February 2008). The tension in the policy frame and the scope for contestation of the 'meaning' of Europe in the Greek domestic setting was also made evident to us by discussion with our interviewees about the contemporary framing of Greek immigration policy. A senior Interior Ministry official noted that 'This new migration policy is consistent with the Lisbon strategy and aspires to social cohesion. It is based on the conviction that migration is not a problem but a benefit, which enables the destination state to derive benefits from the people who reside in them and enrich their culture' (interview, 20 February 2008).

This view was, however, contested from the Ombudsman's Office: 'Migration is viewed as a natural disaster, as a historical accident and as something temporary . . . nowhere is there a sense of these people being here to stay' (interview, 21 February 2008). The same interviewee did note some positive developments, which were seen as arising from the EU context and incorporation of EU laws, such as the directives on family reunion and long-term residence and the gradual embedding of a legal and regulatory framework accompanied by a change of mentality that does not see migrants simply as temporary factors of production, but as members of Greek society.

EU funds have been made available to deal with the settlement of migrants. For example, EU funds supported projects such as EQUAL (managed by DG Employment and Social Affairs), which offered support to asylum seekers and refugees, and worked with the three key players in Greece: the Ministries of the Interior, Employment and Justice, and created a point of engagement with NGOs. An official working in Greece for EQUAL identified work with NGOs and liaison with international organisations as a way in which EU resources could be used to strengthen civil society engagement in a country where such engagement is traditionally weak. Thus, 'Transnational networking and mainstreaming is responsible for creating a mechanism to evaluate which actions are best implemented and to help incorporate them into national policies' (interview, 10 February 2008). The same official argued that there had been some temporal readjustment that had affected the process of learning and adaption:

> it's not like before when you felt like a student and the Commission was the teacher who came to scold and correct you. Nowadays there is the principle of partnership between the member states and the Commission and the member states demand that this partnership – which is engrained in the directives – be respected.
>
> (Interview, 10 February 2008)

Sources of change

There is clear evidence of EU influence on the development of policy, but potential too for dissonance when 'on-the-ground' realities are factored into the analysis. We can now extend this discussion to explore how we see a particularly important role for local government in the administration of Greek immigration policy, which allows us to see the scaling of policy. The basic picture is a hierarchical centralised structure with over-burdened municipalities because of the concentration of the migrant population in particular areas such as Athens. This induces significant capacity problems. As Adam and Devillard explained, 'The immigration department personnel in local administration authorities admit that there is a lack of the necessary human resources for the provision of services envisaged in the current legislative framework on migration' (2008: 272). As the interviewee from the Ombudsman's Office put it:

> The decisions about residence permits are made at the level of the peripheries. In each periphery there is a small core of regular staff with an overload of work. And the rest of the staff are seasonal with contracts ranging from six to eight months. There is no permanence and durability, and that creates many disruptions . . . There are many clashes because some institutions represent a sense of rationality while others represent the not necessarily rational demands of local centres of power or financial power, like, for example, the big agricultural lobbies that primarily use migrants as a workforce and play a crucial role in exercising pressure on policy-makers.
>
> (Interview, 21 February 2008)

There have been efforts to build capacity and here too we see some role for EU funding to support particular projects. The Hellenic Agency for Local Development and Local Government (EETAA) provides training and support to local authorities (interview, 20 February 2008). In 2008 it was running five EQUAL projects to promote mechanisms of cooperation and networks within the local government structures on migration matters, plus there was INTERREG funding for a project with Morocco, Tunisia, Greece, Italy and Spain to run information campaigns for potential migrants in North African source countries. EETAA was also involved in a return migration programme with Albania funded through the AENEAS programme working with other agencies such as IMEPO, the Ministry of the Interior and IOM in Albania. Our EETAA interviewee saw an important role for the EU:

> learning definitely is motivated by the EU; in a way it is an obligation that stems from our participation in the EU. This whole experience of intergovernmental cooperation, networks and programmes brings about new experiences and learning . . . The effect of learning is also obvious

in the language used by NGOs, local government, technical agencies etc.
It is the jargon of the EU.

(Interview, 10 February 2008)

Can this absorption of EU jargon stimulate deeper rooted change? As our
EETAA interviewee put it:

> There is always some kind of clash . . . For example, between the ministries
> and local government: the latter claim to have more concrete goals, to be
> closer to the people and in a better position to implement policies and they
> demand more power, more competencies, but also more funding in order
> to implement policies . . . Also, immigration is a very sensitive issue for
> the local authorities in terms of political pressure and political cost. It is
> much easier for the central government to legalise migrants without
> receiving such intense criticism and reactions as in municipalities or
> communities where the mentality is hostile towards immigrants.
>
> (Interview, 10 February 2008)

The political dynamics at play in the relationship between central and local
government provide an important insight into policy development change in
Greece and to the mediation of EU laws and practices. The migrants themselves
are, of course, in a very weak position. They cannot vote and are not well
organised and rely on pro-migrant organisations, which themselves are in a
structurally weak position. The EU can provide some resources and new ideas,
but the impacts of these are still quite limited.

A basic tension exists between the 'need' for migrant workers and hostility
to migrants. It must be emphasised that this was not only an aspect of the
situation in Greece. In this sense, Greece is not exceptional, but an exemplar
of some of the more general dynamics of migration in Europe. Greek employers
benefit from the use of migrant labour, particularly in certain key sectors. They
may want a more liberal approach. Migration policies are often the subject of
a range of competing interests. In order to satisfy competing demands, policies
could often reflect an intentional jumble, or 'fudging', of different goals and
priorities. Legislation or programmes may be designed to keep different
interests happy, with the result that policies appear to be quite inconsistent or
contradictory (Boswell and Geddes 2010). The issues at play were identified
to us in an interview with a Greek-based IOM official:

> Two years ago on the island of Lesvos there was a fight between some
> locals and some Albanians who were working in their village, so the
> municipal council decided that all Albanians would be *persona non grata*
> in their village and sent them away. And then the season came when they
> needed to collect the olives. So, this is the confusion in public opinion.
> And in the policy-makers this is reflected as a conflict between recognising
> that they need migrants, but having to face a public that doesn't want them.
>
> (Interview, 20 February 2008)

The practical effect was that the same people supported an increase in the number of migrants during harvest time and then, a few months later, they advocated stricter migration controls.

Slovenia

Migration to and from Slovenia is located within an SEE migration system with the three leading source countries in 2010 being Bosnia, Croatia and Macedonia. As Table 5.1 showed, foreign nationals accounted for around 3.5 per cent of the total Slovenian population. As would be expected in a country that joined the EU in its May 2004 enlargement, Slovenian immigration legislation has developed in accordance with the EU *acquis*. Adaptation to EU requirements also coincided with a more distinct European orientation of Slovenian migration policy, which can be seen as evidence of Europeanisation. However, we also see limited traces since 2004 of direct influence on Slovenian policy. The peak period for EU influence was between 1998, when accession negotiations began, and 2004, when accession occurred. As a Ministry of Labour official put it, 'There hasn't been much EU influence since 2004' (interview, 24 June 2008). We would, however, distinguish between direct influence and the profound impact on the framing of the policy problem and thus the setting within which Slovenian policy-makers operate. Evidence for this is the fact that Slovenia managed a swift and relatively trouble-free adaptation to the requirements of Chapter 24 of the accession framework (Adam and Devillard 2008: 425).

The migration picture in Slovenia cannot be understood without accounting for the country's place in the former Yugoslav Republic. From the 1950s, there was emigration by 'guest workers', particularly to Austria and Germany, and movement within the Yugoslav federation. From the mid-1970s onwards, increasing numbers of Bosnians, Croats and Serbs moved to Slovenia, leading to a 'turbulent period in the history of migration to Slovenia, above all because of the break-up of the former Yugoslavia' (Thomson 2006: 2). When Slovenia gained independence in 1991 the effect was to deprive tens of thousands of migrants from other Yugoslav Republics of their legal status in Slovenia. In addition, there were flows of refugees from Croatia and Bosnia-Herzegovina fleeing civil war, to be followed by an influx from Kosovo in 1999.

Institutions

A SEE intraregional migration system linked Slovenia with Croatia, Bosnia, Macedonia, Serbia and Montenegro. Migration flows to Slovenia can be divided into three periods since the country became independent in June 1991 (Adam and Devillard 2009: 418). Between 1991 and 1999 there were large numbers of refugees from Bosnia. The Employment and Work of Aliens Act of 1992 sought to respond to the labour market consequences of Slovenian independence in 1991 and the presence of ex-Yugoslavian people in Slovenia and allowed long-term (at least ten-year) resident foreign nationals to acquire a work permit. In 2000 the Employment and Work of Alien's legislation was amended in line with EU legislation to create three types of work permit: for long-term residents; for employers to bring in workers and for temporary migrant workers. Between 1999 and 2004 there were relatively high levels of irregular migration. The third period, since accession in May 2004, has seen a strong focus on IBM and the 'fight against illegal immigration'. Slovenian immigration policy was thus framed by the EU setting and reflects core EU priorities, particularly the focus on border security and the 'external' dimension of the 'fight against illegal immigration'.

The legislative framework for our analysis was the Aliens Act of 2006 and, prior to that, two resolutions on Immigration Policy passed by the National Assembly in 1999 (Resolution 40/1999) and 2002 (Resolution 106/2002). These formed the national legislation regulating the entry of foreigners and the return of emigrants at the time of our study. The EU focus has been on the border with Croatia as a point for non-EU migrants to enter Italy via Slovenia. Slovenia has signed readmission agreements with Croatia and Bosnia-Herzegovina.

The network

Figure 5.2 shows a centralised network with the Ministry of the Interior playing a key role in managing relations with the EU and other departments of state. In contrast with Greece, the Slovenian network is less 'dense', which may reflect the timing and scale of immigration. Slovenia is a new immigration country and, as we see, has not experienced large immigration flows. It pre-emptively introduced quite severe restrictions on labour migration after accession in 2004, which may have hindered its ability to attain labour market objectives. IMOs are present too, although, as in Greece, they have played an auxiliary role in providing migration management services. The Commission and other EU institutions are less directly present in Greece than in other case countries, but the interview material does help to illustrate how the EU plays a profound role in shaping policy content.

Attention in Slovenia has turned to the management of labour migration, an area where the EU has minimal involvement. It is also an area where we see a role for other central government institutions, particularly the Ministry of Labour. A quota system for labour migrants was introduced in 2004 with the apparent intention of protecting the domestic labour market in an enlarged EU, but 'expectations were too high', as a Ministry of Labour official put it to us and the lesson drawn was that 'Slovenia is not as attractive for economic migrants [from other EU member states] (interview, 24 June 2008). The Interior Ministry remains particularly focused on security. We found a more rights-based approach in the work of the Ministry of Labour, Family and Social Affairs (MLFSA). Funds from the EU EQUAL and PROGRESS programmes have facilitated the MLFSA playing more of a role in migration, but the Interior Ministry remains the key player and the interlocutor with the EU.

Slovenia seems to have quickly and relatively easily adapted to the prevailing EU frame for migration management but faced criticisms about policy content. An interviewee from a Slovenian NGO explained that

> EU policy is welcomed by the Ministry of the Interior, but is less welcomed by civil society . . . Common EU policy has measures regarding integration and other beneficial matters, but in practice more effort is put into restrictive provisions such as border controls.
>
> (Interview, 21 June 2008)

As another NGO interviewee put it, 'EU policy is used as an excuse not to think about migration – for copying EU directives into Slovene legislation without thinking about what adopted legislation would really bring' (interview, 3 June 2008). We detected a growing role for emerging forms of European agency governance focused on the development of border control capacity. FRONTEX has been particularly present in SEE and has been involved in projects with the Slovenian government, which has been an active participant in a number of FRONTEX projects, such as joint FRONTEX operations at the Italy–Slovenia border.

Sources of change

There was little elite-level contestation of EU policy in Slovenia and we did not find the emphasis on the 'exceptionalism' that was evident in the statements of some of the Greek interviewees. The Greek case is obviously very different because of its location and the scale of migration, which has led to dynamics of contestation and resistance with a significant local dimension, as well as the involvement of a wide range of interests affected by migration, particularly work. Instead, we found some evidence that the country was becoming a 'normal' European country of immigration with a strong focus on control and evidence of hostility to migrants (particularly those from outside SEE).

We also found evidence from our interviews with NGOs of criticism of the direction of travel of Slovenian asylum and refugee policy under the influence of EU-originated measures. These are important in the context of border security because it has been argued that a stronger focus on denying territorial access to asylum seekers as a result of tougher border control actually negates the commitments made by member states to respect international standards (Morrison and Crosland 2000).

Some interviewees expressed concern that Slovenian asylum policy had begun to regress since accession with a lowering of standards, an uncritical adoption of EU legislation and a watering down of protection standards (Toplak 2006). This negative framing of asylum policy is consistent with that in other member states, with the relatively small number of asylum seekers represented as abusers of the welfare state. This was evident in the hostility to Iranian migrants who entered Slovenia via Bosnia in 2000 who were vilified

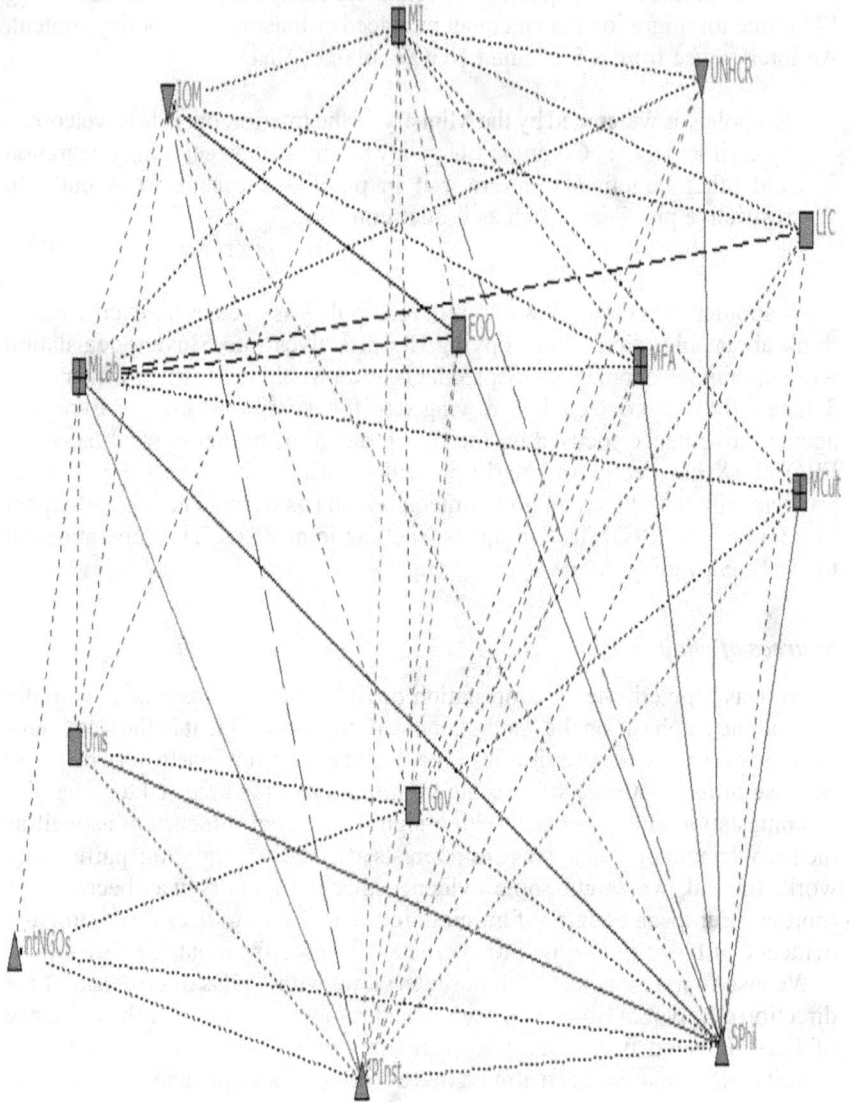

Figure 5.2 The migration and border security network: Slovenia

Organisation	SNA abbreviation
Ministry of Interior	MI
Ministry of Culture	MCult
Ministry of Labour, Family and Social Affairs	MLab
Ministry of Foreign Affairs	MFA
Municipalities	LGov
UNHCR	UNHCR
International Organization for Migration	IOM
International NGOs	IntNGOs
Slovene Philanthropy	SPhil
Peace Institute	PInst
Universities and research institutions	Unis
Legal Informative Centre	LIC
Equal Opportunity Office	EOO

and sometimes physically attacked (Thomson 2006: 11). Questions were also raised about whether EU standards are in conformity with international law as outlined in the Geneva Convention (Pajnik *et al.* 2006).

Croatia

In relation to countries classified by the OECD as 'high income', Croatia is in the top ten for both immigration and emigration. The Croatia–Germany route is one of the world's leading migration corridors and reflects the continuing effects of the recruitment of guest workers from ex-Yugoslavia from the 1950s until early 1970s. In 2000, 24.1 per cent of Croatia's tertiary educated population lived abroad. In 2010, remittances accounted for 2.4 per cent of Croatia's GDP (World Bank 2011). Croatia is also located within an intra-regional SEE migration system with strong connections to Slovenia, Bosnia and Macedonia. In Croatia, we found a strong focus on rapid adaptation to the EU migration and border security *acquis*, but we also found a strong and important role for other member states and IMOs as transmitters of ideas and practices about border control and migration management.

Institutions

Negotiations between the EU and Croatia were opened on Chapter 24 of the accession framework on 24 October 2009 (CEC 2006c). Important components of the Accession Partnership Agreement of February 2008 were measures to tackle corruption and also the need to enter into readmission agreements for the return of migrants to neighbouring countries. An interview with a senior Interior Ministry official (interview, 16 April 2008) pointed to the influence of the EU in quickening the process of policy development. The EU, he said, 'has brought in changes that Croatia would have to bring in anyway [but] has quickened the adoption and enforcement of legislation'. A Foreign Affairs and European Integration Ministry official reiterated the point when noting that 'The question is whether Croatia could regulate its society by itself. Of course it could. However, this process is quickened and time frames as well as goals are set that oblige us to act' (interview, 20 December 2007).

The development of migration and border security policy in Croatia is dominated by an EU frame, which includes development of IBM and the 'fight against illegal immigration', as well as measures to tackle people smuggling and human trafficking. The US State Department's Trafficking in Persons report identified Croatia as a source, transit and increasingly destination country for women and girls trafficked for the purpose of sexual exploitation. It found that

> Croatian females are trafficked within the country, and women and girls from Romania, Bulgaria, Serbia, Bosnia and Herzegovina, and other parts of Eastern Europe are trafficked to and through Croatia for the purpose of sexual exploitation. Croatian men are occasionally trafficked for forced labour. Victims transiting Croatia from SEE are trafficked into Western Europe for commercial sexual exploitation. IOM reported continued seasonal rotation of international women in prostitution to and from the Dalmatian coast during high tourist seasons, raising concerns about trafficking.
>
> (US State Department 2008: 101)

Legislative development in Croatia has been strongly focused on adaptation to Chapter 24 requirements. The Act on the Amendments to the State Border Protection Act, which entered into force on 25 December 2008, and the Act on the Amendments to the Aliens Act, which entered into force on 31 March 2009, aligned Croatia with the EU *acquis* and Schengen Border Code.

The network

The political lead on accession is taken by the Ministry of Foreign Affairs and European Integration (Figure 5.3), which leads at EU level, and by the Ministry of Interior, which is responsible for legislative adaptation. There was high-level coordination of the accession process with weekly meetings designed to facilitate a rapid ability at high political level to respond to issues. This reflects both the political sensitivity of the issue and the demands of accession. Those in more day-to-day roles did report to us that they encountered a strongly hierarchical administrative culture within key ministries that meant that there could be a delay as issues filtered up to the senior level, at which decisions could be made and then back down again. Thus, we need to factor into the analysis Croatia's politicised and hierarchical administrative system.

Figure 5.3 shows the Ministry of the Interior as the key domestic player with a strong tie with the EU delegation. In terms of its 'density', the network in Croatia is more similar to that in Greece than in Slovenia (albeit with a more important role for local government in Greece). In terms of a more general comparison, the similarity with Greece is not surprising and reflects historic patterns of centralisation in both countries, as was also evident in Chapter 4 on Croatian cohesion policy. The migration and border security network in Croatia does, however, differ from that in Greece and Slovenia because of the more direct and intense involvement by IMOs and other member states. Migration management services from organisations such as IOM and UNHCR have been an important part of policy development, as too has twinning with a range of EU member states providing technical expertise and support.

The EU also structures the scope for interventions by IMOs. EU delegations do not have the staff, resources or expertise to undertake detailed, technical policy work and training. The Commission delegation tends to focus on overview, management, working with organisations and institutions in Croatia, and with international organisations. The EU also secures input from EU member states through twinning. International organisations deliver expertise but do not participate actively in policy-making. One reason for this was that laws could be developed very rapidly. An IOM official based in Zagreb (interview, 6 February 2008) reported that the 2008 legislation was developed very hurriedly and that the Parliamentary committee dealing with the legislation called on IOM for its views at only one day's notice. An official from the Commission Delegation specified their role:

> If there is some kind of resistance at the Ministry, or things are working slowly, then we come in and we come in from a little bit of a higher perspective. We nail them down. You are never going to be able to credibly argue that this chapter can be closed unless you have done this and these changes in, let's say, border law.
>
> (Interview, 12 February 2008)

The core executive was seen as secretive and centralised, but there was a positive take on development of IBM from the Commission's point of view when it was noted that 'they have developed a pretty good integrated border management strategy and action plan on the basis of western Balkans guidelines' (interview, 12 February 2008).

Sources of change

We found typical patterns associated with regulatory policy as the Croatian state sought to develop enhanced border control capacity in line with EU expectations and standards. What we also found was a key role played by a

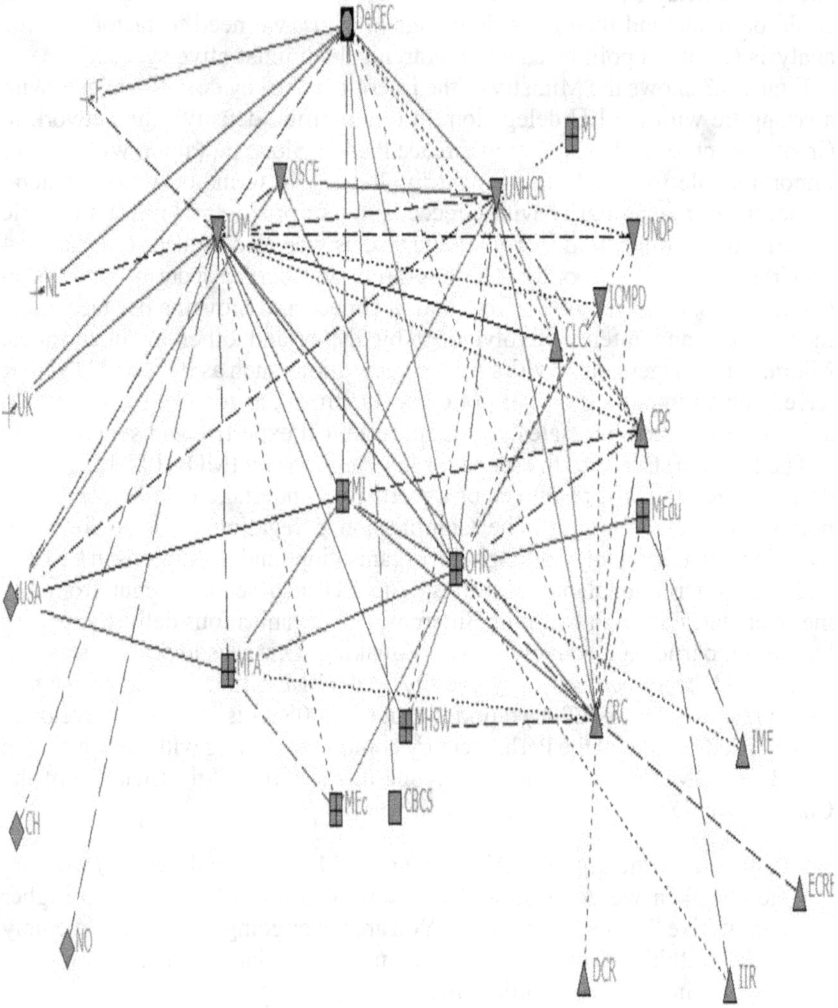

Figure 5.3 The migration and border security network: Croatia

wide range of international organisations that help with this capacity-building. The organisation of the Border Police was determined in 2002 and within Border Police Directorate of the Ministry of the Interior were the following units: State Border Protection Department; Neighbouring Countries Department; Illegal Migrations Department; Maritime and Airport Police Department; Aliens Reception Centre; and Mobile Unit for State Border Surveillance.

There was active cooperation with FRONTEX. A Working Agreement for the Establishment of Operational Cooperation between FRONTEX and the Ministry of the Interior was signed on 15 April 2008. This provided for cooperation in the following fields: exchange of information, education, joint

Organisation	SNA abbreviation
Ministry of the Interior	MI
Ministry of Justice	MJ
Ministry of Health and Social Welfare	MHSW
Ministry of Foreign Affairs and European Integration	MFA
Ministry of Science, Education and Sports	MEdu
Ministry of Economy, Labour and Entrepreneurship	MEc
Cross Border Co-operation Service	CBCS
Office of Human Rights	OHR
Institute for International Relations, Zagreb	IIR
Croatian Legal Centre	CLC
Institute for Migration and Ethnicity	IME
Centre for Peace Studies	CPS
Croatian Red Cross	CRC
European Commission	DelCEC
Organisation for Security and Co-operation in Europe	OSCE
International Organization for Migration	IOM
United Nations High Commissioner for Refugees	UNHCR
United Nations Development Programme	UNDP
International Centre for Migration Policy Development	ICMPD
European Council for Refugees and Exiles	ECRE
Dutch Council for Refugees	DCR

operations, technical cooperation and risk analysis. Croatia has also participated in a range of FRONTEX operations. In 2008 and 2009, these included the Europol/Frontex 'Task Force' for improvement of border management and the combating of organised crime; joint operations DRIVE IN, KRAS (2008) and NEPTUNE (2009); and participation in FRAN Unit (risk analyses).

International organisations have also a key role. These include DCAF's work on the demilitarisation of borders and civilian control. The ICMPD drew from EU funding from the EU's AENEAS project to develop a memorandum of understanding between countries in the region on establishing a system of statistical information exchange on illegal migration and the participation in a regional early warning system, which was signed on 20 November 2008.

A common theme among all interviewees in Croatia was that the EU was the key policy driver, linking Croatia with international organisations. EU support was provided by CARDS, PHARE and TAIEX. Twinning occurred with the Netherlands, Austria, Slovenia, Germany and Hungary. For example, the Austrian government was the twinning partner for IBM. UNHCR and IOM organised seminars on the role of border guards. This is indicative of how their roles had changed from engaging with refugees and war-related issues to 'European' migration issues of border security and the regulation of migration.

We found only a very limited role for NGOs and expert knowledge from inside Croatia. The Centre for Peace Studies (CPS) secured funding from the Croatian government, but also from CARDS and PHARE to develop a focus on minority rights, which included migrants. The Croatian Legal Centre (CLC) sought to mobilise technical expertise and, after 2002, provided free legal aid to asylum seekers with support from UNHCR. CLC secured funding from the EU's AENEAS project to influence the law-making process; provide legal aid; create a coordination body on asylum to meet on a regular basis and provide input to the legal and policy process. The CLC has also worked with the Peace Institute and Legal Information Centre in Slovenia to run training seminars on border security for officials. The key issue was identified by a CLC staff member who asked why, in 2006, when there were 5,600 people apprehended at Croatia's borders for an irregular entry status, only 98 asked for asylum? Expert knowledge was seen as playing very little role in policy development, not least because of the pace of policy development and the desire for action rather than reflection. As an interviewee at the Ministry of the Interior explained:

> The role of experts has been very small. This might be a practical issue since Croatia receives legal acts from Brussels that have to be implemented and those are usually technical questions . . . Experts usually know very little about the field, for example, in illegal immigration. The Police Academy is used for that matter, but these people are mainly practitioners.
> (Interview, 16 April 2008)

The other side of this was noted by a Commission official: from the Croatian government's point of view, 'Equipment for the police is rather welcomed, while policies are not' (interview, 16 April 2008). A reason for the reluctance to draw on expert knowledge was that this might introduce more critical or reflective elements that could slow the pace of adaptation. As an Interior Ministry official put it, 'Experts have been included in the drafting of migration policy in the working group, but their input has not been as we expected. Very often they appear as criticisers, but not as those who recommend solutions' (interview, 16 April 2008). Respondents from research institutes felt that they had not been included in policy development because of the emphasis on rapid adaptation and 'policy-makers do not gain knowledge from domestic sources . . . but they learn what they are forced to' (interview, 22 April 2008).

Within the Croatian core executive we found little evidence of contestation. Moreover, compared to Greece, the migration issue was very recent and there was a very limited domestic politics of migration. Adaptation was swift, but not particularly reflective. This creates scope for some tension, which may become more pronounced in the future. This tension centres on the issue of irregular migration, which has a strong sectoral focus in areas such as tourism. There was thus a 'pull' factor drawing migrants to Croatia and a willingness on the part of employers to use migrant workers whether their status is regular or irregular. This gave rise to tensions between the Interior and Economics Ministries about the 2008 foreigners' law. The Interior Ministry prevailed, but a senior Foreign Affairs Ministry official observed that the Interior Ministry had been 'the leading institution, which I personally consider a big mistake because migration policy as they perceive it is a policy of repression' and argued for a stronger role of the Economics Ministry to reflect labour market concerns (interview, 20 December 2007).

Macedonia

With 21.9 per cent of its population living abroad in 2010 (including 29.1 per cent of its tertiary-educated population), Macedonia is one of the world's leading emigration countries and has experienced only very small-scale inflows. As a result of emigration, 4.5 per cent of Macedonian GDP in 2010 derived from migrant remittances (World Bank 2011). Macedonia does, however, have contested border issues. One of these is the relationship with Albania. Proposals for 'permeable' borders to defuse the Albanian question are best seen as political rhetoric with little chance of acceptance in the two states (Berg and van Meurs 2002: 69). The other is the emerging EU frame, development of IBM and of migration management, which all occur in the context of adaptation to the EU *acquis*.

Institutions

Despite its status as an emigration country, Macedonia is required to develop sophisticated migration and border security policies. The EU is the main driver of policy development and change in Macedonia. As a senior Ministry of the Interior official put it:

> Every adjustment of our legislation is made in accordance with the EU *acquis*. The Schengen borders code at the moment is the basic literature on the basis of which all migration-related legislation is prepared and they are all to be in accordance with the European legislation. Here the EU influence is extraordinary . . . really huge.
>
> (Interview, 10 March 2008)

The Commission's role was to monitor, not to make policy. As a senior official of the Macedonian National Commission for IBM noted:

> I tell them [the Commission] that The Republic of Macedonia is exclusively responsible for the process. But if you provide benchmarks

that need to be fulfilled and if you participate in the process – although the accountability is on the domestic side – the responsibility for the international side is also relevant. If they also sit at the table and discuss with domestic institutions, they also bear some responsibility.

(Interview, 17 March 2008)

There was a strong international influence, particularly of the EU both in resources and monitoring. As was the case in Croatia, there was little frame disjunction because of the strong interest among the Macedonian elite in meeting EU requirements.

The 'transit' frame and the focus on irregular migration prompted a strong focus on IBM. Macedonia is understood in the EU context as a transit country for irregular migrants. It is also seen as a component part of smuggling and trafficking networks. In 2008, the US State Department identified Macedonia as a source, transit and destination country for women and children trafficked for the purpose of commercial sexual exploitation. Macedonian women and children were found to be trafficked internally, mostly from eastern rural areas to urban areas in western Macedonia. Victims trafficked into Macedonia were primarily from Serbia and Albania. Victims transiting through Macedonia are trafficked to South Central and Western Europe, including Bosnia, Serbia, Italy and Sweden. Macedonia re-entered the Tier 1 group of countries listed by the US State Department in 2008 (after falling into Tier 2 in 2004) because it was seen to have made greater efforts to tackle and prosecute traffickers, but was also seen to need to make greater effort to protect victims. We found evidence that international, non-EU standards were important too because a senior official at the Macedonian National Centre for Border Management was very keen to flag this external validation of Macedonian efforts from the US State Department in its 'Trafficking in Persons Report' (US State Department 2008).

Macedonian IBM strategy received EU aid in various forms. This was first from PHARE, then CARDS, then from IPA. There are now IPA units within all key ministries. There is direct Commission involvement in developing the national IBM strategy. Technical support was provided by the Italian government and by the Brandenburg police with a resident police expert present. The main issue for IBM has been domestic coordination with the need to work across six or seven ministries and multiple agencies.

The network

Our research showed that the Ministry of Foreign Affairs and European Integration (Figure 5.4) provided the negotiation lead, while the Ministry of Interior was responsible for domestic adaptation of migration and border security policy. The network was highly centralised with a key role played by other EU member states and IMOs in the deployment of technical expertise to support policy development. An EU Secretariat within the Ministry of the Interior comprised three units: negotiations and integration, IPA funds and international cooperation. The negotiations and integration unit, for example, worked with the Commission on the agreement for visa facilitation and re-admission. As a senior Ministry of the Interior official said, 'The role of the Ministry of the Interior as a main policy-maker of migration policy is uncontested' (interview, 10 March 2008).

The Interior Ministry coordinated the national response through the creation of the following institutional and organisational venues: a National Strategy for Integrated Border Management in 2003, an Action Plan for Integrated Border Management in 2005, a National Strategy for Police Reform in 2003, an Action Plan for implementing police reform in 2005, and a police training strategy in 2007.

Within the Interior Ministry, the Macedonian National Commission of IBM was responsible for policy, while the National Centre for Border Management (NCBM) was the operational body promoting interagency work under the control of the government. A senior official in the NCBM described its role thus: 'This is not a political body, but an analytical and operational body' (interview, 17 March 2008). It promotes the intra- and interagency work called for by IBM and the international cooperation that is also a key component. Relevant internal agencies within Macedonia include the Ministry of Interior, Ministry of Finance, the Customs administration, Veterinary and Phytosanitary inspection, the Ministry of Health and the Radiological Directory.

There was a key funding relationship within the policy network between the NCBM and the European Agency for Reconstruction. The NCBM also received funds from the Macedonian budget. The NCBM was responsible for promoting interinstitutional cooperation, establishing an IT infrastructure, establishing structures for gathering and exchange of intelligence data (with similar mechanisms also being created in other Western Balkan states). Previously, there was an absence of cooperation and even the 'hiding of data' as an official from the National Centre for Border Management put it to us (interview, 17 March 2008).

The EU was central to the network in the sense that it provided the frame for legislative adaptation, but did not have the resources to provide technical expertise and input. It is here that we see the role of international organisations acting as transmission belts for the development of functional, political and administrative capacity. These included the IOM, ICMPD, UNHCR, Democratic Control of Armed Forces (DCAF), plus the EAR (European Agency for Reconstruction), UNDP and OSCE. DCAF played a particularly important role, because the introduction of IBM meant that the Ministry of the Interior took over responsibility for border security from the armed forces. The Law on State Border Control enacted in 2006 and entered into force in April 2007 transferred around 1,500 army staff into the Ministry of the Interior.

Sources of change

There is clear evidence of the development of efforts to develop functional, political and administrative capacity to support policy development in

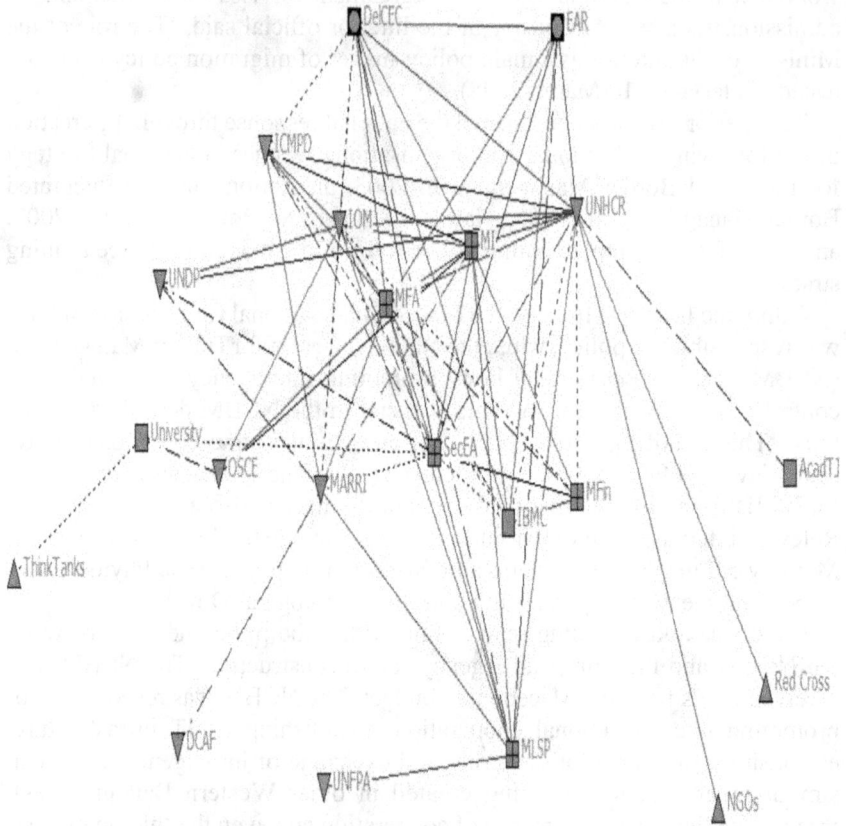

Figure 5.4 The migration and border security network: Macedonia

Macedonia. Through analysis of these projects we can see how EU-led support has been deployed, but has also relied on additional resources from other member states and IMOs. For example, between 2005 and 2007 the CARDS project *Support to and Coordination of Integrated Border Management Strategies* provided an example of the range of advice and expertise that can be brought to bear. This was carried out on behalf of the European Commission and led by the *Service de Coopération Technique Internationale de Police* (SCTIP) within the French Interior Ministry in consortium with the *France Coopération Internationale* (FCI), the Agency for European Integration and Economic Development (AEI) within the Austrian Ministry of Finance, the International Centre for Migration Policy Development (ICMPD) and the Organisation for Security and Cooperation in Europe (OSCE).

Similarly, the IOM worked closely with the Macedonian government to develop the following: the Action Plan 2009–14 on the Country's Resolution on Migration Policy; the National Strategy and Action Plan for Combating

Organisation	SNA abbreviation
Ministry of the Interior	MI
Ministry of Foreign Affairs	MFA
Ministry of Labour and Social Policy	MLSP
University of Skopje	University
International Organization for Migration	IOM
UNHCR	UNHCR
Commission Delegation	DelCEC
MARRI	MARRI
Secretariat for European Affairs	SecEA
European Agency for Reconstruction	EAR
Ministry of Finance	MFin
ICMPD	ICMPD
Centre for the Democratic Control of Armed Forces (DCAF)	DCAF
UNDP	UNDP
Integrated Border Management Commission	IBMC
Macedonian Red Cross	Red Cross
United Nations Partnership Framework	UNFPA
OSCE	OSCE
Think Tank Network	ThinkTanks
NGOs	NGOs

Trafficking in Human Beings and Illegal Migration 2009–12; the National Action Plan for Development of the Established Integrated Border Management System 2009–14; and the Programme for Reintegration of Returnees in Macedonia under the Readmission Agreements. A senior Interior Ministry official noted that there are risks of information overload and cognitive dissonance:

> in the EU in many regards, there is no specific defined standard. If you talk to a French police officer, from the French border police, he has one experience and will say one thing on a subject while the German police officer will say something else, the Swedish one will say something completely different. I think that it can sometimes create a problem for us. With the IT system, let's say, it is most certainly not the same in Italy, France, Slovenia, Germany. Imagine now that you're getting for the one database a German expert, for another database an English expert, for a third one French or a Spanish or maybe an Italian one. It is not so easy when you will have to put all of that together in one single frame.
>
> (Interview, 10 March 2008)

The same official went on to note that

> We cannot copy-paste something which was successful in Germany here in our country and think that it is successful. We can write hundreds of laws, but what matters most is how we implement them. Macedonia still has certain specifics which must be respected and I think that we are aware that we have taken into consideration these specifics and implemented them in our everyday work, as well as in the laws that we adopt.
>
> (Interview, 10 March 2008)

The revised version of the IBM Guidelines (January 2007) included a number of substantial and formal changes to the ways in which the main agencies in the field of border management operate, as well as to data protection and risk management. Furthermore, a part of cooperation and coordination with other actors, including other state actors, included a new subchapter on cooperation in the fields of migration, visa and asylum, and other non-state actors, including relations with carriers/operators, trade facilitators and the general public. Again, we see how the definition of IBM promoted forms of cooperation within and beyond the state that are indicative of the multi-level scaling of policy responses to migration in SEE.

We found little evidence of elite level contestation or resistance in Macedonia. This was probably because there is a virtually non-existent domestic politics of immigration. Macedonia experienced emigration, but very small-scale inflows. Macedonia seems unlikely to become a major destination country. Of far greater significance was the extension of visa-free travel from January 2010 within the Schengen area to Macedonians with biometric passports. Such a concession offers tangible benefit to citizens of candidate countries and can be a far more real expression of the EU's power and lure than the more technical components of adaptation to the *acquis*.

The only significant evidence of contestation that we found centred on budgets and resources, which were obviously central to the development of functional, political and administrative capacity. A Commission official put it thus: 'Of course you need budgetary support, which also depends on the persons involved in the ministries – how they are pushing for their objectives' (interview, 20 March 2008). We also found evidence that adaptation in this field is being prioritised and that funding streams have been available to develop IBM and associated migration policy measures.

Conclusions

In all four cases, adaptation to the migration and border security *acquis* (reflected in the creation, composition and operation of the capacity bargain networks) has contributed to the centralisation of authority, or confirmed existing patterns of centralisation, which is one of the central features identified by SNA and revealed by the capacity bargain networks. This is hardly a surprise as the management of migration and border security in other EU states tends to conform to such a pattern. The chapter has, however, shown that MLG is more than a metaphor for complexity and that there is a clear sense in all four case countries of both the sharing of competencies and interconnectedness. This interconnectedness can be seen subregionally within SEE, through links to the EU and member states and also through connections with international organisations. The key Europeanisation dynamic has been shown to be an elite-focused absorption of EU measures with the capacity bargain and, moreover, the form and content of these EU measures have played an important role in framing domestic action. At the very least, EU action has speeded up domestic adaptation, but the effects are probably more powerful because the EU-wide policy focus on border controls, while the 'fight against illegal immigration' has provided a powerful cognitive frame both for understanding policy challenges and for policy- making itself. What is also clear is that the 'external' focus of policy on border controls addresses only one component of the capacity bargain. This becomes most evident in the Greek case, with traces in Slovenia and Croatia too, in the sense that the 'external' capacity bargain focuses on seeking to regulate access to the state territory. Once immigrants are 'in', then the dynamics become more complex and involve both regulatory and distributive issues that are far more complex and difficult to resolve and with which the EU capacity bargain does not deal.

Greece is the major SEE destination country for immigrants. It is very much to the fore in the EU 'fight against illegal immigration', which has led to a strong focus on external frontier controls. The EU influence on the policy frame is clear, but it could easily be argued that the adaptation in the face of migration flows that Greece has undertaken would have occurred irrespective of the EU role given the location of Greece and domestic pull factors from the informal economy. Our analysis of Greece shows the mediation of EU effects in a complex domestic setting where a 'need' for migrants is tempered by public hostility to immigrants, as well as by the major adaptation pressures placed on central and local government. The capacity bargain network provides the framework for dealing with policy complexity. In terms of laws, we see EU influence on the frameworks introduced in 2001 and, particularly in 2005, we see too the importing of the EU's basic principles on integration, as well as specific EU-funded project work that seeks to promote engagement with civil society, build policy capacity and engage with non-EU states. We see too a multi-level scaling of policy, although, as would be expected, in a regulatory policy type, these can be better understood as principal-agent relations in a setting where authority to manage the residence implications of migration is devolved to municipalities.

There has been relatively swift adaptation to the EU *acquis* in Slovenia indicative of high levels of administrative capacity, as well as the readiness to accept the EU framework. The Ministry of the Interior is the key player in the capacity bargain network and provides the link from the Slovenian government to Brussels. As Slovenia has become more officially aware of its status as a country of immigration, there is also a debate about the development of an admissions policy linked to labour market requirements. Here we see a role for the Labour Ministry. However, we found that this awareness of immigration is also framed by the EU setting, which since 1998 has given meaning to migration as a debate about border security and an attendant suspicion of the motives for migration, particularly by asylum seekers and refugees. In terms of the multi-level scaling of policy, we see engagement with FRONTEX as a means for Slovenia to participate in a subregional setting, engage with its non-EU neighbours and also to work with a range of international organisations. In the next two sections, exploring Croatia and Macedonia, we saw how there is a subregional dimension to the governance of border security and migration within SEE, within which Slovenia plays a role. This also provides a way for us to see both EU influence on policy – a key driver in Slovenia – but also the role played by a range of international organisations in developing policy capacity.

In Croatia we see swift adaptation to the EU *acquis*. The prospect of membership provides a strong impetus to domestic change. We found key roles for the Ministry of Foreign Affairs in negotiations with the EU and of the Ministry of the Interior in domestic adaptation. We saw too the strong and important role played by international organisations providing specialist expertise and advice in the capacity bargain network. This shows how the Commission sets the framework but how international organisations intervene to provide specialist guidance and support. This also shows how this dimension of the MLG of migration and border security helps states such as Croatia develop their functional, political and administrative capacity in line with EU expectations. These international organisations serve as transmission belts for EU migration and border security policy and practices.

In Macedonia, as in Croatia, we see efforts to adapt to the EU *acquis*. In Macedonia we found an even more nascent policy setting with major efforts by the EU and international organisations to promote the development of functional, political and administrative capabilities within the capacity bargain network. We saw again how international organisations provide the transmission belt for communicating EU priorities into the domestic setting and providing the templates needed for adaptation.

6   Environment

Introduction

This chapter analyses adaptation to the environmental *acquis* in our four countries. The environment was chosen for two reasons: first, it is a policy sector where MLG is, because of the scale and complexity of the issues involved, considered the default setting. Jordan, for instance, described environmental policy as a 'sophisticated, multi-level governance system in which policy-making powers are shared between supranational and subnational actors to a unique extent' (1999a: 2). Environmental policy is focused on the management of non-rival public goods, some of which, such as lakes or rivers, may be common pool resources and therefore potentially excludable, but common sink resources, such as the atmosphere, are non-excludable.[1] It is a technically challenging policy area and this is reflected in Chapter 27 (Environment) of the *acquis* with over 300 directives and regulations, which is the second largest after agriculture. Not surprisingly, 'Environmental policy is the second-most studied policy in connection with multi-level governance' (Piattoni 2010: 139). Such technical demands bring strong disciplinary pressures to bear on member and would-be member states alike, but for SEE states with limited administrative capacity and specialist knowledge, it is a particular challenge that profoundly influences the capacity bargain. Environmental policy is a major and growing aspect of EU activity, and has major implications for capacity and governance at all levels, from the local to the supranational, drawing in international organisations other than the EU and is also an important arena for the mobilisation of civil society (Fairbrass and Jordan 2004: 147–64).

Second, the environment is a politically complex policy type. In contrast to cohesion (distributive), and migration and border security (regulatory), environmental policy is a 'mixed' type. By origin it is clearly regulatory and so is specific and focused; it targets individuals behaving in ways that decision-makers deem requires regulation in order to limit the impact of that behaviour on others. Unlike a 'pure' regulatory policy, however, the costs of regulation are not borne solely by those subject to that regulation (despite principles such as 'the polluter pays'), but are also borne collectively and benefits are collective. The environment as a policy sector has, therefore, elements of redistribution flowing from the encompassing nature (environmental issues are mainstreamed in all EU legislation) of many environmental issues. Spill-over is further encouraged by the often highly technical nature of environmental problems and the policy responses, which are likely to be costly. These features place considerable emphasis on creating scientific, technical and political consensus, and mobilising and coordinating resources in complex ways and for extended periods. In her study of MLG, Piattoni notes that 'protection of the environment has been the policy terrain on which local, national, and transnational social movements and non-governmental organisations mobilized most intensely' (2010: 135). The environment poses, therefore, extremely demanding problems that require sophisticated governance and as such environmental policy is a major reflection of the EU's governance principles.

This chapter, like its two predecessors, explores how engagement with the EU has altered (or created) domestic modes of governance dealing with the governance of the environment as an outcome of Europeanisation. We see strong elements of down-loading in the development of policy in all four countries as well as significant roles for non-EU international actors; particularly noteworthy is the emphasis placed on civil society engagement. The capacity bargain's functional, political and administrative dimensions enable us to assess types of adaptation and forms of policy approach.

The political and technical complexity of environmental policy shows the actual role and potential significance of transboundary and civil society actors as sources of legitimacy and expertise (Haverland 2003; Jordan and Liefferink 2004). There is, therefore, a distinct multi-level scaling effect that, like cohesion, draws on levels of government and NGO involvement that feeds into transboundary politics, as is the case with borders and migration (Knill and Lenschow 1998: 595–614; Knill 2007; Knill and Tosun 2008: 147–71). Piattoni's work on MLG, which only deals with member states but is none-theless suggestive, argues that environmental policy is two-level (state–EU) which, in contrast to cohesion but in common with border security, downgrades the role of subnational governments. Thus, she contends,

> we might say that the 'governance' aspect of MLG is more easily proven than the 'multi-level' aspect. It is not surprising, then, that environmental policy should have triggered debate on the issue of subsidiarities in both its territorial and societal dimensions.
>
> ... An empirical test of MLG, in the case of environmental policy, would seek to demonstrate, at a minimum, that subnational mobilization was significant, and that international and societal dynamics are fully factored in. Moreover, the linkage between subnational institutions and societies is particularly crucial for this policy area.
>
> (2010: 140)

However, and in common with the other two policy sectors, our evidence is that the key role lies with the Ministry of the Environment as policy-maker, coordinator and core implementer.

Finally, the chapter considers policy convergence. Common policies throughout the EU are essential if domestic policy is to be effective and if all actors are to operate on a level playing-field. This is obviously important in the case of the environment where varying standards or enforcement could reduce one producer's costs at the expense of others. As in our other cases, the *acquis* and other EU statements and preferences constitute substantial downward pressure for adaptation, but there is also substantial room for variation. Variation is, in part, the consequence of national administrative traditions, but also flows from differing environmental inheritances, different capacities and capabilities, and the weight accorded the environment among competing priorities, as well as by the way in which the EU makes environmental policy (Golub 1996: 686–703; Jordan 1999b: 69–90; Jordan and Breuker 2003: 555–74; Holzinger *et al.* 2006: 403–20).

EU environmental policy was originally low-salience, tangential to Community objectives and embodied in the 1957 EEC Treaty articles 2 (quality of life, harmonious economic development and balanced expansion), 100 (dismantling barriers to the Common Market) and 235 (allowing the Council of Ministers to take action in areas not covered by treaties). From the 1970s onwards, the EU carved out a distinct set of environmental policy objectives as policy developed alongside the common market (Weale 1996: 594–611; Zito 1998: 671–90; Wälti 2004: 599–634; Scherpercel 2007: 23–46; Knill 2009: 873–94). The reasons for this lock-step were, first, that varying national standards might confer competitive advantage; second, that environmental policy could help demonstrate that integration was about more than economic growth; and, third, that this was reinforced by a recognition that solutions to environmental problems were beyond the capabilities of any single state. Taken together, these three reasons provided the rationale for Brussels to assume a distinctive role. In 1973 the first Community-wide Environmental Action Plan (EAP) laid out fundamental principles and while the EAP's was non-binding it codified policy (Lenschow 2005: 309) and the Single European Act (1986) gave an explicit legal base to the EU's environmental competence. The SEA also placed great stress on civil society and NGO involvement as critical linkages to the subnational as well as to international organisations. Nevertheless, business remains the most influential single interest. These provisions were strengthened further by the Treaty on the European Union (1992) and the Treaty of Amsterdam (1997), and in 1994 the European Environment Agency (EEA) was created (Haigh 1999: 109–12; Lenschow 1999: 39–60; 2005: 306–27; Weale *et al.* 2000; Sbragia 2000: 293–316).

Up until the early 1990s environmental policy goals were pursued by uploading measures associated with environmental 'leaders' (such as the Federal Republic of Germany) but the last two decades have seen a move towards economic instruments and 'soft law' (Flynn 1997; Lees 2005, 2007), characterised by increased levels of discretion exercised by member states. The mixture of top-down regulatory direction and soft law is reflected in, and is also a reflection of, the division between 'leaders' and 'laggards', such as Greece (Lenschow 2005; see, however, Börzel 2000). In the Commission, we find a division of competences between DG Environment, the Industry and Agriculture DGs and, in the case of South East Europe, DG Enlargement and, to a lesser extent, DG Regional Policy (DG Regio). The DGs often differ in their perceptions of the effectiveness of the environmental policy agenda within the wider accession process (Weale 1999). What is clear, however, is that the Commission as a whole regards the environment as very significant in enlargement and Chapter 22 poses a great test for any polity.

In the enlargement process the key institutional player is the Commission. In addition, the EEA acts as a decentralised information-gathering and advisory body, often in concert with the Europe-wide 'European Information and Observation Network' (EIONET). NGO involvement is limited but clearly visible in a number of regional environmental networks cultivated by the EU (Stephenson 2010). This cultivation is consistent with the EU's objectives of drawing on the expertise of NGOs and other civil society actors at the formulation, implementation and monitoring stages of the policy-making process. These objectives are embedded within the *acquis* and enlargement, and are shared by international actors, such as the UN or OECD. They are also reflected in international agreements such as the Espoo Convention on Environmental Impact Assessment in a Trans-Boundary Context (1991), Agenda 21 (1992), the Aarhus Convention (1998) and more recent regional agreements such as the Joint Statements of Skopje regarding the Regional Environmental Reconstruction Programme (2000, 2003), the Kyiv Protocol on Strategic Environmental Impact Assessment (2003), the Athens Energy Community Treaty (2005), the Montenegro Joint Statement of the Regional Ministerial Conference 'Environmental Policies in the Context of European Integration' (2006), the NGO-focused *SEE Regional Declaration on Environmental Cohesion as the tool to EU integration and Sustainable Development* (2006) and the Bucharest Agreement (2008).

The regional context

While the transposition of the environmental *acquis* is homogenising, it occurs within the context of a region that is subject to heterogeneous environmental conditions (Meško *et al.* 2010: 1–10; Tews 2009: 130–9). The specific environmental indicators for our four case countries are discussed later but, as a region, SEE is incredibly diverse. It encompasses four distinct biogeographical areas – the Mediterranean, Central European, Alpine, and the Pannonic salt steppes and marshes (this last is not found in any of our cases) as well as thirteen internationally shared river basins and four transboundary lake basins (Stritih *et al.* 2007). Moreover, the rigours of Titoist economic planning from the late 1940s to the 1970s saw a previously agrarian economy undergo 'rates of industrialisation and urbanisation [that were] amongst the highest in the world' (Clarke 2002: 388). Industrialisation and its legacy of economic development and environmental damage were not evenly distributed across the former Yugoslavia. We see a divide in levels of development within the ex-Yugoslav cases, with Slovenia displaying relatively high levels on all of the key indicators of development compared with Macedonia, for instance, where more challenging conditions are to be found (World Bank 2011). The different developmental tangents of the countries of the former Yugoslavia have added to the environmental diversity of the region today and the subsequent potential for collective action problems in forging a common purpose in the field of environmental policy. Nevertheless, a degree of common purpose has been demonstrated with the Skopje and Montenegro Joint Statements and the other agreements mentioned earlier in this chapter. Of these, the 2000 and 2003 Skopje Joint Statements are particularly relevant in that they were explicitly intended to provide a major framework for collective action, not only for the transposition of the EU *acquis* but also for the broader sectoral integration of EU environmental objectives (Stritih *et al.* 2007: 9).

Starting with policy instruments, the current 6th EU EAP (2002–2012) identifies a number of key environmental instruments[2] but, of these instruments, European standardisation[3] and the community Eco-Management and Audit Scheme (EMAS)[4] are more relevant to existing member states rather than Croatia and Macedonia. However, two voluntary agreements (VAs), the Community Programme for NGOs and the LIFE/LIFE+ programmes, enjoyed a high profile in the period covered by our study. The Community Action Programme for Environmental NGOs (Council Decision 97/872/EC, revised in Decision 466/2002/EC) was created explicitly to expand the geographical scope of the programme to all countries in the region. The programme was designed to cultivate NGO participation in the policy process in order to further EU environmental objectives. LIFE was carried over from the 5th EAP and was given legal force by EP/Council Regulation EC 1655/2000. The instrument co-financed environmental activities in member states and in certain non-member countries, including SEE countries, with a total budget of over €1,500 million. LIFE was replaced in 2007 by LIFE+, which runs until 2013 with a budget of €2,190 million. As will be discussed at greater length in the context of our case countries, the technical challenges associated with the transposition of the *acquis* have unleashed significant centralising tendencies that sit uncomfortably with the EU's stated objective of widening involvement in the policy process. In this context, it is worth noting that 75–80 per cent of LIFE+ resources are directed through a new 'Implementation and Governance' budget strand, which represents a shift from a pure VA focus, albeit formalised, to one with stronger regulatory drivers explicitly aimed at encouraging wider stakeholder involvement. This shift reflects a perception within the Commission in particular that LIFE had failed to cultivate the full participatory role for NGOs and other stakeholders within governance networks that would have off-set these centralising tendencies.

Further conduits for EU influence are found in a number of pre-accession programs such as the Instrument for Structural Policies for Pre-Accession

(ISPA), launched in 2000, PHARE, created in 1989, the Community Assistance for Reconstruction, Development and Stabilisation (CARDS) programme, adopted in 2000, and the Priority Environmental Projects for Accession (PEPA) programme, announced in 1999 and in operation since 2000. Once again the impact of these programmes is not uniform and is dependent upon two factors. The first, not surprisingly, is eligibility. Greece, of course, was excluded from all of these pre-accession programmes, while of the other three countries, Slovenia was a recipient of ISPA assistance until its accession in 2004. By contrast, Croatia and Macedonia have been recipients of CARDS, while Slovenia has not. Similarly, Slovenia and, up until 2000, Macedonia have been recipients of PHARE while Croatia has not, but all three countries have been recipients of PEPA funding as part of their respective accession processes. The second factor is the identity of the different DGs that direct these programmes. Thus, ISPA was controlled by DG Regio, which is primarily focused on economic, social and territorial cohesion, PHARE and CARDS are controlled by DG Enlargement, and only PEPA is controlled by DG Environment. The Commission is not a unitary actor and the incentives provided by the programmes depend on the priorities set by the respective DGs. The implications of this are discussed at greater length later in the chapter.

Moving on to the mediating networks, the key conduits for EU influence are the Regional Environmental Reconstruction Programme for South East Europe (REReP for SEE), the Balkan Environmental Regulatory Compliance and Enforcement Network (BERCEN)/the Environmental Compliance and Enforcement Network for Accession (ECENA), and the more broadly based European Network for the Implementation and Enforcement of Environmental Law (IMPEL), of which the AC IMPEL subnetwork is focused explicitly on the region.

REReP was initiated under the Stability Pact for South Eastern Europe and endorsed by Ministers of the Environment from Albania, Bosnia and Herzegovina, Bulgaria, Croatia, Macedonia, Montenegro, Romania, Serbia and Kosovo at a meeting in Skopje in 2000. REReP draws upon expertise from Central and Eastern Europe, which had undergone the same process a decade earlier. The REReP budget for its SEE subsidiary is estimated to have been at least € 70 million over five years to 2005 and had five components: first, institutional strengthening and policy development (€ 11.2 million); second, environmental civil society building (€ 14.3 million); third, emergency assistance for combating war damage (€ 35 million); fourth, reinforcement of existing cooperative mechanisms and structures, and development of regional cross-border projects (€ 9.5 million); and finally, support to Priority National and Local Environmental Projects (no figures available). With the exception of emergency assistance for combating war damage, four of these components had clear implications for the development of environmental governance in the region. More specifically, the institutional development component included proposals to develop a Joint Environmental Action Plan for the region, a joint regional investment strategy, capacity building for Environmental Impact Assessments and other instruments specified in the 5th and 6th EAPs, membership and cooperation with the EEA, and strengthening capacity for approximation of the environmental *acquis*. The civil society component included the promotion of networking and cooperation of NGOs and the establishment of regional institutions for sustainable development, legal advocacy and the coordination of emergency responses. The cooperative mechanisms/cross-border projects component included plans for participation in international projects such as the International Commission for the Protection of the Danube River and other regional projects. The fifth component included the building of capacity at the municipal level of government.

The terms of reference of REReP and REReP for SEE reflected EU preferences and had clear implications for the development of governance. One of REReP's key outputs was the creation of the BERCEN network, made up of the same countries as those participating in REReP. BERCEN and its successor ECENA were funded by CARDS, although some of BERCEN's activities were funded by PHARE and individual member states such as the Netherlands, as well as EU-associate states such as Norway. The stated aim of both BERCEN and ECENA was to build capacity within the region in order to implement and enforce environmental legislation that emerged as part of the SAP. BERCEN was set up in December 2001 and wound up in 2006, to be succeeded by ECENA, which currently includes Albania, Bulgaria, Bosnia and Herzegovina, Croatia, Macedonia, Montenegro, Romania, Serbia and Turkey, as well as the Commission. REReP's encouragement of the kind of multi-tier, multi-sphere modalities found in the BERCEN and ECENA networks have had a significant potential impact on the development of environmental governance in the region in that they were not only cross-border in nature but also functionally integrated the region into the wider Europe.

IMPEL is another network with multi-tier, multi-sphere features and includes both EU member states and non-members, of which those involved in the regional SAP are integrated into the dedicated subnetwork AC IMPEL. Beyond BERCEN and ECENA, IMPEL has also forged links with other partner networks – INECE, REPIN, the GreenEnforce Network, and the Network of Heads of European Environment Protection Agencies. IMPEL includes representatives from ministries and regulatory authorities, although each country is officially represented by a nominated National Coordinator. Despite its highly networked character, IMPEL's internal governance retains a number of orthodox features, with a system of plenary meetings (officially the main strategic body) and working groups (for individual projects), overseen by an Executive Board. The work of IMPEL is structured around a set of Annual Work Programmes (AWPs), a Multi-Annual Work Programme (MAWP), and a Cluster Multi-Annual Work Programme (CMAWP). Again, both the content and delivery of IMPEL reflects the EU's preferences. Thus, during the period under study, IMPEL had three work clusters that worked to the 6th EAP and were set out in various AWPs and the relevant MAWP. These were, first, improving environmental permitting, inspection and enforcement; second, managing the trans-frontier shipment of waste; and third, developing and benchmarking better environmental legislation. All three place an emphasis upon partnership programming, expert review and the dissemination of best practice.

For Croatia and Macedonia, but not Greece and Slovenia, the demands of accession were the core driver of engagement with the EU at the heart of which is the transposition of the EU *acquis*. To cope with the significant technical and normative demands placed upon accession states by the Environment Chapter, national strategies for the transposition of the environmental *acquis* are set out in National Environmental Action Plans (NEAPS). Local Environmental Action Plans (LEAPs) have also assumed increasing importance in the local implementation of the environmental *acquis*. The Environmental Action Programme for Central and Eastern Europe (EAPCEE) encouraged the shifting of responsibilities from the central state to the regional and/or municipal tiers of governance and LEAPs emerged as a means of responding to this steer. Thus, the capacity bargain is struck at all levels of governance and the *quid pro quo* is the disciplinary impact of the EU's Annual Reports on accession states' progress.

However, it is important to enter a caveat here and ask how significant this regional dimension to domestic networks really is. Our research shows that regional actors and networks are not identified as significant in domestic networks. The EU has placed considerable emphasis on regional cooperation, reflecting its conviction that SEE has enough in common to constitute a distinct region and that regional interaction could mitigate historical legacies of conflict. States are required to participate in a wide range of regional networks; these are regarded by the EU as important and candidates have no option other than to engage with these networks. Given the importance of this regional dimension for the EU, their domestic impact is meagre.[5] This is because engagement with the EU is *primarily* intergovernmental and through country-Commission bilaterals, with regional interaction subordinate to both, so the latter is not critical to engagement with the EU. Any state will have a myriad of interconnections, some regional, but many are nested within the primary relationship with the Commission. This can be seen in the (non)relationship between the regional and domestic environmental policy networks. This is not to suggest there are no connections or that what exists is unimportant but they are not identified as such by domestic capacity bargain networks and so are not picked up by the SNA. Our methodology, remember, required actors to identify their most significant interactions. The political implications of this non-visibility is to reinforce the centrality of bilateral engagement with the EU and Commission, and the dominance of the domestic core executive which are, of course, present in the regional networks. While states recognise that they must engage with regional environmental networks for political and implementation reasons, their primary focus is the relationship with the EU and Commission. A side-effect of this is to reinforce the 'renationalisation' of environment policy.

So, to sum up, this section of the chapter has described what does appear to be impressive progress in terms of declarations of intent in the field of environmental policy and protection, the provision of roadmaps by which these intentions are put into practice, the identification of the appropriate policy instruments, and the cultivation of regional networks to manage and negotiate the pressures of integration in a cooperative fashion. We now turn to the case countries.

Greece

Greece has an indifferent environmental record, despite the fact that it has been an EU member state since 1981 and has therefore been compliant in and subject to the development of the environmental *acquis* over the last three decades. Analyses of Greek environmental policy stress complexity and bureaucratic fragmentation compounded by a weak history of environmental policy, weaknesses in state capacity, a failure to draw on available expert knowledge and a lack of public participation. In the absence of external EU enforcement, the result is policy failure with decision-making favouring business and other economic elites (Pridham *et al.* 1995: 244–70; Apostolou and Pantis 2009: 221–37).

Table 6.1 sets out a number of key environmental indicators that chart Greece's progress since 1990. The table provides pooled data for twenty-nine categories of indicator, including the obvious candidates such as CO_2 emissions (kilotons (KT) and metric tons per capita), agricultural emissions (methane and nitrous oxide) and other greenhouse gasses (hydroflurocarbons (HFC), perflurocarbons (PFC) and sulphur hexafluoride (SF6). Taken together these indicators are considered by international organisations such as the World Bank (from where these data were sourced) as providing a reliable picture of states' environmental performance. A detailed analysis is beyond the scope of this chapter but even a cursory examination demonstrates that Greek environmental performance is not impressive. Thirteen indicators show a marked deterioration from the 1990 baseline, including a rise in CO_2 emissions from 75,441.8 kilotons in 1990 to 1994, to 97,191.3 in 2005 to 2009 and 790, 000 metric tonnes to 1,620 metric tonnes CO_2 equivalent in other greenhouse gasses over the same period. By contrast, only five indicators – covering agricultural methane emissions, nitrous oxide emissions, aspects of water pollution and the extent of forested land area – have shown clear improvements. Most of the other indicators display trendless fluctuation but, worryingly given Greece's long-standing status as an EU member state, what is also striking is the amount of missing data across the series. Moreover, this not just a case of a relative environmental laggard being guilty of poor data collection in the early years, for much of the missing data (relating to aspects of water pollution) indicates that major problems remain in monitoring Greek environmental performance. Given that much environmental reporting and data collection is reliant on the subnational tiers of government, it also casts doubt upon the

Table 6.1 Environmental performance indicators: Greece (1990–2009)

Indicator	1990–94	1995–99	2000–04	2005–09
Agricultural methane emissions (% of total)	48.4	47.5	41.2	39.1
Agricultural nitrous oxide emissions (% of total)	90.8	91.0	90.9	91.3
CO_2 emissions (KT)	75,441.8	84,502.8	93,593.2	97,191.3
CO_2 emissions (metric tons per capita)	7.3	7.8	8.5	8.7
Fish species (threatened)	–	–	–	62
Forest area (% of land area)	26.1	27.2	28.4	29.3
Forest area (sq km)	33,594.0	35,104.0	36,614.0	37,822.0
GEF benefits index for biodiversity (0 = no biodiversity potential to 100 = maximum)				3.0
Industrial methane emissions (% of total)	7.8	8.2	10.0	9.7
Industrial nitrous oxide emissions (% of total)	5.4	4.9	4.4	3.3
Mammal species, threatened	–	–	–	10
Marine protected areas (number)	–	–	–	12
Marine protected areas (% of total surface area)	–	–	–	2.4
Methane emissions (kt of CO_2 equivalent)	6,390	6,490	7,070	7,410
Nitrous oxide emissions (thousand metric tons of CO_2 equivalent)	13,230	13,230	13,190	13,090
Organic water pollutant (BOD) emissions (kg per day)	50,857.1	46,291.1	58,639.7	–
Organic water pollutant (BOD) emissions (kg per day per worker)	0.19	0.20	0.20	–
Other greenhouse gas emissions, HFC, PFC and SF6 (thousand metric tons of CO_2 equivalent)	790	1,040	1,170	1,620
Plant species (higher) threatened	–	–	2	11
Terrestrial protected areas (number)	–	–	–	111
Terrestrial protected areas (% of total surface area)	–	–	–	3.4
Water pollution, chemical industry (% of total BOD emissions)	12.5	13.3	10.3	–
Water pollution, clay and glass industry (% of total BOD emissions)	6.9	6.9	6.7	–
Water pollution, food industry (% of total BOD emissions)	20.3	22.5	23.1	–
Water pollution, metal industry (% of total BOD emissions)	–	4.5	4.4	–
Water pollution, other industry (% of total BOD emissions)	21.7	22.4	28.6	–
Water pollution, paper and pulp industry (% of total BOD emissions)	6.6	7.9	9.0	–
Water pollution, textile industry (% of total BOD emissions)	–	20.5	15.3	–
Water pollution, wood industry (% of total BOD emissions)	2.1	1.9	2.7	–

Source: World Bank, 2011.

administrative capacity of environmental governance networks in Greece. Actors working within these networks recognise the problem and the need for Greece to enhance its administrative capacity. As one interviewee put it: 'the Greek public system and its bureaucracy have a specific logic which has big problems in adapting to change [and] this will take time to overcome' (interview, TEDKNA (Local Union of Municipalities and Communes of the Prefecture of Attica), 5 June 2008).

Inasmuch as Greece has made progress in environmental protection and enforcement, most of the impetus (in terms of the direction of policy, details of legislation, main sources of funding and the still flawed monitoring of performance) has come from the EU rather than been generated domestically. According to an interviewee from one of Greece's key environmental NGOs, 'more than 95 per cent, I would say, of all the laws which are introduced are in response to EU legislation, in order to harmonise the Greek situation with the EU's directions' (interview, Pan-Hellenic Network of Ecological Organisations, 3 June 2008). Coercive pressure has often come from the ECJ but, because of its relatively early accession, Greece has not been subject to the same degree of disciplinary pressure as that brought to bear on newer member states and the current candidate states. As a result, domestic environmental actors welcome the political pressure generated by Greece's engagement with the ECJ (interview, Hellenic Society for the Protection of the Environment and the Cultural Heritage, 4 June 2008).

Institutions

Article 24 of the 1975 Greek Constitution underlines the obligation of the State to take all preventive measures required to protect the environment, with special provisions for the protection of forested areas. In order to achieve this, the National Council for Spatial Planning and the Environment was founded in the following year and in 1980 it was replaced by the Ministry for the Environment, City Planning and Public Works (YPEXODE). YPEXODE was in turn replaced in 2009 by the Ministry of Environment, Energy and Climate Change, following the victory of the Panhellenic Socialist Movement (PASOK) in elections but, during the period of our study, YPEXODE was the key institutional actor in the governance of Greek environmental policy at both the formulation and implementation stages. We shall refer to YPEXODE as the Ministry of the Environment. The ministry's environmental protection role did not sit comfortably with its planning and public works functions, and these have now been hived off into a new Ministry for Infrastructure, Transport and Networks. Moreover, in a pattern that will be seen in our analysis of the other case countries, the ministry's competencies as the environment ministry were not exclusive but were shared with other ministries.

The involvement of ministries such as Agricultural Development, Development, Health and Transport, and Mercantile Marine were, given the nature of environmental policy, to be expected and not particularly controversial.

For instance, due to the increasing importance of energy policy for environmental protection, the Ministry of Development, which headed the Regulatory Authority for Energy and the Centre for Renewable Energy Sources and coordinated national energy policy, became an increasingly important actor. More notable was the increasing involvement of the Ministry of Interior, which was responsible for local government and represented the main link between the state and the local authorities. This meant that a number of decisions (e.g. those regarding the monitoring and control of atmospheric pollution) were subject to a co-decision process involving the environment ministry and the Ministry of the Interior. With this spread of competencies, interviewees from the co-responsible ministries suggested that there were increasing coordination issues between the environment ministry and other ministries in the core executive, as well as notable differences in the degree to which different ministries were willing to consult non-state actors. As one NGO activist explained:

> we are still quite far from having sufficient civil society participation. The Ministry of the Environment is quite opposed to any culture of consultation. The Ministry of Agricultural Development is quite different; in fact, it has invited us to informally consult them . . . . The Ministry of Economics also followed a type of 'consultation procedure' . . . The Ministry of Mercantile Marine and Island Policy has also expressed interest in cooperation . . . so we are in touch with some ministries, but all this depends on the individual minister's will; nothing is formalised and obligatory.
>
> (Interview, WWF, 15 February 2008)

Attempts at central steering by the Ministry of the Environment occurred at both the formulation and implementation phases of the policy process. In terms of policy formulation, our interviewees referred to the environment ministry's insistence that initiatives generated within, for instance, the Ministry of Development or the Ministry of Transport had to be signed off by the environment ministry. If unresolved, coordination issues were often taken to the Greek State Council, which ruled on interpretations of national laws, as well as International Environmental Agreements and Conventions. In terms of implementation, attempts at central steering were made more difficult because the peripheries and the municipalities, were key players. The thirteen Greek peripheries were responsible for executing policies formulated by the Ministry of the Environment and subsequently monitoring their implementation by the municipalities and communes. The emergence of a significant governance tier around the peripheries and fifty-four prefectures was the result of the decentralisation measures noted above and also the impact of EU-funded programmes such as LIFE and GreenMed. Other ministries involved in environmental policy, such as the ministries of Development, Transport and Agriculture also worked closely with local authorities, but this was more on a project basis, rather than the strategic cooperation that existed with the Ministry of the Environment and the Ministry of the Interior.

The emergence of a significant local tier of governance inevitably also introduced a new dimension of political conflict into the governance networks. As a Ministry of Environment official observed:

> conflict . . . exists on the basis of benefits and disadvantages that come with implementation . . . in a specific locality. On the one hand economies of scale are created . . . but on the other there is suspicion and scepticism on behalf of the public and that can damage the local politicians.
> (Interview, Ministry of the Environment, 19 February 2008)

Key local players at the implementation phase included the HSLGO, a joint stock company whose stockholders included Greek central government (the Ministry of the Interior was the main shareholder, along with the Ministry of the National Economy), the Union of District Government of Greece, the Consignments and Loans Fund, the Central Union of Municipalities and Communes of Greece KEDKE), Local Unions of Municipalities and Communes (e.g. TEDKNA), the Technical Chamber of Greece, the Pan-Hellenic Confederation of Unions of Agricultural Cooperatives (PASEGES) and other social sector actors.

For instances when conflict required adjudication, the Ombudsman for the Environment was set up as an arbitrator in interjurisdictional and state–civil society disputes such as when NGOs referred environmental policy violations for review. An interviewee summed up the role of the Ombudsman:

> the paradox is, in the case of the environment, that there are conflicting pressures, especially in the local societies, among the elected representatives which stall the implementation of environmental legislation, for example, on issues of habitat development, protection of environmental goods, and so on.
> (Interview, Ombudsman for the Environment, 15 February 2008)

The interviewee continued by pointing out that

> There is a clash between economic development and environmental protection in Greece which should not be the case. Our role in all of this is to try and ensure the rule of law and to point out that the two aforementioned issues are not irreconcilable, that this is a really obsolete way of thinking.
> (Interview, Ombudsman for the Environment, 15 February 2008)

In terms of NGOs and other societal actors, our respondents indicated that the involvement of civil society remained limited, although there was a consensus that their influence on policy-making would and should increase over time. As an interviewee from Greenpeace pointed out, 'I think there has been change [and] an increased mobilisation of all related actors' (interview, Greenpeace, 5 June 2008). NGOs increasingly exercised influence through the provision of expertise at the policy formulation phase; for example, through advisory bodies such as the National Committee for the Application of Law 2939 on Recycling. As one participant said:

> through this committee we are in the centre of decision-making and we try to make certain proposals so that recycling can be developed faster. We definitely have a lot of contact with the ministries, especially with the environment ministry. We are in constant contact with the local government, which reaches out to us.
>
> (Interview, Ecological Recycling Society, 13 February 2008)

In addition, environmental NGOs police the implementation of environmental policy though the referral of environmental policy violations to the Ombudsman for the Environment. To sum up this section, our respondents discerned a process through which NGOs and other societal actors were increasingly gaining leverage over the environmental policy-making process, not just through access to Ombudsman but also through the establishment and gradual development of consultation processes at various levels of governance, largely as a result of the ongoing impact of the Aarhus Convention, which stipulated the increased involvement of NGOs and other civil society actors, as well as through access to funding via the LIFE and INTERREG programmes (interview, Hellenic Society for the Protection of the Environment and the Cultural Heritage, 4 June 2008).

In addition, respondents pointed to the increasing significance of public opinion as an influence upon the framing and contestation of environmental policy, through the increased salience of environmental issues in electoral politics. As a government official observed:

> citizens also participate through the prefectural councils, where they have the right to submit their opinions and suggestions. For example, during the procedure for the establishment of environmental terms for industries and big works like roads, fisheries, mines, hotels, when the proposals are sent to the prefectures for consultation. The citizens' proposals are taken into consideration when they are justified.
>
> (Interview, Ministry of the Environment, 2 June 2008)

The network

Figure 6.1 reveals a well-developed network with vertical and horizontal ties between key nodes that span all potential levels of governance. Transnational actors have a strong presence, including the Representation of the EU in Greece

(RepEUG), the DGs for Agriculture (DGAgr), Environment (DGEnv), Energy (DGEnergy) and Research (DGRes), representatives from LIFE/LIFE+, and non-EU actors such as the World Wildlife Fund (WWF), the UN and OECD. The differentiated nature of the EU presence is a result of Greece's long-standing status as an EU member state. Network density appears to be reasonably strong and, on the basis of our respondents' perceptions, interaction is intense, with many strong ties between actors.

Interestingly, it is not a core government ministry but rather the Hellenic Network of Ecological Organisations (PHNEO) – an NGO – that was identified by our respondents as being the critical actor within the network because of its connections to other participants. Of the EU institutions, DG Environment had very close ties with PHNEO and another NGO, the Ecological Recycling Society (RS), as well as with the Ministry for the Environment (MEnv).[6] In addition, DG Energy had an intense tie with the Ministry of Development (Med) and LIFE had an intense tie with another NGO, the Ecological Recycling Society. None of the other EU actors had intense ties of this kind, despite the fact that other international actors with such ties included the UN, Greenpeace and WWF, all of which had intense ties with the Hellenic Society for the Protection of the Environment and the Cultural Heritage (HSPECH in the Figure 6.1). WWF also has an intense tie with PHNEO.

The environment ministry was, obviously, a key domestic actor. As already noted, the Ministry of the Environment had close ties with the most significant international actor, DG Environment, as well as with PHNEO, the Recycling Society, and the environmental Ombudsman. It is harder to portray the Ministry of the Environment as the gatekeeper, given that the Ministry of the Interior (MI in Figure 6.1) had the most intense tie with local government. In addition, there were a number of intense ties between nodes that bypassed the core executive completely, such as those between local governments and the Recycling Society, Hellenic Agency for Local Development and Local Government (EETAA, or HSLGD in the figure), Municipal Environmental Companies (MunEnvC), and the Central Union of Municipalities and Communes of Greece (KEDKE, or CUGM in the figure). These linkages point to a mature pattern of civil society interaction that was welcomed by our interviewees. As one interviewee commented:

> other actors involved are Local Government (Prefectures and Municipalities) and the various ENGOs which are definitely a form of institution which motivates and activates local and central government to act. The work that they do is increasingly important in the past decade and the fact that all levels of administration have been sensitised regarding the environment is largely attributed to them. Things that NGOs were proposing some years ago and seemed beyond the realm of policy are now central in policy debates.
>
> (Interview, TEDKNA, 5 June 2008)

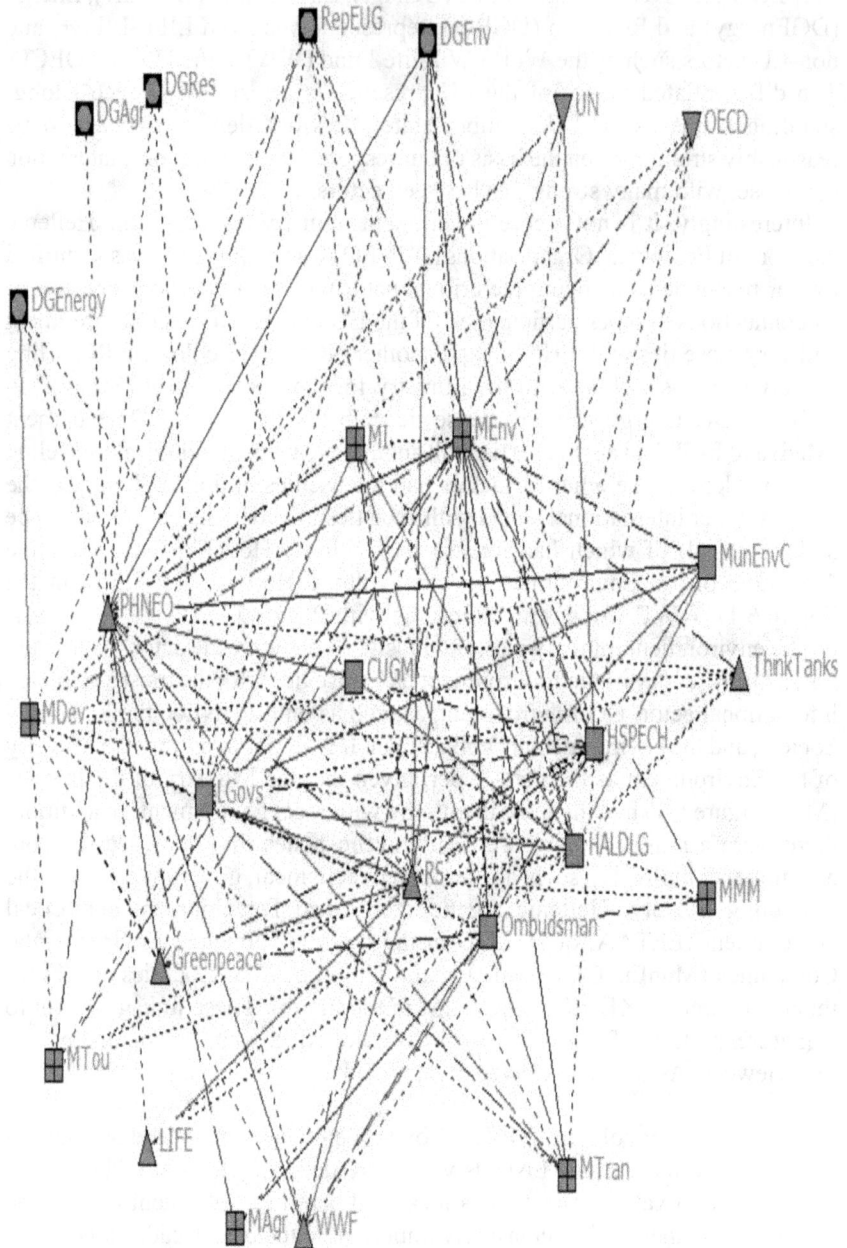

Figure 6.1 The environment network: Greece

Organisation	SNA abbreviation
DG Environment	DGEnv
DG Energy	DGEnergy
DG Research	DGRes
DG Agriculture	DGAgr
Ministry of Environment, Physical Planning and Public Works	MEnv
Ministry of Tourism	MTou
Ministry of Agricultural Development	MAgr
Ministry of Mercantile Marine	MMM
Ministry of Transport	MTran
Ministry of Interior	MI
Municipalities	LGovs
Municipal Environmental Companies	MunEnvC
Hellenic Agency for Local Development and Local Government	HALDLG
Greenpeace	Greenpeace
WWF	WWF
Hellenic Society for the Protection of the Environment and the Cultural Heritage	HSPECH
Recycling Society	RS
Representation of the EU in Greece	RepEUG
LIFE-Greece Team	LIFE
OECD	OECD
UN	UN
State Ministry of Development/Regulatory Authority for Energy	MDev
Think Tanks	ThinkTanks
Pan-Hellenic Network of Ecological Organizations PANDOIKO	PHNEO
Ombudsman	Ombudsman
Central Union of Municipalities and Communes of Greece	CUGM

Sources of change

Although Greek environmental performance and reporting remains patchy, progress has been made in terms of the functional, political and administrative capacity of the state. Functional capacity has increased and the transposition of the EU *acquis* is now relatively unproblematic. Political capacity has also improved and NGO involvement in particular has become more extensive in recent years. Indeed, our SNA demonstrated a reasonably complex governance network in which respondents reported more critical ties for an NGO (PHNEO) than for the core environment ministry. Even if we allow for the fact that the operationalisation of our SNA is reliant on perceptions, this does suggest a redistribution of power and resources across the governance network and away from the core executive. Even in the context of this redistribution, however, administrative capacity is more of a problem, as demonstrated by both the deterioration of some aspects of environmental performance and by Greece's failure to provide full and comprehensive environmental data. So, drawing upon our analytical framework, although in Greece the capacity bargain originates much earlier than our other cases and has had longer to embed itself, the capacity bargain remains unbalanced and incomplete for largely domestic reasons. To quote one interviewee:

> all of these processes of consultation emanate from EU pressures but sometimes their realisation is very problematic. There is a tendency by the central administration in Greece to want to keep a monopoly of power and not share it with civil society as the EU prescribes.
> (Interview, Hellenic Society for the Protection of the Environment and the Cultural Heritage, 4 June 2008)

Within the capacity bargain, the EU has acted as a provider of direction, legislation, funding and monitoring in environmental policy. Respondents in our study noted an overlap in the form and content of EU and Greek environmental policy, albeit with an understandable emphasis in the latter on national priorities, needs and challenges. The EU has also encouraged a more pluralistic policy community and EU funding has contributed to the development of activities by NGOs, local governments and municipal companies (e.g. DEPEVA) as well as actors such as EETAA. The influence of the EU is seen by domestic actors as a source of authority against those refusing to comply with the environmental legislation. The EU was also seen as a welcome source of pressure on the Greek authorities, especially in those instances – such as when Greece was successfully taken to the ECJ for the issue of hygienic waste management in a number of areas – where Greece has been sanctioned by the EU.

The ECJ's role as *deus ex machina* in Greek environmental politics is a reflection of the failure of the rise in environmental consciousness during the 1970s and 1980s to transpose itself into the domestic party system. Reasons given for the low salience of environmental concerns and Greece's poor environmental record span explanations stressing a lack of capacity to those emphasising the failure of the Greens within the Greek party politics (O'Neill 1997). At the same time, however, the emergence of PHNEO in the mid- to late-1990s was instrumental in pressuring the Ministry of the Environment to announce a six-year Environmental Protection Action Plan in 1994 to enact the principles of the EU's fifth EAP. As part of this first Greek NEAP, 730 billion drachmas (including EU funds) were pledged for the five-year period to 1999 (Ministry of the Environment Law 2204/1994). More recently, a new Law on Spatial Planning and Sustainable Development was passed to replace the 1999 Law (Law 2742/1999). It includes the Special Plans Framework, designed to encourage governance networks and clarify their social and administrative responsibilities (Law 3661/2008).

Nevertheless, we can also detect inertia and resistance. The main manifestation of this phenomenon is the reluctance of the environment ministry to embrace a more pluralist and polycentric policy community. This is an artefact of the traditional centralised model of the Greek state and its institutions, as well as Greece's 'simple polity' nature until the early 1990s. These old practices are slowly being eroded through the pincer effect of top-down (EU to state/substate) and bottom-up (civil society to state/substate) pressures partly motivated by the interaction between the EU and civil society level bypassing the intermediary state level. Beyond the state level, respondents recognised the central role of the EU and, to a lesser extent, the roles of international organisations such as the UN and the OECD, as well as the disciplinary effects of long-established International Conventions such as the Kyoto Protocol, and the Ramsar and Aarhus Conventions (interview, Pan-Hellenic Network of Ecological Organisations, 3 June 2008).

The impact of engagement with the EU has led to moderate MLG effects in Greece in which capacity has become more dispersed, but on a task-specific basis. The EU's principles and practices have encouraged a culture of consultation that is arguably alien to the established SOPs of Greek governance and the result has been a process by which power and resources have moved towards NGOs, local governments, scientists and semi-private actors. This is matched by the cultivation of debate and openness of environmental information, despite the failures of data collection. Nevertheless, much remains to be done to enhance the openness of Greek environmental networks:

> the institutional aspect and decision-making is a crucial point. The participation/consultation process has been broadened to include a number of actors (peripheries, municipalities, ENGOS, scientists), but the final decision-making authority still resides with the ministry, it is very concentrated. Consultation is an important step but it's not a panacea.
>
> (Interview, TEDKNA, 5 June 2008)

Slovenia

Slovenia's environmental policy performance has improved enormously, with progress made in enhancing air quality, Kyoto compliance and industrial pollution (Sotlar *et al.* 2011: 11–40). Slovenia inherited its environmental policy stance from the former Yugoslavia and it was not until the mid to late 1990s that the country's preparations for EU accession in 2004 began to impact upon environmental legislation. The Environment Chapter of the accession negotiations was opened in December 1999 and closed in December 2001 (Decision 2002/94/EC). Slovenia possessed relatively high levels of administrative capacity and as a result made good progress in the transposition and implementation of the environmental *acquis*. Progress was especially good in the fields of horizontal legislation, air quality, waste management, nature protection, industrial pollution control and risk management, noise, civil protection and climate change. Less progress was made in the fields of water quality, GMOs and radiation protection. Recent research indicates that the pace of reform is slowing (Detlef and Müller-Rommel 2010: 23–44) and there was a feeling among some of our interviewees that it might even be going into reverse (interview, REC Country Office Slovenia, 18 December 2007).

Table 6.2 demonstrates that Slovenian environmental performance is more impressive than that of Greece. Only eight indicators show a marked deterioration from the 1990 baseline, including a rise in CO_2 emissions from 12,336.7 kilotons in 1990–94, to 15,158 in 2005–09, a modest rise in industrial methane emissions as a percentage of total emissions over the same period, and rises in some aspects of water pollution, particularly those emitted by the metals industry, which doubled over the period from 2 per cent to over 4 per cent of total emissions. Five indicators show improvement, notably in the extent of forested land area and water pollution. The other indicators display trendless fluctuation but, unlike in Greece, although there are missing data in the early years of the series, the most recent data are complete. This indicates that Slovenia's mobilisation of subnational tiers of government in the field of data provision has been quite successful, which points to the existence of considerable administrative capacity within environmental governance structures in Slovenia.

Institutions

The key environmental policy institution in Slovenia is the Ministry of Environment and Spatial Planning (MESP). The Ministry was and remains divided into four directorates: the Secretary General Directorate, Directorate for Environment, Directorate for Spatial Planning, and Directorate for EU Matters and Investment. The MESP is the main instigator of environmental policy, proposing environmental legislation to parliament and formulating secondary legislation. It is responsible for core functions of environmental policy-making, such as nature protection, energy efficiency and renewable energy support, environmental health and spatial development, the security of adequate water resources, the maintenance of water quality, and the sustainable management of surface, underground and seawater. The MESP has four supporting agencies: the Environmental Agency, Environment and Spatial Planning Inspectorate, Survey and Mapping Authority, and the Slovenian Nuclear Safety Administration. These are semi-autonomous agencies modelled on the US and German templates, and are responsible for the practical implementation of environmental policy. The Environmental Agency's mission is to monitor, analyse and forecast natural phenomena and processes in the environment, and to reduce natural threats to people and property. The Environmental Inspectorate is responsible for monitoring and assessing the implementation stage of the policy cycle. The Survey and Mapping Authority implements administrative, professional, technical and supervisory assignments,

Table 6.2 Environmental performance indicators: Slovenia (1990–2009)

Indicator	1990–94	1995–99	2000–04	2005–09
Agricultural methane emissions (% of total)	58.0	53.1	50.6	47.9
Agricultural nitrous oxide emissions (% of total)	90.7	93.5	91.7	88.2
CO_2 emissions (KT) (1992)	12,336.7	15,887.1	14,630.4	15,158.0
CO_2 emissions (metric tons per capita) (1992)	6.2	8.0	7.3	7.6
Fish species (threatened)	–	–	–	24
Forest area (% of land area)	59.5	60.8	62.0	76.2
Forest area (sq km)	11,985.0	12,239.0	12,492.0	12,695.0
GEF benefits index for biodiversity (0 = no biodiversity potential to 100 = maximum)	–	–	–	0.2
Industrial methane emissions (% of total)	16.7	17.5	21.0	20.9
Industrial nitrous oxide emissions (% of total)	0.0	0.0	0.0	0.0
Mammal species, threatened	–	–	–	4
Marine protected areas (number)	–	–	–	3
Marine protected areas (% of total surface area)	–	–	–	0.4
Methane emissions (kt of CO_2 equivalent)	1,740	1,600	1,620	1,630
Nitrous oxide emissions (thousand metric tons of CO_2 equivalent)	1,080	1,080	1,080	1,100
Organic water pollutant (BOD) emissions (kg per day)	–	28,261.8	29,178.7	28,156.9
Organic water pollutant (BOD) emissions (kg per day per worker)	–	0.13	0.13	0.13
Other greenhouse gas emissions, HFC, PFC and SF6 (thousand metric tons of CO_2 equivalent)	580	310	140	210
Plant species (higher) threatened	–	–	0	0
Terrestrial protected areas (number)	–	–	0	30
Terrestrial protected areas (% of total surface area)	–	–	–	6.6
Water pollution, chemical industry (% of total BOD emissions)	–	11.6	11.1	11.9
Water pollution, clay and glass industry (% of total BOD emissions)	–	4.4	3.9	3.9
Water pollution, food industry (% of total BOD emissions)	–	7.7	9.0	8.9
Water pollution, metal industry (% of total BOD emissions)	–	2.0	1.9	4.1
Water pollution, other industry (% of total BOD emissions)	–	41.2	45.9	48.1
Water pollution, paper and pulp industry (% of total BOD emissions)	–	7.8	6.8	6.5
Water pollution, textile industry (% of total BOD emissions)	–	20.0	16.3	12.1
Water pollution, wood industry (% of total BOD emissions)	–	5.4	5.0	4.9

Source: World Bank, 2011.

and also disseminates data and issues permits and certificates. Finally, the Slovenian Nuclear Safety Administration is responsible for nuclear and radiological safety, nuclear trade, transport and handling of nuclear and radioactive materials, accountability and control of nuclear materials.

Unlike our other cases, there is less dispersal of environmental competencies to other ministries within the core executive. Nevertheless, during the period under study there were two more key state-level actors beyond the MESP. First, the Institute for Nature Conservation was tasked with nature conservation, especially within ecologically vulnerable areas in the country. It supported the MESP operationally through the collection of biological data and the provision of expertise when drafting nature conservation legislation. Second, the Council for Sustainable Development had an advocacy and counselling function and constituted a forum for the interests of civil society. The Council was made up of 34 members, drawn from ministries, private enterprise, farming, Roma minorities, NGOs and other civil society actors.

At the subnational level, Slovenia does not have administrative regions, only the 210 municipalities. Of these, only the eleven biggest with city status have statutory responsibility for environmental protection. The municipalities enjoyed a degree of autonomy but LEAPs had to be in line with national legislation. These measures were locally important as they involved, for instance, reducing traffic in city centres. The division of legal competences between MESP and the municipalities were codified in the Environmental Law and associated secondary legislation as a result of criticism from the EU at an early stage of the accession process. As one local authority official explained,

> nowadays the Ministry is very keen to include municipalities in decision-making and consultation, because the Ministry received a negative assessment from the EU regarding the participation of lower levels. The assessment had a positive impact on the Ministry and from then on the ministry involves the Municipalities in consultations regarding legislation.
> (Interview, Municipality of Maribor, 14 January 2008)

Nevertheless, on a more instrumental level, the perceived retention of resources at the centre remained a source of resentment:

> the Ministry should give more funds for environmental and energy investments. The Ministry in many cases promises the funds, but then it can last up to two years before the funds are actually available. Local level organisations are much stressed and they lose confidence towards the Ministry. This should be changed.
> (Interview, Local Energy Agency (Pomurje Region), 14 January 2008)

NGOs and civil society actors had an important advocacy and decision-making role, although only a handful of them had full-time employees during the period of our study. The most important professional Slovenian national NGOs were: the Foundation for Sustainable Development (Umanotera), the Slovenian Energy Forum (SE-F), the Association for Sustainable Development (Focus), the Association of Environmental Movements – Party of Environmental Movements (ZEG/SEG), the Institute for Sustainable Development (ITR) and the CIPRA NGOs. Given Slovenia's relatively recent democratisation, the relative scale of NGO activities in Slovenia was quite impressive, but NGO activists remained dissatisfied with the current modes of governance. The main reason for this was a perceived lack of involvement in the policy formulation phase, with one interviewee declaring 'conflict between government and non-government organisations is related to the governmental conviction that NGOs are not competent and representative partners. NGOs' reproach to government is that government runs the participation process without any real intention to involve NGOs' (interview, Vitra Cerknica NGO, 15 February 2008).

The network

Figure 6.2 indicates a developed network that spans all levels of governance. The key transnational actor according to our respondents was REC. REC's influence was substantial and much of it independent of the MESP, labelled MEnv in the figure. The MESP was the joint key state actor in the network, with two critical ties, the same number as that of the local energy agencies (LEAs). According to our respondents, the actor with the most significant presence was the SE-F, with ties to Umanotera as well as other smaller NGOs, followed by REC. REC also enjoyed significant relationships beyond the critical tie with the MESP. The first was with the SE-F, and the second was with the subnational regional development agencies (RDAs). Elsewhere, the Slovenian Environmental Agency (EARS) was reported to have had strong ties with the Chamber of Commerce and Crafts (CCC).

So, the MESP was by no means the key node of the network. Having said that, the MESP was clearly well networked and the preponderance of relatively weak ties between it and its network partners may be an artefact of our interviewees' responses rather than a true reflection of network dynamics. One explanation for this is that the MESP's activism in encouraging NGO involvement had led to their influence being discounted by respondents as they adapted to the new more pluralistic governance networks to be found in Slovenia. Certainly in our interview data, non-state actors appeared to recognise the opportunities that had opened up to them. For instance, one respondent noted the willingness of MESP officials to include stakeholders at all stages of the policy process (interview, Regional Centre for Central and East Europe, 18 December 2007). Another interviewee, however, indicated that this involvement was sometimes more symbolic than substantive (interview, Energy Agency Pomurje, 14 January 2008). The apparently weak network

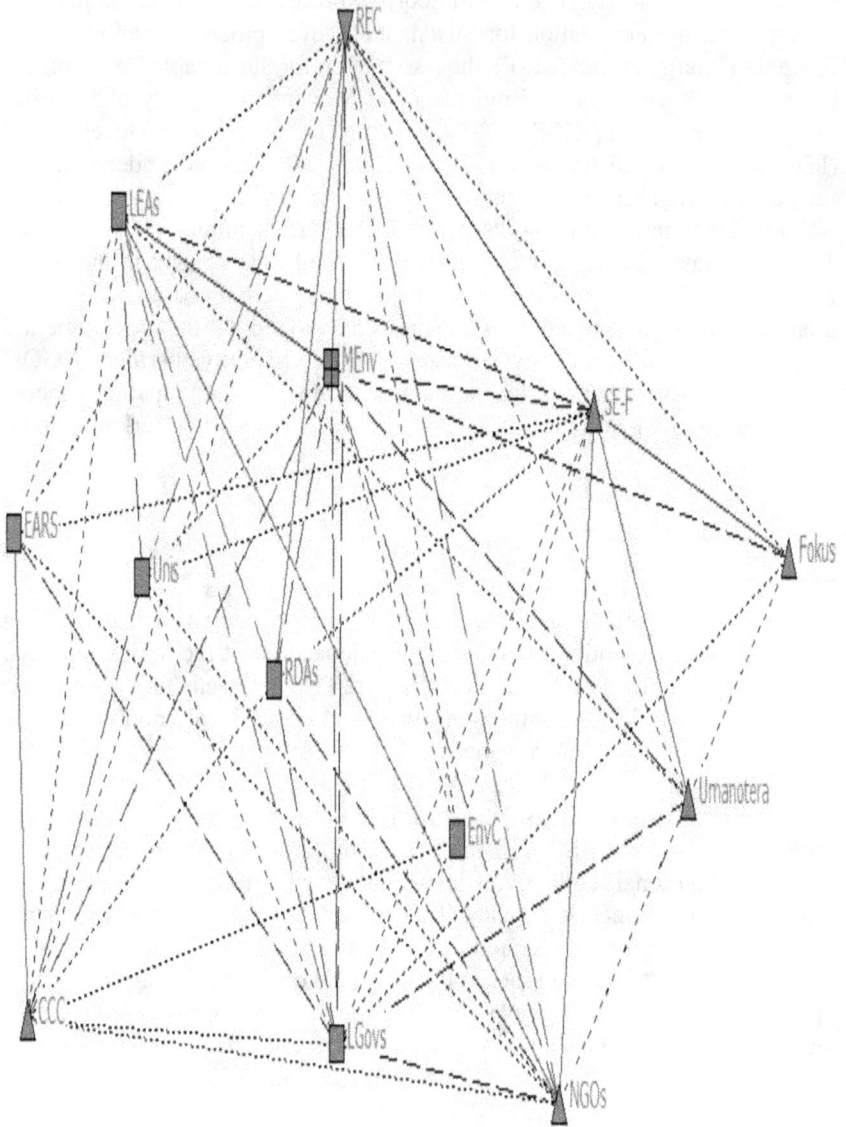

Figure 6.2 The environment network: Slovenia

Organisation	SNA abbreviation
Ministry of Environment and Spatial Planning	MEnv
Environmental Agency of RS	EARS
Regional development agencies	RDAs
Local energy agencies	LEAs
Municipalities	LGovs
Chamber of Commerce and Crafts	CCC
Regional Environmental Centre for Central and Eastern Europe	REC
NGOs	NGOs
Umanotera	Umanotera
Slovenski E-Forum	SE-F
Fokus	Fokus
Universities	Unis
Environmental Council	EnvC

status of the MESP in our SNA is a puzzle. The ministry was and remains the main legislative driver of environmental policy in Slovenia, despite the contrary evidence from our SNA.

Sources of change

The improvement in Slovenian environmental performance over the last twenty years has been marked and real progress been made in terms of the functional, political and administrative capacity of the state. Functional capacity is impressive as reflected in Slovenia's rapid transposition of the EU *acquis*, as is the level of political capacity reflected in our SNA analysis. Indeed, as with Greece, an NGO – in this case SE-F – was identified as the key network node, and a regional network, REC, was also perceived as being more networked than the MESP. This represents a significant redistribution of power and resources away from the core executive that is truly multi-level in nature. Compared with Greece, Slovenia possesses greater administrative capacity, as demonstrated both by its relatively impressive environmental performance and its ability to monitor and enforce that performance. In short, the capacity bargain between Slovenia and the EU appears to be more comprehensive than that in Greece. Given that capacity bargains can lead to a redistribution of power and resources away from the core executive, the apparent scale of this process in Slovenia might also explain the relative decentredness of the MESP within our SNA results.

In terms of the drivers of the changes seen in Slovenia, the desire of elites to meet the transposition requirements led to a period of legislative activism in the fields of industrial pollution, waste-water treatment, nature protection, renewable energy and energy efficiency (Sotlar *et al.* 2011). As one interviewee argued, 'the EU has forced Slovenia to accept legal acts to implement environmental policy. If Slovenia would not have accessed the EU, there would be just some 10 per cent of existing legislation that would have been adopted' (interview, Focus NGO, 4 February 2008). At the same time, however, another interviewee stressed the role of domestic elites in the shaping of Slovenian environmental policy: 'European solutions cannot be the same. Therefore, we cannot say that some solution that was good in one country will also work in Slovenia' (interview, Slovenski E-forum, 1 February 2008). Be that as it may, an Environmental Protection Act was introduced in 2004, becoming operational the following year. Targets on air quality have largely been reached and are in line with the *acquis*. In terms of waste management, a recycling of packaging proposal was adopted in 2002 and intended to cover the five years to 2007. Legislation on air quality is in line with the *acquis*, with policies adopted concerning the collection and treatment of urban waste water and the distribution of water. Management of water has been accounted for under the Water Act of 2002 with allowance for a Water Fund. By and large, nuclear safety policy is in line with the *acquis* and progress has also been made on air quality and water management (CEC 2009). There was also a drive to enhance Slovenia's administrative capacity; the Environmental Agency and the Institute for Nature Conservation were established in April 2001 and January 2002 respectively.

On the minus side, industrial pollution measures are only partly in place and there are few or no measures regarding large combustion plants, emissions ceilings and integrated pollution and prevention control (IPPC). As a result, at the time of writing Slovenia still has transitional arrangements with the EU for the treatment of urban waste water (until 2015), and for integrated pollution prevention and control (until 2011, instead of 2007 for other EU member states).

In terms of the expansion of NGO involvement, the decision of Slovenia to accept the Aarhus Convention in 2003 created a forum for public partici-pation in decision-making in the environmental policy domain. Civil society participation is also encouraged through the EU's LIFE instrument, which has financed a number of projects in the country. By late 2006, there were six ongoing LIFE projects with a total investment of €5.4 million, of which €2.8 million came directly from the EU. The main domestic driver for the inclu-sion of Slovenian NGOs was the adoption of the Law on Access to the Public Information in 2003. No fewer than thirteen articles of the Environmental Law codify the public's right to access information and participate in environmental matters. The Slovenian government has also adopted a Strategy of Cooperation with NGOs, which provides a template for best practice in cooperation with NGOs. Nevertheless, despite these changes we have seen that some NGOs still complained about what they saw as an ongoing lack of influence on the legislative process (interview, Vitra Cerknica, 15 February 2008).

Although the capacity bargain in Slovenia is more comprehensive than that of Greece, it has weaknesses, the main one being the need to build up capacity and resources at *all* administrative levels. In 2008 the EU identified a number of priority objectives including strengthening the Environmental Inspectorate and other enforcement agencies, introducing a credible system of fines and other sanctions, improving coordination between administrative units at all levels, improving environmental monitoring, preparing strategic plans, including financial strategies, developing an environmental investment strategy with realistic costing of the requirements of alignment, increasing levels of investment in environmental infrastructure, particularly in the fields of waste water collection and treatment, drinking water supply, air pollution and waste management (CEC 2008c). The third of these objectives, improving coordination between administrative units, is especially relevant and it is worth noting that in 2007 the newly appointed State Secretary for Environment, Mitja Bricelji, pledged to improve cooperation between the related but institutionally separate sectors of environment, planning and nature. This implies a further decentring of the MESP, thereby generating further pluralisation in the network.

There is evidence of some deeper-seated Type II MLG effects in Slovenia, as demonstrated by a relatively pluralistic and open policy community and the codification of rights that respects the spirit and the letter of the legislation required by the accession process but also in legislation (such as the Strategy of Cooperation) that is above and beyond what is required. On the horizontal dimension, decision-making at the national level remains dominated by the MESP. Conversely, there is more involvement of NGOs and other non-state actors participate at key points, such as during the adoption of the National Environmental Protection Programme and during the codification of Strategic Impact Assessments and Environmental Impact Assessments. There are also informal opportunities for lobbying at the ministerial level. On the vertical dimension, the municipalities have limited powers and responsibilities, the extent of which depends on municipal size, resource base and city status. Municipalities have responsibility for (*inter alia*) water and sewage treatment, refuse collection and disposal, environmental protection and consumer protection. Of these, only refuse collection is exclusively a municipal competence. In addition, as our interviewees have indicated, there is a sense that the new responsibilities of the local tier have not been matched by a timely transfer of resources from central government.

Outside the formal structures of governance, NGOs and other actors exercise their voice through influencing public opinion. In recent years, public opinion has prevented the building of radioactive waste-disposal sites in at least five Slovenian municipalities. It has also led to the cancellation or postponement of major investments, including the building of wind power plants on Volovja Reber, the building of the hydro power plant Moste II and the building of seven hydro power plants on the Mura river. Campaigning is seen as an alternative conduit of influence for NGOs that both side-steps existing governance structures and, over time, will lead to their further pluralisation. Nevertheless, as in Greece, there is still much to be done in this respect. As one interviewee indicated,

> EU membership forced some changes [but] public participation in the last years is getting worse. NGOs are lacking cooperation [*sic*]. The Ministry of Public Administration enabled public participation at the preparation phases of several acts but the system is not working yet.
>
> (Interview, REC Country Office Slovenia, 18 December 2007)

Croatia

The SAA between Croatia and the EU was signed in October 2001, ratified by EU member states in 2004 and came into effect in February 2005, two years after Croatia's formal application for EU membership. Croatia was granted full candidate status in June 2004 (Vlašić and Feketia 2006). The Commission Opinion on Croatia focused on a number of environmental policy goals, notably the development of horizontal legislation, including environmental impact assessment and public participation. Other key issues identified as requiring a response were the strengthening of administrative capacity at the national and regional levels to ensure more effective planning, including the preparation of financial strategies, the strengthening the capacity of regional and national inspection services to enforce environmental legislation, and adopting and implementing a national waste management plan (CEC 2001b).

These priorities were built on in the Accession Partnership Agreement (2006), which identified the need to mainstream environmental policy by integrating environmental protection requirements into the other sectoral policies, develop an environmental investment strategy, speed up the transposition of the environmental *acquis*, especially in the fields of waste management, air quality, water quality, nature protection and integrated pollution prevention and control, enhance environment infrastructure and ratify the Kyoto protocol (Decision 2006/145/EC; see also Decision 2008/119/EC). Progress was monitored through the European Partnership, through the Annual Reports process and, at the domestic level, a National Committee for monitoring accession negotiations forms part of the negotiation structure for Croatian accession.

The predicted cost of Croatia meeting the requirements of the Environmental Chapter is approximately €10 billion by the year of 2025, including around €4.8 billion for water management, €2 billion for air protection and €3.25 billion for waste management. These costs are taken into account in eleven transitional periods set out in the chapter. Croatia has installed a National Environmental Information System (NEIS) as part of the *acquis* compliance process and the available statistics show significant improvements in environmental performance, including air quality and the amount of electricity generated from renewable resources. The immediate priorities going forward are resolving Croatia's waste-management problems and the harmonisation of the remainder of domestic legislation with the *acquis*. At the time of our interviews, the progress that had been made in this respect was recognised by environmentalists:

> significant progress is evidenced in the drafting and adoption of legislation, and in the development of national environmental institutions. Also, most of the international agreements have been ratified and there are clear indicators of the integration of environmental and sustainable development objectives in other sectors.
>
> (Interview, Heinrich Böll Foundation, 19 December 2007)

Table 6.3 demonstrates that Croatia's performance is more similar to that of Slovenia than of Greece. Eight indicators show a deterioration from the 1990 baseline, including a sharp rise in CO_2 emissions from 12,336.7 kilotons in 1990–94 to 23,665.8 in 2005–09, a less alarming rise in industrial methane and nitrous oxide emissions as a percentage of total emissions over the same period, and – as in Slovenia – rises in some aspects of water pollution, in this instance by the clay and glass, metal, and paper and pulp industries. Eight indicators show improvement, for instance in methane and nitrous oxide emissions, industrial nitrous oxide emissions and the extent of forested land area. Four other indicators display trendless fluctuation but, as in Slovenia, the most recent data are complete. This indicates that Croatia's mobilisation of subnational tiers in the field of data provision has been successful, implying a growing administrative capacity in environmental governance.

Institutions

The key institutional actor in the field of environmental policy is the Croatian Ministry of Environmental Protection, Physical Planning and Construction (MZOPU). The ministry was established in 2000 with the merging of the State Directorate for the Protection of Nature and the Environment and part of the Ministry of Physical Planning, Construction and Housing. Along with other ministries and governmental bodies, the ministry underwent major changes with the reorganisation of the Croatian administration in 2004. The largest and most important directorate was and remains the Directorate for Environmental Management, coordinating the bodies responsible for Environmental Assessment and Industrial Pollution and for Atmosphere, Sea and Soil.

Beyond the environment ministry, the Ministry of Culture had responsibility for nature protection, through its Nature Protection Directorate and the State Institute for Nature Protection (2002), while responsibility for water management lay with the Ministry of Agriculture, Forestry and Water Management, the Ministry of Health and Social Welfare, and the Ministry of Economy, Labour and Entrepreneurship as well as Croatian Waters (Hrvatske Vode), a government agency responsible for the whole of water resource management. Although water management deals with coastal waters, responsibility for it lay with the Ministry of Sea, Transport and Infrastructure. Drafting of

Table 6.3 Environmental performance indicators: Croatia (1990–2009)

Indicator	1990–94	1995–99	2000–04	2005–09
Agricultural methane emissions (% of total)	38.0	32.6	29.0	29.8
Agricultural nitrous oxide emissions (% of total)	67.3	66.1	65.3	63.8
CO_2 emissions (KT) (1992)	12,336.7	19,763.6	23,372.4	23,665.8
CO_2 emissions (metric tons per capita) (1992)	3.8	4.3	5.0	5.3
Fish species (threatened)	–	–	–	46
Forest area (% of land area)	37.9	38.0	38.1	39.4
Forest area (sq km)	21,186.0	21,251.0	21,314.0	21,362.0
GEF benefits index for biodiversity (0 = no biodiversity potential to 100 = maximum)	–	–	–	0.5
Industrial methane emissions (% of total)	39.2	42.8	47.2	44.2
Industrial nitrous oxide emissions (% of total)	27.4	27.0	25.7	22.3
Mammal species, threatened	–	–	–	7
Marine protected areas (number)	–	–	–	19
Marine protected areas (% of total surface area)	–	–	–	4.4
Methane emissions (kt of CO_2 equivalent)	3,950	3,410	3,450	3,690
Nitrous oxide emissions (thousand metric tons of CO_2 equivalent)	3,070	3,070	3,310	3,590
Organic water pollutant (BOD) emissions (kg per day)	–	48,493.5	42,802.3	41,825.8
Organic water pollutant (BOD) emissions (kg per day per worker)	–	0.17	0.17	0.17
Other greenhouse gas emissions, HFC, PFC and SF6 (thousand metric tons of CO_2 equivalent)	670	300	180	720
Plant species (higher) threatened	–	–	0	1
Terrestrial protected areas (number)	–	–	–	177
Terrestrial protected areas (% total surface area)	–	–	–	7.5
Water pollution, chemical industry (% of total BOD emissions)	–	11.2	10.3	9.5
Water pollution, clay and glass industry (% of total BOD emissions)	–	5.6	5.5	5.9
Water pollution, food industry (% of total BOD emissions)	–	16.6	17.9	17.9
Water pollution, metal industry (% of total BOD emissions)	–	3.7	3.6	3.3
Water pollution, other industry (% of total BOD emissions)	–	31.0	32.4	35.1
Water pollution, paper and pulp industry (% of total BOD emissions)	–	6.2	6.7	7.2
Water pollution, textile industry (% of total BOD emissions)	–	20.9	18.8	16.2
Water pollution, wood industry (% of total BOD emissions)	–	4.8	4.8	4.8

Source: World Bank, 2011.

environmental legislation was mainly undertaken by the Committee on Physical Planning and Environmental Protection in the Croatian Parliament. The committee defined strategic priorities for environmental protection, and was therefore a key target for lobbying by societal interests. Coordination and interest aggregation issues, especially between economic and environmental actors, were taken to the Sustainable Development and Environmental Protection Council.

Two arms-length institutions operated at the national level: the Croatian Environmental Agency (CEA) and the Environmental Protection and Energy Efficiency Fund (Environmental Fund). As in Slovenia, these autonomous agencies were modelled on the US or German template and were established by the National Environmental Action Plan (2002) as a means of institutional strengthening. The creation of the CEA was a direct result of the signing of the SAA, in which Article 81 of the Implementation Plan for the SAA foresaw the creation of the Agency by the end of 2002, and Article 103 stipulated the creation of an EIS (CEC 2001b). The Environmental Fund, by contrast, was set up in 2004 by the Ministry of Environment and the Ministry of Economics in consultation with the Energy Institute, and provided an additional budget line to support projects and activities in the areas of environment protection, energy efficiency and renewable energy. It was intended to be the main conduit for the administration of the IPA funds in the field of environmental protection.

The 20 regional counties (plus Zagreb city) and 429 local municipalities played and continue to play a role in the governance of environmental policy. Croatia had adopted 30 LEAPs but, at the time of our fieldwork, no more were under development. In addition to the LEAPs, the government, in cooperation with different donor organisations, had also undertaken training and capacity building at the subnational level in order to meet EU standards and require-ments that local municipalities would have to comply with as EU accession approached.[7]

The network

Figure 6.3 outlines a network less developed than those in Greece or Slovenia. The network spanned all spheres of governance, with many ties to the international or regional level (through agencies such as the UNDP, the World Bank or REC) linking to the subnational administrative levels as well as environmental NGOs.

Looking at the network in more detail, there were important ties between the UNDP and the regional and local tiers of government (RGovs and LGovs), as well as between the European Commission Delegation to Croatia (DelCEC) and the environment ministry (MEnv). For its part, the environment ministry had strong ties with the Croatian Environmental Agency (CEA), which in turn had strong ties to the universities (Unis) and to the State Institute for Nature Protection (SINP). As would be expected, the environment ministry was tied

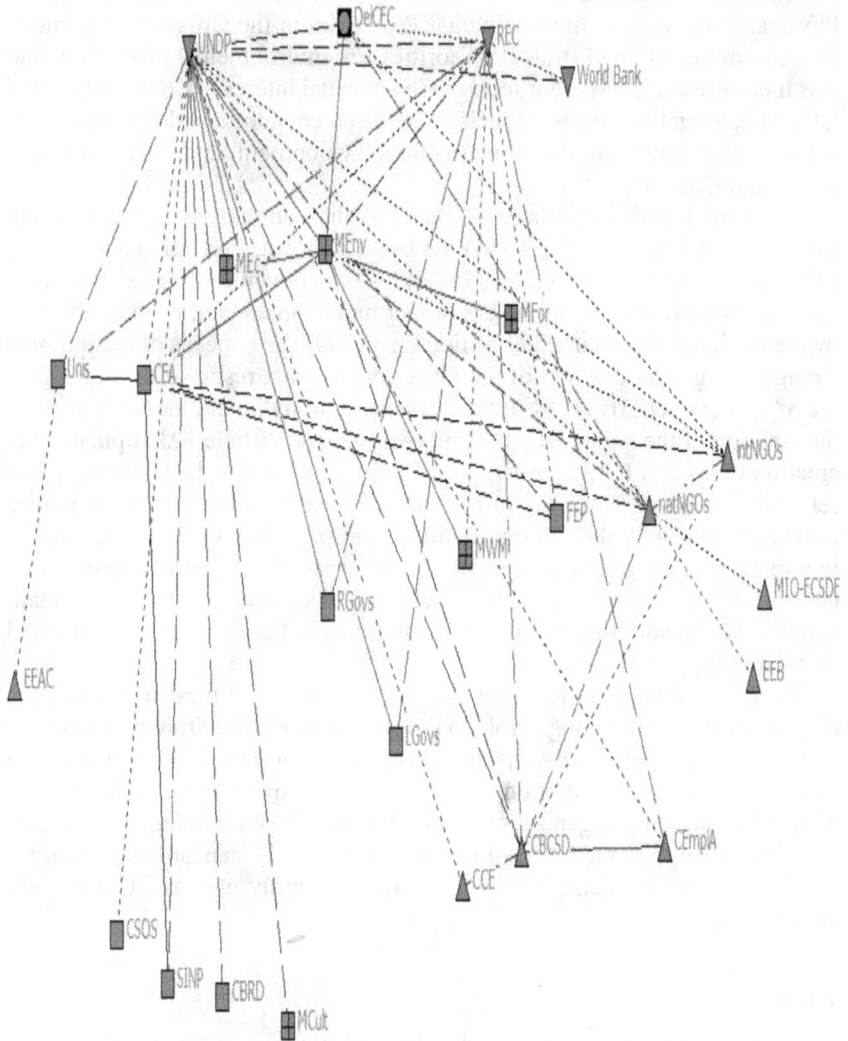

Figure 6.3 The environment network: Croatia

to the Ministry of Economy, Labour and Entrepreneurship (MEc) and the
Ministry of Foreign Affairs and European Integration (MFor). There was also
a strong connection between the Croatian Business Council for Sustainable
Development (CBCSD) and the Croatian Employers Association (CEmpA).

We find a network that is visually complex but which remained strongly
hierarchical in the sense that the majority of key relationships were 'vertical'
(for example, between the EU and the environment ministry), or 'horizontal',
between core ministries or core societal interests (for example, between the

Organisation	SNA abbreviation
Ministry of Environment	MEnv
Ministry of Economy	MEc
Ministry of Culture	MCult
State Institute for Nature Protection	SINP
Fund for Environment Protection and Energy Efficiency	FEP
Croatian Environment Agency	CEA
Central State Office for Strategy	CSOS
Croatian Bank for Reconstruction and Development	CBRD
European Commission Delegation Croatia	DelCEC
Regional and local governments	RLGovs
Croatian Business Council for Sustainable Development	CBCSD
Universities	Unis
World Bank	World Bank
Regional Environment Centre	REC
UNDP	UNDP
National NGOs	natNGOs
International NGOs	intNGOs
Ministry of Forestry	MFor
Ministry of Water Management	MWM
Croatian Employers' Association	CEmplA
Croatian Chamber of Economy	CCE
European Environmental Advisory Councils	EEAC
European Environmental Bureau	EEB
United Nations Industrial Development Organisation	UNIDO
United Nations Environmental Programme	UNEP
Mediterranean Information Office for Environment, Culture and Sustainable Development	MIO-ECSDE

Croatian Business Council for Sustainable Development and the Croatian Employers Association). In other words, the core network was characterised by a small number of strategic linkages, based on resource dependency or common socio-economic interests. Beyond the core was an outer circle of actors with little purchase on the core network and low levels of interaction between themselves.

The key actor, therefore, was the environment ministry, which acted as the gatekeeper to EU engagement and was located at the centre of the governance network. This is a qualitatively different finding from those for Greece and Slovenia, and indicates that the transformation of Croatian governance structures as a result of engagement with the EU is incomplete and the network is still being constructed. The capacity bargain has not (so far) led to a significant redistribution of power and resources largely as a result of the demands for effective central capacity as part of the accession process and because of weaknesses in capacity subnationally and among civil society organisations. As one civil society interviewee explained, a little vividly: 'the Ministry for Environmental Protection is absolutely the biggest authority . . . and it is very difficult to question their decisions and survive' (interview, Croatian Business Council for Sustainable Development, 19 December 2007).

Sources of change

We can identify weak MLG effects as a result of engagement with the EU and, because there has been less change, it is more difficult to identify the sources of the limited change that has taken place. In our interviews, the EU was identified as highly influential in setting up both the policy priorities and the policies themselves. It was clear from responses that the priority given by Croatian authorities to the EU accession process not only had consequences for the content and quality of the policies adopted, but also in terms of the formal inclusion of a diverse set of actors in setting up those policies, albeit within clear jurisdictional parameters. This is closest to the MLG Type II. Paradoxically, however, respondents in the region claimed that the designation of a particular policy initiative as being of 'European' importance often had the opposite effect in that it shut out non-state actors and interests in a 'fast-track' process (respondents at the EU level were sceptical about this claim). As one interviewee said: 'the pace of change is too fast because of the accession to the EU – so they can't cope with it properly, or there is not enough capacity to cope with it in ways that we should' (interview, UNDP, 8 February 2008), while another blamed 'the stampede of European legislation . . . for instance, each law that has this "EU stamp" goes into fast procedure, not a normal reading' (interview, Green Action NGO, 14 May 2008). To counter the centralisation stimulated by EU accession, respondents representing actors that perceived themselves as being shut out of the process had constructed a rival narrative to justify their future inclusion, arguing that centralisation (and their exclusion) would pose an obstacle to accession. Beyond the EU, respondents also recognised the roles of international organisations such as the UN and the OECD (interview, Croatian Environmental Agency, 15 May 2008).

Along the horizontal dimension, we have a picture of a state-centric architecture of governance: a centralised but fragmented horizontal dimension with jurisdiction spread across five ministries, exercising competencies over distinct policy segments, with a lack of coordination between the actors. There are similar issues along the vertical dimension. Despite some formal devolution of powers, municipalities are perceived to lack both a culture of inclusion and consultation, resources and administrative capacity, and expertise. Where capacity and know-how is lacking, the traditional sources of external expertise have been NGOs and other societal actors (Lees 2000). In Croatia, NGO representatives saw their inclusion as formal and symbolic, rather than substantive, although some NGOs, such as Green Action (Zelena Akcija), Zagreb and the Green Forum (a network of around forty environmental NGOs, including Zelena Akcija) and Eko Kvarner, had a substantive input into the process of environmental governance (interview, Green Action NGO, 14 May 2008).

Macedonia

Macedonia's environmental policy strategy during the period of this study was set out in its 1997 and 2004 NEAPs (NEAP 1 and NEAP 2), which charted its strategy for compliance with the environmental *acquis*. NEAP 2 set out targets for the five years until 2009 that included improving the quality of the environment in urbanised areas by reducing sulphur dioxide pollution and particulate concentrations, as well as adopting comprehensive waste-management systems, improving water supply by enhancing water resources management and improving surface water quality by eliminating the discharge of untreated industrial effluent, enhancing protection for flora and fauna, and strengthening environmental management capacity by developing appropriate regulations, and increasing the capacity of institutions responsible for monitoring and enforcement (Republic of Macedonia 2004). Macedonia has prioritised the role of LEAPs in order to achieve these targets.

The Commission's Analytical Report found Macedonia's environmental legislation to be almost entirely incompatible with the *acquis* (CEC 2005: 109). Successive Progress Reports indicated that Macedonia has made reasonable progress in areas such as horizontal legislation (particularly on strategic environmental assessment), air quality (implementing legislation assessing ambient air quality, and a recovery and recycling system for ozone-depleting substances), and waste management (implementing legislation for landfills etc., introducing a national strategy for waste management and the process of issuing waste permits), but has had less success in areas such as water quality, nature protection, industrial pollution and risk management, noise and GMOs. The Macedonian NEIS was also set up in 1998.

The obvious point to be made from the data in Table 6.4 is that there has been a failure in environmental monitoring and data collection, despite the setting up of the NEIS. There are only four complete runs of data and while all are either positive or neutral in their implications, it is impossible to assess environmental performance. What we can say with more certainty is that these missing data reflect the failure of municipalities to provide such data. However, it is important to remember that the structure of municipal government in Macedonia is very new and politically highly contentious. The municipalities'

Table 6.4 Environmental performance indicators: Macedonia (1990–2009)

Indicator	1990–94	1995–99	2000–04	2005–09
Agricultural methane emissions (% of total)	–	–	–	–
Agricultural nitrous oxide emissions (% of total)	–	–	–	–
CO_2 emissions (KT) (1992)	12,336.7	10,625.6	10,926.0	10,867.4
CO_2 emissions (metric tons per capita) (1992)	6.2	5.4	5.4	5.3
Fish species (threatened)	–	–	–	14
Forest area (% of land area)	35.6	35.6	35.6	35.6
Forest area (sq km)	9,060.0	9,060.0	9,060.0	9,060.0
GEF benefits index for biodiversity (0 = no biodiversity potential to 100 = maximum)				0.2
Industrial methane emissions (of total)	–	–	–	–
Industrial nitrous oxide emissions (% of total)	–	–	–	–
Mammal species, threatened	–	–	–	5
Marine protected areas (number)	–	–	–	0
Marine protected areas (% of total surface area)	–	–	–	–
Methane emissions (kt of CO_2 equivalent)	–	–	–	–
Nitrous oxide emissions (thousand metric tons of CO_2 equivalent)	–	–	–	–
Organic water pollutant (BOD) emissions (kg per day)	–	–	–	–
Organic water pollutant (BOD) emissions (kg per day per worker)	–	–	–	–
Other greenhouse gas emissions, HFC, PFC and SF6 (thousand metric tons of CO_2 equivalent)	–	–	–	–
Plant species (higher) threatened			0	0
Terrestrial protected areas (number)	–	–	–	61
Terrestrial protected areas (% total surface area)	–	–	–	–
Water pollution, chemical industry (% of total BOD emissions)	–	–	–	–
Water pollution, clay and glass industry (% of total BOD emissions)	–	–	–	–
Water pollution, food industry (% of total BOD emissions)	–	–	–	–
Water pollution, metal industry (% of total BOD emissions)	–	–	–	–
Water pollution, other industry (% of total BOD emissions)	–	–	–	–
Water pollution, paper and pulp industry (% of total BOD emissions)	–	–	–	–
Water pollution, textile industry (% of total BOD emissions)	–	–	–	–
Water pollution, wood industry (% of total BOD emissions)	–	–	–	–

Source: World Bank, 2011.

newness means they are extremely weak in terms of their capacities in a highly technical area such as environment policy; resources have been devoted to establishing core functions (such as revenue raising) and service delivery as part of the OFA decentralisation process.

Institutions

The main institutional actor in Macedonia is the Ministry of Urban Planning, Construction and Environment (MEPP). MEPP is organised into four departments covering Legislation and Standardisation, Sustainable Development, European Integration, and Environmental Information. There are also two field-based project implementation divisions covering the Lake Ohrid conservation project and the Lake Doiran salvage project. The ministry administers three further units: the State Environment Inspectorate, the Office of the Environment, and the Fund for the Environment and Nature Protection and Improvement. MEPP is responsible for the drafting of legislation in line with EU requirements and other agreements. There are also smaller roles for the Ministries of Agriculture, Transport and Telecommunications, and Health and Forestry. In addition, there is some input from administrators responsible for the Environment Chapter within the Secretariat for European Affairs, as well as the Agency for Development and Investments, and the Parliamentary Commission on Environment, Youth and Sports. There is no stand-alone Environment Agency and the Environmental Fund was replaced by mainstream budget programming in 2003.

At the time of our fieldwork, twenty-four municipalities had developed LEAPs and all municipalities are now obliged to do so. The environment ministry has recognised the need for cooperation between the state and substate levels and between the municipalities themselves. The key obstacle to empowering the substate level is administrative capacity and expertise, not least the lack of English-speaking staff capable of accessing international networks and know-how. As one government official explained: 'we draft the laws, but the weak link here is the implementation, so the most negative influence in this area comes from the people, the individuals because of the low consciousness level about the environment . . . also an important factor are the low sanctions, low punishment payments that are set by the laws' (interview, Ministry of Urban Planning, Construction and Environment, 8 March 2008). It is here that the capacity bargain with the EU is particularly needed and will have the most impact.

The involvement of NGOs and other civil society actors in Macedonia is weak but growing. Respondents identified NGOs such as the Association of Environmentalists, or the Institute for Sustainable Communities as being reasonably influential, although there was a perception that NGOs were less active than they had been in the past. Expertise was still offered but this was more on a task-specific basis than one of partnership.

The network

Figure 6.4 outlines an extremely sparse network composed of few actors and a limited degree of interaction, but in which a small number of central actors were very closely interconnected.

In contrast to, for example, Croatia, the UNDP did not appear to enjoy particularly high levels of purchase at the state and subnational levels and, of the trans-state actors in the region, our respondents indicated that it was REC that enjoyed the most influence at the national level. Once again, this external influence was subject to a gatekeeper in the shape of the environment ministry, MEPP (MEnv), which enjoyed a very close tie with REC, local government and with the Movement of Ecologists of Macedonia (MEM). This is a relatively small number of critical linkages compared with the numbers seen in our other case countries, but there were relatively fewer key actors in the network than in our other cases. This is a small dense network that reflects the historic weakness of environment as a policy sector in Macedonian politics and the small number of (central) actors involved in this network.

Sources of change

In as far as there have been changes in the structures of governance in Macedonia and the distribution of power and resources within governance networks, our respondents indicated that Macedonia's EU-funded projects aimed at capacity building, strengthening environmental management, air quality improvement and the management of transboundary water resources have been the key sources of change. REC also appears to have played a key role.

In fact, despite, or perhaps because of, the obvious weaknesses of environmental governance in Macedonia, the influence of external organisations is disproportionately strong on both government and civil society. As a government official argued,

> regarding different projects we cooperate and communicate with EU members, for example Italy, Austria, or Switzerland, which it is not in the EU but it supports a lot of projects in Republic of Macedonia in the field of bilateral cooperation ... the World Bank, regarding project implementation and financing. The stability pact is also present [and] we have cooperated with them [sic]. Then there are the neighbouring countries and regional ones, like Greece ... then bilateral cooperation with Albania, Bulgaria, Turkey and others. I am mentioning these countries regarding the financial assistance that has been provided, and all the projects implemented'.
>
> (Interview, Secretariat for European Affairs, 7 March 2008)

This sentiment was echoed by an NGO activist who stated that 'we cooperate with many such organisations from Spain, Germany, Switzerland, Bulgaria and Greece. Mainly from the non-governmental sector – professional NGOs.

We cooperate less with domestic organisations' (interview, Macedonian Ecological Society, 6 March 2008).

It is this penetration of the domestic level by the international commmunity that presents us with a paradoxical empirical and analytical puzzle for at first glance, evidence from Macedonia demonstrates the weakest MLG effects of our four case countries. On the horizontal dimension, there is less evidence of the mainstreaming of environmental policy and, as a result, competences are mainly confined to the environment ministry, albeit with limited input from the Ministries of Agriculture, Transport and Telecommunications, Health and Forestry, the Secretariat for European Affairs, the Agency for Development and Investments, and the Parliamentary Commission on Environment, Youth and Sports. There are very limited MLG effects on the vertical dimension beyond the usual municipality competencies for sewage, garbage, local environmental protection, etc. NGO involvement is limited and expertise is provided on a task-specific basis rather than through partnership agreements, which is consistent with Type II MLG. The key point to note, however, is that respondents indicated a willingness, indeed a determination, to open up governance networks and practices along the lines envisaged by the EU (interview, Secretariat for European Integration, 7 March 2008). At present, however, the key problem is the need to enhance administrative capacity and expertise at the centre and at the substate level in order to transpose the environmental *acquis* and also sectorally integrate environmental objectives. As one respondent put it:

> all directions are coming through the EU. . . from the DG, so we are trying to follow everything that is going on in the EU, as fast as we can to adopt it, to implement it properly . . . it is crucial because we want to become an EU member.
>
> (Interview, Secretariat for European Affairs, 7 March 2008)

There is no zero-sum relationship between acquiring expertise and moving towards MLG, but at present the latter objective is subordinate to increasing capacity. It is through this that the puzzle is revealed for, although the 'governance' dimension of the MLG is exceptionally weak, 'multi-levelness' is quite pronounced. Strictly speaking, the MLG effects in Macedonia are weak *and* strong, depending on the weighting of the two dimensions, and as the capacity bargain between Macedonia and the EU impacts upon the structures, norms and processes of governance, not only will governance structures become more robust, but multi-levelness will remain in place and increase as the accession process continues. As one interviewee memorably explained:

> I think other countries in the region and especially those who are ahead of them in the track to the EU – Bulgaria, Romania, Croatia, Czech Republic and Slovakia. They look at those countries as places for learning . . . the EU is not seen as a place of learning but as a place of standards.
>
> (Interview, Institute for Sustainable Communities, 6 March 2008)

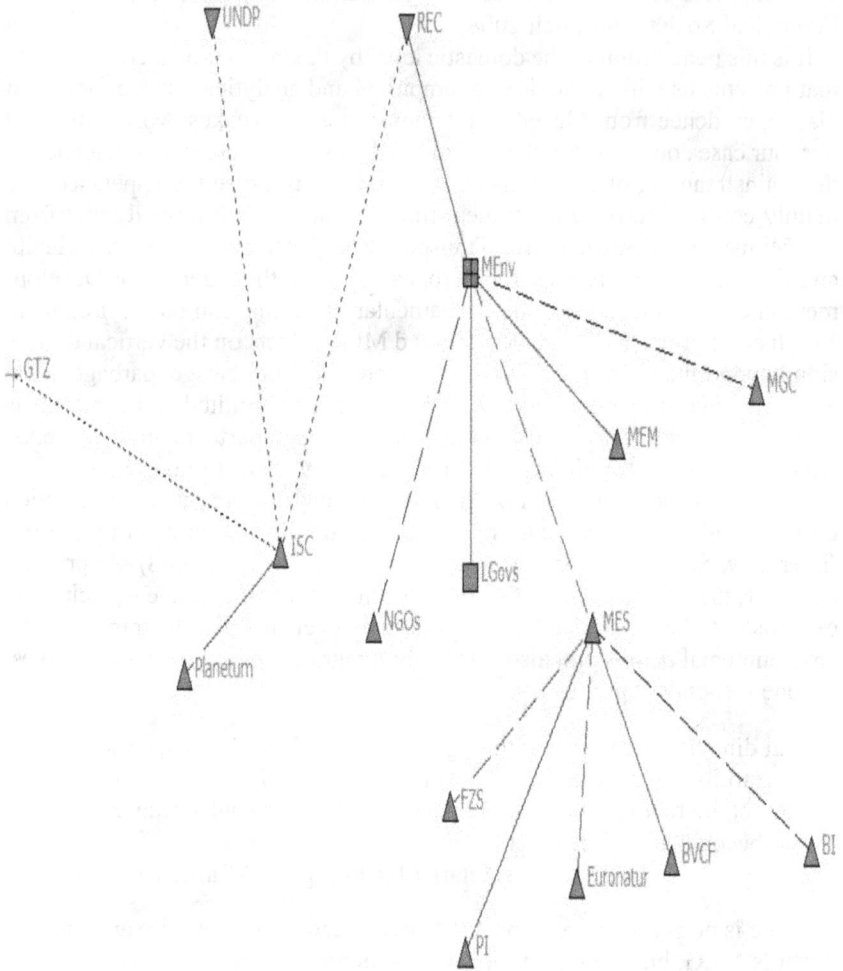

*Figure 6.*4 The environment network: Macedonia

Conclusions

SEE is a region with varied bio-geographic attributes and transboundary environmental issues, noted variance in levels of development and in the nature and extent of environmental degradation. This chapter has described the degree to which regional agreements have been put in place and the types of policy instruments deployed by the EU and the associated regional networks cultivated to manage the pressures of integration. Indeed, the degree of horizontal cooperation between environment ministries distinguishes this policy sector compared to other *acquis* chapters (Stritih *et al.* 2007: 260).

Organisation	SNA abbreviation
Regional Environmental Center for Central and Eastern Europe	REC
Movement of Ecologists of Macedonia	MEM
Macedonian Ecological Society	MES
Macedonian Green Centre	MGC
NGOs	NGOs
Municipalities	LGovs
Frankfurt Zoological Society	FZS
Euronatur	Euronatur
Plantlife International	PI
Birdlife International	BI
Ministry of Environment and Physical Planning	MEnv
Black Vulture Conservation Foundation	BVCF
Gesellschaft für technische Zusammenarbeit	GTZ
UNDP	UNDP
Planetum	Planetum
Institute of Sustainable Communities	ISC

It has examined four states confronted by similar sets of integrative pressures but with differing national governance styles that generate different responses to those pressures as a result and that are reflected in the SNA. These networks are by and large isolated from the regional framework on which the EU places great emphasis.

At first glance, the SNA suggest three patterns of network. The first is found in Greece and Slovenia, where respondents reported EU-related networks that were dense in both linkages and interaction. In contrast to Croatia and Macedonia, our respondents in Greece and Slovenia did not clearly identify the environment ministries as the pre-eminent actor but rather reported NGOs and/or NGO peak associations (the PHNEO and SE-F) as having the most significant role within the capacity bargain networks, which is consistent with a significant redistribution of power and resources as a result of engagement with the EU. The second pattern, found in Croatia, is distinguished by an EU-inspired network in which the environment ministry was identified as the critical actor. Although engagement with the EU has brought about changes in the modes of governance, any redistribution of power and resources within the network had been limited and insufficient to decentre the power of the core executive. Finally, a third pattern is to be found in Macedonia. This capacity network was weak in density but *relatively* intense because of a high level of interaction between a small number of actors. This network was dominated by the environment ministry and this implies a very limited redistribution of power and resources. The lack of capacity was pronounced, hence the degree of penetration by external actors.

There are two reasons, however, why we do not rely on these broad patterns. First, as a cursory glance at the network maps demonstrate, the Greek and Slovenian networks are, in fact, different because Greece's longer engagement with EU environmental policy produced an extensive and dense network. Although there was evidence of resistance to further pluralisation in Greece, in Slovenia the opposite applied as legislation encouraging NGO involvement went beyond that required by the accession criteria. Second, our analyses are interrogations of actors' perceptions and it could be argued that where state actors such as the Slovenian environment ministry have actively encouraged NGO involvement in the process of environmental governance, this has led to a weakening of its perceived centrality. So, the more activist a ministry is in encouraging pluralisation, the more it might seemingly 'paint itself out of the picture'.

So what do the findings discussed in this chapter tell us about the dynamics of Europeanisation and MLG within the environmental policy domain in our four case countries? It will be recalled that we take a non-deterministic position on the scope and scale of Europeanisation. We assume that there will be variance in the degree of Europeanisation, depending on first, the time, timing and sequencing of the process of engagement; second, on the nature of existing structures and SOPs, and, finally, on the demands and logic of the particular policy area. A comparative statistical analysis of 21 European countries (plus Mexico, the US and Japan) after 1970, covering 40 environmental issues at 4 sampling points (1970, 1980, 1990 and 2000) found EU membership to be the most important factor in explaining domestic policy change (Liefferink *et al.* 2009). The policy transfer involved in *acquis* transposition and the enlargement process is therefore highly visible. Europeanisation's influence on environmental policy cannot be doubted; what of MLG?

In this chapter, our four country cases demonstrate that adherence to or the transposition and incorporation of the environmental *acquis* has had an impact on modes of governance. However, we also find variance in the degree of impact, depending on the first two of these factors, which offsets the harmonising impact of the demands and logic of environmental protection as a transboundary policy problem as well as the technical demands of the environmental *acquis*. Although all of our four cases faced common technical demands presented by the environmental *acquis*, these demands were addressed within national institutional contexts that generated different constellations of actors, which in turn shaped and constrained the outcomes of the sectoral politics in each state.

As environmental policy requires the involvement of a multitude of actors in a dispersed decision-making process, Fairbrass and Jordan identify environmental policy as 'an excellent vehicle' for analysing MLG and 'decision-making across territorial levels' (2004: 148). A key feature, and which cohesion and environment share, is opening policy to societal groups and subnational governments; moreover, this openness is a defining characteristic of MLG. Following the agenda suggested by Piattoni (2010: 140) we find evidence that environmental groups tend to be more actively engaged than subnational governments. In environmental policy there is a strong ethic of subsidiarity but this is indeterminate, acting as a political influence on the production of flexible national solutions reflecting national circumstances. This is reinforced by EU policy (see for example the 5th EAP 1992–2000), which tends to define broad objectives and leave national authorities to develop their response and which means environmental and social groups can have a significant presence.

However, conventional policy mechanisms continue to dominate (Holzinger *et al*. 2006), all the more so in candidate countries. While there are national variations, this reflects three common traits: first, the importance of the national level and the core executive; second, the absence of capacity and capability at all levels; and third, a need to create and sustain institutions capable of undertaking complex coordination. This and wider experience in the EU makes MLG the default setting for environmental policy. In both cohesion and environmental policy MLG is seen as essential to 'good' policy and normatively desirable. In the case of borders and migration the normative dimension is less visible, but in all our policy sectors MLG seems better at describing processes and institutions rather than explaining why policy is made in a particular way. We have already noted the 'mixed' nature of environmental policy, but what sort of politics is generated? In all our cases MLG is closest to the Type II MLG, characterised by specific jurisdictions, intersecting memberships, no limit to the number of jurisdictional levels and a relatively flexible design. How powerful have these MLG effects really been? The critical actors in Croatia and Macedonia, the environment ministries, are in the core executive, while in Slovenia and Greece the NGOs/NGO peak associations are perceived to be the most influential. In *all* of our cases many actors considered critical by our respondents are located outside the core executive, encouraging a significant dispersal of power and resources.

Some of that power has dispersed to the subnational level, but there has also been a dispersal of power beyond the state to civil society. This is more pronounced in Slovenia and Greece. In Slovenia the vast majority of critical actors reported by our respondents operated outside the core executive and more than half of these were actually located outside the state altogether. Similar dynamics, albeit on a less pronounced scale, can be seen in Greece. Croatia demonstrates more moderate effects and Macedonia the weakest. In Croatia we noted the (contested) claims of perverse consequences in which the 'fast-tracking' process led to greater centralisation, as well as the modest input from NGOs and actors from the business sector. In Macedonia we found the weakest network of all and, not surprisingly, significant direct EU input as well as substantial involvement from INGOs and NGOs, reflecting the lack of administrative capacity and resources. Here the capacity bargain reflects an attempt to 'fill-in' a 'hollow' state. The EU's purpose has not just been to enhance the transposition of the environmental *acquis*, but also to cultivate MLG effects to encourage deep learning and a pluralisation of governance. Interviewees in DG Enlargement and DG Environment regarded these effects as a desirable ends in themselves, despite misgivings among DG Environment officials about the Commission's ability to monitor the implementation and enforcement phases of the environmental policy-making process (interview, DG Environment, 25 May 2009). However, in all our cases, the core executive, particularly the environment ministry, continues to exercise de facto control over the process of governance even if, as in the case of Slovenia, *de jure* control appears to have been relaxed or, as in Macedonia, control is partially franchised out to international agencies and other external actors. Core executive actors displayed an ability to harness the adaptational pressures for their own strategic ends, which have tended to be congruent with the EU's objectives for governance and policy.

Over a decade ago Börzel identified considerable variance in compliance with EU environmental law that could not be explained by northern 'leaders' versus southern 'laggards'. Non-compliance was much more likely when EU policy caused significant misfit and where domestic actors are not mobilised to pressure national authorities to resolve the misfit, hence Börzel (2000) argues that this explains both the variation *between* countries as well as variation between policies *within* countries. MLG undoubtedly offers insights into policy-making but this chapter, as the two previous ones, confirms the critical role of the core executive as gatekeeper and coordinator of implementation. This chapter again confirms that MLG overstates the autonomy of subnational governments and civil society organisations and NGOs, but in contrast to cohesion (albeit to a lesser degree than is the case with borders and migration) IOs are quite significant in contrast to the wider MLG literature that tends to downplay their role. The salience of environmental issues, their technical complexity and inherent transnationalism means they have substantial implications for governance. These are, however, grounded on a paradox: the tendency for policy to be *re-nationalised* despite powerful downward pressure for convergence. Environmental cooperation in member states has led, broadly, to 'intensive transgovernmentalism' (Wallace 2004) but what we see in SEE is a mix of this, regional cooperation, the specifics of the policy sector capacity bargain and the region's mixed relationships with the EU. Forty years' experience with environmental policy has shown that governments cannot easily resist pressure for improvement but they do complain about regulation (both its laxity and strictness) in support of flexibility in implementing EU policy.

So the scope of the capacity bargain in the environmental sector has widened in our cases, albeit with specific dynamics in each. The functional aspect of the capacity bargain appears the most complete in all four countries, as the input side of EU rule-making (i.e. *acquis* transposition) is relatively unproblematic, except in Macedonia's case. The political bargain is more contested, particularly where the externalities of the functional bargain (i.e. the fast-tracking of legislation) have sustained a tighter distribution of power and resources. This was a particular source of complaint from NGOs in Croatia, although the premise was rejected by Commission officials in Brussels; in Slovenia in particular and to a lesser extent in Greece, the political bargain has been less contested. In Macedonia, by contrast, the underdevelopment of civil society makes the political bargain less salient than the other two dimensions. Also, efforts here have tended to focus on completing the OFA process. It is in the administrative dimension of the capacity bargain that we see the greatest degree of variance, despite a consensus (also embracing the EU) on deepening the capacity bargain.

The result is a complex, indeed tortuous, policy process where standards can be agreed but implementation delayed, which is one reason why environmental policy was linked to the single market for member states and in enlargement for candidate states in an effort to bypass or neutralise national (non-)regulatory traditions. Three of our cases (Greece, Slovenia and Croatia) are centralised polities and (theoretically) likely to have fewer implementation problems, but all have experienced serious capacity and capability problems, particularly at the lowest levels of the polity (a particular problem in Macedonia given the governance load placed on municipalities). In each of our cases there are factors pushing 'Europeanisation' through the lens of domestic politics that encourages renationalisation irrespective of the state's formal relationship with the EU. Paradoxically, there is an inherent tendency for national variations to be reinforced despite the coherence of the downward pressure from the EU (Knill and Tosun 2008: 149).

Two aspects of the capacity bargain have the potential to transform environmental governance. The first is cost. *Acquis* transposition is relatively inexpensive compared with the enormous costs associated with environmental infrastructure (Stritih *et al*. 2007: 25). In this regard, accession and pre-accession countries are reluctant or unable to spend scarce resources on such long-term projects and may secure opt-outs (Slovenia) or become reliant on external actors (Macedonia), or even pool resources and expertise as with, for example, the Regional Environmental Reconstruction Programme. This leads us to the second aspect: all of these developments are technically demanding and have their own disciplinary effects that promote further integration. Indeed, this disciplinary dynamic was recognised and welcomed by Commission officials (interview, DG Enlargement, 25 May 2009). The diffusion of expertise will inevitably lead to greater interaction between tiers of government, between government and NGOs, between domestic networks and external actors, and between the domestic and the regional. It is where existing governance structures are weakest that the transformative potential of this dimension of the capacity bargain is most apparent, leading to a fundamental redistribution of power and resources within the environmental policy sector.

7 Conclusions

This book has explored the European Union's engagement with Greece, Slovenia, Croatia and Macedonia, comparing governance in three policy sectors and synthesising material on the four countries and three policy sectors to distil broad comparative conclusions about the EU's impact on domestic governance. The Copenhagen Criteria (1993) require applicants to achieve the stability of institutions guaranteeing democracy, the rule of law, human rights and respect for and protection of minorities; a functioning market economy, as well as the capacity to cope with competitive pressure and market forces within the Union; and to have the ability to take on the obligations of membership, including adherence to the aims of political, economic and monetary union. The Copenhagen Criteria only apply currently to two of our cases and previously to Slovenia; they never applied to Greece, but they represent a distillation of what the Commission (and member states) conceptualise as the essence of the European state and its governance. SEE is, therefore, at the core of the debates about what the EU is and what it will be. While the region clearly represents a major challenge for the EU (and the EU for the region), we do not believe there is anything exceptional about SEE that renders it and the EU incompatible. In the book we have demonstrated the importance of the capacity bargain (which is integral to the wider sovereignty bargain) in promoting change in the functional, political and administrative dimensions of engagement with the EU.

Governance is a difficult concept to pin down but the EU has identified five principles of good governance: openness, participation, accountability, effectiveness and coherence that apply to accession and member states. There are, therefore, powerful elements pushing convergence in European governance, over and above the 200,000 pages of *acquis communautaire*; these include the body of EU law as expressed in the Treaties, secondary legislation and the jurisprudence of the European Court of Justice. Cumulatively, these represent a Europe-wide move towards a particular mode of network governance and our project is, in part, an examination of emerging EU governance in the context of SEE. The transposition of the *acquis* requires considerable investment in strong and capable administrations at all levels of the polity to ensure implementation and enforcement. If Europeanisation is a macro-process of adjustment and adaptation, we also have to recognise the importance of the micro-politics of implementation – hence the focus on policy sectors and their capacity bargains. Complex multi-actor processes inevitably produce a gap between implementation and compliance. When the implementation chain is long in a context where there are no implementation *acquis* and implementation is a national competence for both accession and member states, implementation is most likely to be driven forward by the national centre.

However, irrespective of any specific shortcomings in the capacity bargain networks we have examined, the processes we have explored hold out considerable potential for the future growth of infrastructural power at the expense of bureaucratic power. As such, the changes explored in this book testify to the possibility of dramatic and irreversible change in the relationship between state and society.

The EU's view of governance emphasises mutual dependence but there are no Community rules regarding administrative organisation or public management. Candidate countries must create the conditions for integration by adjusting their administrative structures and the Commission stresses the need for administrative learning and effective implementation of EU law as a matter of common interest. Despite a lack of direct powers, the EU does profoundly and extensively influence governance; future and current members are required by the EU to have a reliable system of governance able to incorporate Community standards and decisions into their legal systems, effectively implementing these and securing enforcement. Implementation remains a national competence and this underpins diversity. Other factors reinforcing diversity are, first, the absence of formal 'governance' *acquis*, other than within the conditionality criteria and the principles of European law, and a reliance on soft instruments (exchanges, twinning, etc.) to encourage learning. Second, there is no Community competence or institutional responsibility for governance issues, which tends to fall into the intergovernmental area. Third, governance issues are often accorded a low, or secondary, status by domestic governments; and finally, there is evidence of poor sustainability after accession as a country's priorities change and domestic politics orient themselves to membership.

Europeanisation entails change in national government in two respects: first, the grafting on of a supranational layer produces a shift of power upwards; and second, it entails a significant change in the architecture of the polity at the national and subnational levels reflected in a move towards a more plural-participatory politics and a more diffuse distribution of power. As a highly compound polity the EU, after making due allowance for national peculiarities, will inevitably have major consequences for centralised states: those closer to the compound polity are more likely to adapt with relative ease (Slovenia), with adaptation more problematic in highly centralised states (Greece and Croatia). Macedonia's historical inheritance as a simple polity was modified by Ohrid and engagement with the EU that established a trajectory towards a more compound polity. Engagement with the highly compound EU pulls domestic politics away from the simple end of the continuum. Aspirant and member states are obliged to ensure that Community tasks and policies are effectively and properly fulfilled to achieve the outcomes sought by the Union and the member states. This means that current and future member states must have reliable systems of governance capable of promptly and effectively transposing Community standards and decisions into national law, and then implementing and enforcing them, thus maintaining consistency between domestic and EU policies as they evolve in tandem. Again, the capacity bargain plays a central role, a role that implies social learning built on national traditions. Formal compliance is not enough as actors are expected to engage with normative assumptions (*inter alia*, reliability, predictability, certainty, efficiency) about how government should work.

The methodological problem we addressed was how to explore the effects of these changes on polity, politics and policy. Our understanding of the EU's impact on polity, politics and policy relies on interview data, but in order to obtain a more systematic understanding of each policy sector and network, data was gathered from interviewees to undertake Social Network Analysis. SNA provided more systematic insight into motivations, preferences and perceptions, as well as network architecture, by generating maps of each policy sector in each country, which we have termed the capacity bargain network. The network maps are not definitive, as we have stressed repeatedly; they do *not* represent *the* policy network because definitive mapping would have required greater time and resources than those at our disposal. We do contend that the range of interviews and the reputational approach enabled us to map a plausible distribution of power and influence that was not obtainable from interviews or documentary evidence. SNA enabled us to move beyond, or more accurately add depth to, our understanding of the consequences of engagement with the EU in each national context and policy sector.

Three overall conclusions stand out from this methodology. First, SNA identifies the existence of a 'core', or strategic, network responsible for resource mobilisation and programme determination. This inner network shades often imperceptibly into the wider implementation network. Second, over time our evidence is that these networks not only become more complex (in terms of the numbers of participants) but also more intense (in terms of the number of interactions); moreover, and as a result, the norms governing their operation shift (albeit with varying speed) from grudging acceptance of NGOs and civil society involvement as necessary to an acceptance (with varying degrees of enthusiasm) that the pluralisation of the network offers the prospect of 'better' policy. Third, SNA demonstrates (confirmed by other evidence) that there is no direct connection between a more plural network and a more diffuse power structure. EU governance preferences and norms pass through a domestic filter – the state – which translates (or transposes) these preferences as well as policy into the domestic context, and the overall effect of this is to keep power centralised. As all our states have a history of centralisation, which points to the utility of historical institutionalism, the question of whether or not engagement with the EU constitutes a juncture sufficiently critical to transform this centralisation remains moot. SNA provides a visualisation of the extent, shape and operation of both Europeanisation and MLG, and as heuristic devices provide an opportunity to explore and address issues of power and influence.

Engagement with, and membership of, the EU requires the pooling of sovereignty to be better able to achieve national policy goals and deal with transboundary issues. This constitutes a state's overall sovereignty bargain with the EU, which does not necessarily compromise its sovereignty. The sovereignty bargain is the basic building block of the state–EU relationship and depends on states with the capacities and capabilities to meet the obligations of membership, which has a specific manifestation (the *acquis*) in each policy sector. This book focuses on three capacity bargains – cohesion, migration and environment – all of which are intended to augment and extend the state's infrastructural power via supranational transboundary cooperation and resource mobilisation producing governed interdependence. The capacity bargain, moulded by the unique characteristics of each policy, constitutes an attempt to increase both the state's institutional depth and breadth. The overall effect of engagement with the EU and the capacity bargain(s) has been to strengthen the four states to achieve political and policy objectives not achievable with their current resources and capabilities. Each SNA map therefore represents the architecture of each sectoral capacity bargain. The significance of the capacity bargain's functional, political and administrative dimensions should not be underestimated as it represents the cutting edge of Europeanisation and the mechanism for dealing with 'misfit' and the gap between EU and domestic policy.

The existence of a policy and capability gap between the European and domestic is not a sufficient condition for Europeanisation because of the role of the state as a 'filter'. Engagement with the EU has encouraged the Europeanisation of governance but as divergence persists there is always 'misfit' because of domestic politics and history. Despite a bias towards inertia, national institutions and policy adapt and change over time because of changes in the external environment, changes in the actual (or perceived) performance of institutions and the social learning that flows from engagement with the EU. Our evidence from the SNA and the interview data is that enlargement and integration (separate but interconnected processes) constitutes a process of member-state building involving convergence on an EU governance model. Our evidence shows unequivocally that extensive Europeanisation has occurred – defined as efforts to overcome the perceived and identified gap between EU preferences and domestic conditions – and that a characteristic feature of engagement has been the growth of multi-level governance. Given the nature of our case countries' relationship with the EU as a long-standing member, a new member that passed through the enhanced post-Copenhagen Criteria enlargement procedure, and as two states subject to a conditionality regime even more rigorous than this, finding extensive evidence of Europeanisation should not come as too great a surprise.

While many interviewees, especially in Brussels and those nationals often in closest touch with the Commission, argued that in the absence of the EU many of the changes attributed to Brussels would have happened as a result of their modernisation or as a response to policy complexity, the overwhelming majority of in-country interviewees saw the EU's influence as fundamental for policy content and for how policy was made. Despite its imperfections, Europeanisation as a concept provides valuable insights into the dynamics of policy and politics. The position with respect to MLG is less clear.

The growth of multi-level governance would seem to be the inevitable result of the EU's governance preferences (such as participation, partnership and accountability) and policy strictures, with MLG as the kernel of 'good' governance. This is reinforced by a consensus embracing international institutions other than the EU, favouring governments 'steering' rather than 'rowing', allied to changes in the international political economy encouraging a smaller but more effective state. Not surprisingly, therefore, we identify a broad move towards Type II MLG in all cases, even in migration and border security. Multi-levelled-ness is also the outcome of the increased complexity of policy that, in many cases, requires transboundary approaches for responses to be effective. In three of our cases, radical changes in governance were the result of the break-up of Yugoslavia and consequent democratisation and marketisation. Our evidence suggests that growing compoundness, Europeanisation or MLG do not necessarily result in significant diffusion of power from the centre and there are powerful forces at work, some paradoxically stimulated by engagement with the EU, pulling in the opposite direction.

In the case of cohesion policy, engagement with the EU has generated obvious MLG effects, but in the wider literature the tendency is to see MLG as a universal attribute of EU-influenced governance. Alternatively, and on a wider canvass, MLG can be seen as a characteristic of modern governance in general. However, our research (even in the foundational case of cohesion) devalues MLG as an explanation of politics. MLG is not a theory but a description of surface features and elements of process, and to penetrate further we must ask broader questions relating to MLG's effects (or non-effects) on the distribution of power as well as on structure and process. Our cases show we are dealing with 'multi-level' politics: how could it be otherwise when the overarching institutional framework is supranational and the policy problems transboundary? What matters most, however, is the distribution of power and the consequences of engagement with the EU for that distribution. In all our cases – both polities and policies – we find, in contrast to the tenets of MLG a process of continued, and in many cases, reinforced centralisation within a multi-level system. Type II MLG becomes, in other words, a metaphor for policy complexity and its management. This is so even when opportunities for NGO/civil society involvement have increased because their influence is invariably confined to the details of policy or is seen by participants as symbolic but necessary to satisfy the EU and ensure domestic tranquillity. Our conclusion is, therefore, that MLG's explanatory power is limited.

Perhaps the most difficult question to assess is the degree to which engagement with the EU leads to convergence in governance. In rejecting Balkan exceptionalism we placed great emphasis on historical legacies and the importance of domestic variables and their interaction with engagements with the EU. What we see is quite complicated but familiar: the policy case studies show a marked degree of convergence in policy. While the institutional specifics vary from country to country (as do the policy specifics) a broadly comparable set of policy networks (as demonstrated by the SNA) exist, however, and this is our key point, while the specifics of the networks vary, they function in remarkably similar ways both vertically (the three networks in a single country) and horizontally (the same network in all four countries) in that the network and its governance are dominated by a limited core of actors. The Commission may not be a participant in a network but nevertheless it determines in a large part the network's activities. Again, therefore, we note the persistence of centralisation (and reinforcement) in historically centralised polities coupled with the polities' engagement with a highly compound EU polity, the hypothesised effect of which is to pull constituent polities towards 'compoundness', a key feature of which is a diffusion of power. Is there any indication of this happening?

Implicitly and explicitly, the EU's governance norms and the requirements of specific policies point to the decentralisation of power. This strategic objective was certainly recognised by our interviewees irrespective of country and policy area (and was reflected in the SNAs), and was accepted by interviewees as legitimate, necessary and normatively good. We found no cases of, for example, core executive actors rejecting these norms; equally, many, if not all, of our NGO/civil society actors concede, with varying degrees of enthusiasm, that over the course of the involvement with the EU opportunities for participating in networks and thereby contributing to policy development and implementation have increased. Equally, virtually all of our interviewees – public or private – concede that the effectiveness of participation was questionable. In most cases this was due to (*inter alia*) unfamiliarity with the policy, complexity, a lack of technical expertise and resources, competing political loyalties, and the decoupling of policy formation and implementation. None of these are insurmountable given time but, from a historical institutionalist perspective, this is the problem.

Early patterns of network engagement and resource distribution are extremely hard to alter. Networks, in this sense, represent 'hardened power', reflecting a particular set of relationships and rewards that can prove remarkably resilient, often requiring a powerful exogenous shock to trigger radical change. Our evidence is that only in very exceptional circumstances (for example, the eurozone crisis) is such a shock likely to come from EU institutions. The most likely time for such a shock, or something analogous to it, is during the accession process when the Commission's influence (via conditionality) is at its height, but our evidence is that the Commission prefers to trade power distribution for effectiveness and thereby reinforce centralised power. While engagement with the EU undoubtedly stimulates change in the content of policy and the contours of governance, we remain pessimistic that engagement will result in a significant shift of power away from the centre at any time in the near future.

Surveying the impact of the EU on governance in our four cases, we can identify a number of common features. First, the states experienced few problems in developing the appropriate laws. Obviously, there were some variations with the candidate states experiencing more difficulties than either Greece or Slovenia. In all cases, however, an appropriate legal framework was established.

Second, and again with a varying degree of difficulty, these states developed appropriate strategies, drew up regulations and transposed the *acquis* into domestic law. Related to this was that the appropriate institutions were established, institutions approved by the Commission and EU.

Third, the capacity bargain policy network is invariably dominated by a single ministry. However, the central ministry heads a multi-level structure involving subnational governments, NGOs and other ministries; these networks are both vertical and horizontal. Coordination problems and difficulties are frequently cited by our interviewees and the overall effect of MLG is to reinforce central control.

Fourth, within each capacity bargain policy network there is a core of actors who have a determining influence over the network's strategy. This core also reacts with a wider set of actors in the implementation of policy.

Fifth, resource shortages and variable capacities and capabilities at different tiers of government and between actors in the capacity bargain network represented major obstacles to effective implementation and enforcement. Technical expertise, for example, was often in short supply and tended to be concentrated at the centre with the severity of shortages increasing the further away from the centre. All our three policy areas required substantial front-line investment in order to ensure that policy is implemented effectively but the existence of an implementation gap was remarked upon frequently in our interviews.

Sixth, citizen and NGO participation are regarded as both intrinsically good and in the interests of better public policy. In all our four cases citizen/NGO participation is seen as legitimate and welcomed, but interviewees frequently questioned whether participation had any substantial effect on policy or policy-makers. This was because NGOs were often small and lacked the resources and capabilities to engage effectively. In candidate states participation came second to the overriding goal of EU membership; some groups (notably business) enjoyed good access whereas 'citizen' NGOs were often seen as a problem and even obstructionist.

Seventh, learning was identified by our interviewees as desirable, important and common. There was, obviously, a tendency to see learning as a particular feature of the candidate states, but it was also identified as a major exercise in member states, especially in complex policies that required multilevel and multinational solutions. Where there was more debate was whether or not this constituted 'deep learning', or real attitude and preference change. Broadly, our evidence suggests that in the candidate states there is some evidence of 'deep learning' but this is not universal in all policy sectors. This may be a function of length of engagement with the EU and the evolution of the capacity bargain policy network. Indeed, it would be remarkable if this were not the case. In member states, the problem was distinguishing between the effects of integration into the EU (equivalent to the candidate states' drive for membership) and the socialisation of elites into a 'European' governance value system as a result of engagement.

At the start of this book we suggested that SEE and our four cases symbolised a major test for the EU's transformative power and the model of integration it represents. Our countries and cases present a broad perspective on both the region and the literatures surrounding multi-level governance and Europeanisation. The crisis in the eurozone and Greek political economy point to a much higher level of Commission surveillance of domestic polities generally and particularly of those using the euro. This also implies that it will be much harder in the future for members to join the eurozone. The legacy of the 2004 enlargement (a more rigorous and tightly policed enlargement process) and on-going difficulties with Romania and Bulgaria point to the expansion of post-accession conditionality. This also implies an enhanced Commission role in monitoring domestic policy. So, in many ways SEE poses a more complex set of problems for the EU than did CEE and the future is likely to see a continuation, and expansion of, engagement with the EU. In this way SEE, as so often in the past, is playing a pivotal role in the politics of Europe.

Notes

2 Europeanisation and multi-level governance in South East Europe

1 The network maps were created using UCINET/Netdraw (www.analytictech. com/ucinet) and we gratefully acknowledge the help and assistance of Dr Daniel Wunderlich in preparing the maps. The analyses and the errors are, of course, entirely our own. The nature and type of relationships is shown by the style of the line connecting different actors. The ties are represented thus:

1 = occasional business relations/work contacts: dotted line
2 = regular contacts, often confined to individual projects: dashed line
3 = permanent and strategic: solid line
The following symbols represent the nodes:

Organisation	Symbol
Central ministries	box
Para-governmental agencies	square
EU actors	circle in box
NGOs	upward pointing triangle
International organisations	downward-pointing triangle
Member state agencies	plus
Non-member state agencies	diamond

3 History and governance

1 The Herfindahl index (or Herfindahl-Hirschman index measures market fragmentation and competition, ranging from 0.0 (monopoly) to 1.0 (free competition) and which gives more weight to larger firms. This index is used widely in the study of ethnic politics to calculate an index of fragmentation – the Ethno-Linguistic Fragmentation Index, or ELF. The formula is () where S_i is the percentage share of total population of each ethnic group, n is the number of ethnic groups and indexes the ethnic groups; the closer to 1, the greater the fragmentation, and vice versa.

2 The Copenhagen Criteria continue: 'Membership requires that the candidate country has achieved stability of institutions guaranteeing democracy, the rule of law, human rights and respect for and protection of minorities, the existence of a functioning market economy as well as the capacity to cope with competitive pressure and market forces within the Union. Membership presupposes the candidate's ability to take on the obligations of membership including adherence to the aims of political, economic and monetary union' (European Council 1993: 7.iii).

3 Rokkan's work is closer to the political development model criticised by Tilly (1984: 129–39, especially 137–9) but is nonetheless valuable because of the emphasis laid by Rokkan on interaction between states as central to state formation (Rokkan 1975, 1982).
4 The ESI report identified three state-building strategies: authoritarian, traditional capacity building and member state-building. The first applies to Bosnia and Herzegovina, and Kosovo; we are concerned with the last two strategies.
5 After 1941 Slovenia was partitioned between Germany, Hungary and Italy, with the largest part merging with the Ostmark (Austria) and so no puppet regime was established. There were pro-fascist organisations such as the Slovenian Home Guard which fought against the partisans.
6 Tudjman's *The Horrors of War* (1989) challenges the number murdered in the Jasenovac concentration camp complex. Estimates range from 500,000 to 1,000,000, whereas Tudjman estimates 30,000–60,000. As many of these victims were Serbs, this was inevitably controversial and historical memories of the Independent State of Croatia resonated powerfully in contemporary politics (Ramet 2007). This was a Nazi puppet state ruled by the Ustaša, the virulently nationalist Croatian Revolutionary Movement led by Ante Pavelić as *Poglavnik* ('Headman') and which was responsible for Jasenovac (Mann 2005: 294–8). The Ustaše sought an ethnically pure independent Croatia; its racial laws (modelled on those of Nazi Germany) focused on Serbs, Jews and Roma, although the regime tolerated Bosniaks (Muslims of Croatian descent). Tudjman was not seeking to re-establish the Ustaša state, but in the febrile atmosphere of the late 1980s and early 1990s it is not surprising that parallels were drawn and Tudjman was increasingly seen as Milošević's analogue.
7 Delegation of the European Union to the Republic of Croatia (no date). *Croatia and EU – Prejudices and Realities*. Available from: www.delhrv.ec.europa.eu/?lang=en&content=61 (accessed 4 September 2010).
8 To a degree unique in our cases, the academic literature on Macedonia concentrates on identity. For example, Cowan (2000), Roudmetof (2000), Pettifer (2001), Rossos (2008), Shea (2008) and Szajkowski (2009).
9 The Internal Market Scoreboard, analysing the degree to which a state has (or has not) transposed internal market directives into national law, is useful in comparing Greece and Slovenia's effectiveness. Though a crude measure of Europeanisation, it does explore 'downloading' policies and the development of the capacities and capabilities to sustain the obligations of membership. However, as it applies to only two of cases (and for one of these only since 2004) there is little to be gained by a detailed analysis of this data.
10 In 65 per cent of all cross-country pairwise comparisons using the 2007 WGI, results are statistically significant at the 90 per cent significance level; 74 per cent are statistically significant at the 75 per cent significance level. The WGI project has attracted both plaudits and brickbats. This is not the place to explore these but for the debate, see, for example, Kurtz and Schrank (2007a, b) and Kaufmann *et al.* (2007a, b).

4 Cohesion

1 Our usage and understanding of multi-level governance differs from Piattoni's. First, we see MLG and Europeanisation as complementary because our cases cover both member and candidate states. Piattoni's criticism that Europeanisation is (to paraphrase) 'everywhere and therefore nowhere' that produces a complex and contradictory political process with more in common with political change sums up what we see in SEE (2010: 100–1). Second, Piattoni focuses on member states and three aspects of MLG: the intensified mobilisation of regions at the EU level,

the increased presence of transnational civil society organisations and increased regional empowerment. Only the last of these is significant in our work. Piattoni's conclusion that the linkage between political authorities and civil society organisations 'remains rather superficial' (2010: 125) corresponds to our findings. We also concur that 'MLG can and should be interpreted and discussed also as a theory of European integration and of the transformation of the nation-state' (2010: 108).

6   Environment

1   Public goods are non-rival when one agent's consumption of the good does not of itself limit the consumption of the good by other agents. Public goods are non-excludable when the benefits generated by one agent's restraint cannot be limited to that agent alone.
2   These policy instruments are: (1) a Community Action Programme promoting NGOs in the environmental field; (2) the LIFE financial instrument; (3) the Environment and Health strategy; (4) an integrated product policy; (5) environmental agreements; (6) environmental taxes and charges in the Single Market; (7) the European Environment Agency (EEA); (8) the Eco-label scheme; (9) European standardization; (10) the community eco-management and audit scheme (EMAS); (11) environmental impact assessment; (12) assessment of the effects of plans and programs n the environment; (13) environmental inspections; (14) state aid; (15) the European Investment Bank; (16) the European Pollutant Release and Transfer Register (PRTR); (17) scientific committees for consumer safety, public health and the environment; (18) and global monitoring for environment and safety (GMES).
3   A Communication from the Commission, EP, and Economic and Social Committee of 25 February 2004 (CEC 2004) set the objective of integrating environmental aspects in the broader process of European standardisation, stressing the need to open up the standard-setting process to civil society and the scientific community. Two caveats are necessary. First, this instrument only becomes relevant towards the end of our research and, second, it only directly impacts upon Greece and Slovenia. Nevertheless, the potential MLG effects of this initiative are self-evident.
4   The Community eco-management and audit scheme (EMAS) was set up by EP/Council Regulation EEC No 761/2001. It replaced a previous scheme that had run from 1993 (EEC No 1836/93). EMAS is a voluntary scheme, albeit with a number of incentives for joining it, and thus coverage of the implementation, monitoring and enforcement of the scheme is patchy. Nevertheless, the scheme encourages regulatory flexibility and the inclusion of private sector actors within the regulatory framework.
5   Only the Regional Environment Centre for Central and Eastern Europe is identified as important in national networks and then only in Slovenia and Macedonia.
6   The original website is now closed. The new website is www.ypeka.gr/.
7   See the Environmental Management in Local Governments training organised at Zadar University 8–12 May 2006, financially supported by the USAID: http://isite23.isite.com.hr/Download/2006/04/27/Environmental_Mngmt_Course_Design_041206ENG.doc.

References

Adam, C. and Devillard, A. (2008) *Comparative Study of the Laws in the 27 EU Member States for Legal Migration*, Brussels, European Parliament Directorate General Internal Policies of the Union, Policy Department C: Citizens' Rights and Constitutional Affairs.

Allen, J. and Hamnett, C. (1995) *A Shrinking World: Global Uneveness and Inequality*, Oxford: Oxford University Press.

Analytica (2005) *The End of a Long Transition? Macedonia's Readiness for EU Candidacy*, Skopje: Analytica.

Analytica (2006) *Conceptualizing Decentralization Trends in Macedonia*, Skopje: Analytica.

Anderson, J. (2002) 'Europeanization and the Transformation of the Democratic Polity, 1945–2000', *Journal of Common Market Studies*, 40: 793–822.

Anderson, P. (2006) *Imagined Communities: Reflections on the Origin and Spread of Nationalism* (revised edn), London: Verso.

Andreas, P. (1998) 'The Escalation of US Immigration Control in the Post-NAFTA era', *Political Science Quarterly*, 113: 591–615.

Ansell, C. (2004) 'Restructuring Authority and Territoriality', in C. Ansell and G. di Palma (eds) *Restructuring Territoriality: Europe and the United States Compared*, Cambridge: Cambridge University Press.

Ansell, C. (2006) 'Network Institutionalism', in R.A.W. Rhodes, S.A. Binder and B.A. Rockman (eds) *The Oxford Handbook of Political Institutions*, Oxford: Oxford University Press.

Ansell, K.G., Parsons, A.C. and Darden, A.K. (1997) 'Dual Networks in European Regional Development Policy', *Journal of Common Market Studies*, 35: 347–75.

Apostolou, E. and Pantis, J.D. (2009) 'Conceptual Gaps in the National Strategy for the Implementation of the European Natura 2000 Conservation Policy in Greece', *Biological Conservation*, 142: 221–37.

Arango, J. (2000) 'Becoming a Country of Immigration at the End of the Twentieth Century', in R. King, G. Lazaridis and C. Tsardanidis (eds) *Eldorado or Fortress: Immigration in Southern Europe*, London: Macmillan.

Arsova, T. (no date) *Financing of Regional Development in the Republic of Macedonia*. Available at: http://mls.gov.mk/dokumenti/int_conference/12_Impulse%20to%20WG%203,%20Tatjana%20Arsova.pdf (accessed 12 December 2010).

Avery, G. and Batt, J. (2007) '*Balkans in Europe: Why, When, and How?*', Policy Brief 1, March, Brussels: European Policy Centre.

Bache, I. (2008) *Europeanization and Multi-level Governance: Cohesion Policy in the European Union and Britain*, Lanham, MD: Rowman & Littlefield.

Bache, I. and Taylor, A. (2003) 'The Politics of Policy Resistance: Reconstructing Higher Education in Kosovo', *Journal of Public Policy*, 23: 279–300.

Badie, B. (1995) *La fin des territoires: essai sur le désordre international et sur l'utilité sociale du respect*, Paris: Fayard.

Baganha, M. (1997) *Immigration in Southern Europe*, Lisbon: Celta Editora.

Bailey, D. and De Propris, L. (2002) 'EU Structural Funds, Regional Capabilities and Enlargement: Towards Multi-level Governance?', *Journal of European Integration*, 24: 303–24.

Baldwin-Edwards, M. (1999) 'Where Free Markets Reign: Alien in the Twilight Zone', *South European Society and Politics*, 3: 1–15.

Baldwin-Edwards, M. (2009) 'Greece', in M. Baldwin-Edwards and A. Kraler (eds) *REGINE: Regularisations in Europe*, Amsterdam: Amsterdam University Press.

Banac, I. (1984) *The National Question in Yugoslavia: Origins, History, Politics*, New York and London: Cornell University Press.

Barnett, M. and Duvall, R. (2005) 'Power in Global Governance', in M. Barnett and R. Duvall (eds) *Power in Global Governance*, Cambridge: Cambridge University Press.

Bartlett, W. (2002) *Croatia: Between Europe and the Balkans*, London: Routledge.

Bartolini, S. (2005) *Restructuring Europe: Centre Formation, System Building and Political Structuring Between the Nation-State and the European Union*, Oxford: Oxford University Press.

Bebchuck, L.A. and Roe, M.J. (1999) *A Theory of Path Dependence in Corporate Governance and Ownership*, New York: Columbia Law School Working Paper Series No. 192414.

Benz, A. and Eberlin, B. (1999) 'The Europeanization of Regional Policies: Patterns of Multi-level Governance', *Journal of European Public Policy*, 6: 329–48.

Berg, E. and van Meurs, W. (2002) 'Border and Orders in Europe: Limits of Nation- and State-Building in Estonia, Macedonia and Moldova', *Journal of Communist Studies and Transition Politics*, 18: 51–74.

Berkowitz, S.D. (1982) *An Introduction to Structural Analysis: The Network Approach to Social Research*, Toronto: Butterworth.

Bianchi, G. (1992) 'The IMPs: A Missed Opportunity', *Regional Politics and Policy*, 2: 47–70.

Bibič, A. (1993) 'The Emergence of Pluralism in Slovenia', *Communist and Post-Communist Studies*, 26: 367–86.

Bigo, D. (2001) 'Migration and Security', in C. Joppke and V. Guiraudon (eds) *Controlling a New Migration World*, London: Routledge.

Blavoukos, S. and Pagoulatos, G. (2008) *Fiscal Adjustment in Southern Europe: The Limits of EMU Conditionality*, GreeSE Paper No. 12. Hellenic Observatory Papers on Greece and Southeast Europe, London: London School of Economic and Political Science.

Blinkhorn, M. and Veremis, T. (1990) *Modern Greece: Nationalism and Nationality*, London: Sage.

Börzel, T. (1999) 'Towards Convergence in Europe? Institutional Adaptation to Europeanization in Germany and Spain', *Journal of Common Market Studies*, 37: 573–96.

Börzel, T. (2000) 'Why there is no "Southern Problem": On Environmental Leaders and Laggards in the European Union', *Journal of European Public Policy*, 7: 141–62.

Börzel, T. (2002) 'Pace-setting, Foot-Dragging and Fence-Sitting: Member State Responses to Europeanization', *Journal of Common Market Studies*, 40: 193–214.

Börzel, T. (2005a) 'Europeanization: How the EU Interacts with its Member States', in S. Bulmer and C. Lesquesne (eds) *The Member States of the European Union*, Oxford: Oxford University Press.

Börzel, T. (2005b) 'The Europeanisation of National Policy', in S. Bulmer and C. Lesquesne (eds) *The Member States of the European Union*, Oxford: Oxford University Press.

Börzel, T. and Head-Lauréote, K. (2009) 'Networks in EU Multi-Level Governance: Concepts and Contributions', *Journal of Public Policy*, 29: 135–51.

Börzel, T. and Risse, T. (2003) 'Conceptualising the Domestic Impact of Europe,' in K. Featherstone and C. Radaelli (eds) *The Politics of Europeanisation*, Oxford: Oxford University Press.

Börzel, T. and Risse, T. (2007) 'The Domestic Impact of EU Politics', in K.E. Joergenson, M.A. Pollack and B. Rosamund (eds) *Handbook of European Politics*, London: Sage.

Börzel, T., Pamuk, Y. and Stahn, A. (2008) *Good Governance in the European Union*, Berlin Working Paper on European Integration No. 7, Free University of Berlin: Jean Monnet Lehrstühl Integration.

Boswell, C. (2009) *The Political Use of Expert Knowledge: Immigration Policy and Social Research*, Cambridge: Cambridge University Press.

Boswell, C. and Geddes, A. (2010) *Migration and Mobility in the European Union*, Houndmills: Palgrave Macmillan.

Brandes, U. and Erlebach, T. (eds) (2005) *Network Analysis: Methodological Foundations*, Berlin and Heidelberg: Springer-Verlag.

Breiger, R.L. (2004) 'The Analysis of Social Networks', in M. Hardy and A. Bryman (eds) *Handbook of Data Analysis*, London: Sage.

Brubaker, R. (1996) *Nationalism Reframed: Nationhood and the National Question in the New Europe*, Cambridge: Cambridge University Press.

Brunsson, N. (2003) *The Organization of Hypocrisy: Talk, Decision and Action in Organizations*, 2nd edn, Copenhagen: Copenhagen Business School Press.

Brusis, M. (2002) 'Between EU Requirements, Competitive Politics, and National Traditions: Re-creating Regions in the Accession Countries of Central and Eastern Europe', *Governance*, 15: 531–59.

Brusis, M. (2005) 'The Instrumental Use of European Union Conditionality: Regionalization in the Czech Republic and Slovakia', *East European Politics and Societies*, 19: 291–316.

Bruszt, L. (2008) 'Multi-level Governance – the Eastern Versions: Emerging Patterns of Regional Developmental Governance in the New Member States', *Regional and Federal Studies*, 18 (5): 607–27.

Bruunbauer, U. (2002) 'The Implementation of the Ohrid Agreement: Ethnic Macedonian Resentments', *Journal of Ethnopolitical and Minority Issues in Europe*, 1, University of Graz: Centre for the Study of Balkan Societies and Cultures.

Bucar, B. and Brinar, I. (2005) 'Slovenia – Political Transformation and European Integration', in A. Skuhra (ed.) *The Eastern Enlargement of the European Union: Efforts and Obstacles on the Way to Membership*, Innsbruck, Vienna and Munich: Studienverlag.

Bulmer, S. (2007) 'Theorizing Europeanization', in P. Graziano and M.P. Vink (eds) *Europeanization: New Research Agendas*, Houndmills: Palgrave Macmillan.

Bulmer, S. and Radaelli, C. (2005) 'The Europeanization of National Policy', in S. Bulmer and C. Lesquesne (eds) *The Member States of the European Union*, Oxford: Oxford University Press.

Cameron, F. and Kintis, A. (2001) 'Southeastern Europe and the European Union,' *Journal of South Eastern Europe and Black Sea Studies*, 1: 94–112.

Carrington, P.J., Scott, J. and Wasserman, S. (eds) (2005) *Models and Methods in Social Network Analysis*, New York: Cambridge University Press.

CEC (1993) *European Council in Copenhagen 21–23 June, Conclusions*, DOC/93/3, Brussels: European Commission, 22 June.

CEC (1998) *Regular Report on Slovenia's Progress Towards Accession*, Brussels: European Commission.

CEC (2001a) *European Governance: A White Paper*, Brussels, COM (2001) 428, 25 July.

CEC (2001b) *Proposal for a Council Decision Concerning the Signature of the Stabilisation and Association Agreement between the European Communities and its Member States and the Republic of Croatia on behalf of the European Community*, COM (2001) 371 final, Brussels: European Commission.

CEC (2003) *Governance and Development*, COM (2003) 615, Brussels, 20 October.

CEC (2004) *Former Yugoslav Republic of Macedonia Stabilization and Association Report*, SEC (2004) 373 final, Brussels: European Commission.

CEC (2005) *A Common Agenda for Integration: Framework for the Integration of Third Country Nationals in the EU*, COM (2005) 389 final, Brussels.

CEC (2006a) *Policy Priorities in the Fight Against Illegal Immigration*, COM (2006) 402 final, Brussels.

CEC (2006b) *The Global Approach to Migration One Year On: Towards a Comprehensive European Migration Policy*, Brussels, COM (2006) 735 final, Brussels.

CEC (2006c) *Screening Report, Croatia, Chapter 24 – Justice, Freedom and Security*, Brussels, DG Enlargement. Available at: http://ec.europa.eu/enlargement/pdf/croatia/screening_reports/screening_report_24_hr_internet_en.pdf.

CEC (2007a) *Understanding Enlargement: The European Union's Enlargement Policy*, Brussels: DG Enlargement.

CEC (2007b) *Croatia's Path Towards the EU: Speech in Zagreb, 5 June*, SPEECH/07/363, Brussels: European Commission.

CEC (2007c) *Screening Report: Croatia. Chapter 22 – Regional Policy and Coordination of Structural Instruments*, Brussels: European Commission.

CEC (2007d) *Guidelines for Integrated Border Management in the Western Balkans*, Brussels: CEC, updated version, January.

CEC (2007e) *Applying the Global Approach to Migration to the Eastern and South-Eastern Regions Neighbouring the European Union*, COM (2007) 247 final, Brussels: European Commission.

CEC (2007f) *Commission Staff Working Document: Croatia 2007 Progress Report*, COM (2007) 663 final, Brussels: European Commission.

CEC (2008a) *Strengthening the Global Approach to Migration: Increasing Co-ordination, Coherence and Synergies*, COM (2008) 248 final, Brussels: European Commission.

CEC (2008b) *Project Fiche: Integrated Border Management – Former Yugoslav Republic of Macedonia*, CRIS number 2008/20–311, Brussels: European Commission.

CEC (2008c) *EU Regionally Relevant Activites in the Western Balkans 2008/09*, SEC (2009) 128 final, Brussels: European Commission.

CEC (2009) *2008 Environmental Policy Review*, Brussels: European Commission.

CEC (2010a) *Report on Greek Government Deficit and Debt Statistics*, 8.1.2010 COM (2010) 1 final, Brussels: European Commission.

CEC (2010b) *Council decision addressed to Greece with a view to reinforcing and deepening fiscal surveillance and giving notice to Greece to take measures for the deficit reduction judged necessary to remedy the situation of excessive debt*, Council of the European Union 9443/10 ECOFIN 250 UEM 171, 7 May, Brussels: European Commission.

CEC (2010c) *Croatia 2010 Progress Report*, SEC (2010) 1326, 9 November, Brussels: European Commission.

CEC (2010d) *The Former Yugoslav Republic of Macedonia 2010 Progress Report*, SEC (2010) 1332, 9 November, Brussels: European Commission.

Clarke, R. (2002) 'Yugoslavia', in Carter, F.W. and Turnock, D. (eds) *Environmental Problems of East-Central Europe*, London: Routledge.

Cohen, L.J. (2007) 'The Milošević Dictatorship: Institutionalising Power and Ethno-Populism in Serbia', in B.J. Fischer (ed.) *Balkan Strongmen: Dictators and Authoritarian Rulers of South Eastern Europe*, London: Hurst.

Committee of the Regions (2008a) *Minutes of the 5th Working Group on Croatia, 8 December 2008*, CdR 17/2009, Brussels: Committee of the Regions.

Committee of the Regions (2008b) *Minutes of the 1st Meeting of the EU-former Republic of Macedonia Joint Consultative Committee, 11 November*, CdR 376/2008, Brussels: Committee of the Regions.

Committee of the Regions (2009) *Minutes of the 2nd Meeting of the Joint Consultative Committee EU – the former Yugoslav Republic of Macedonia, 3 March 2009*, CdR 221/2009, Brussels: Committee of the Regions.

Cowan, J.K. (2000) *Macedonia: The Politics of Identity and Difference*, London: Pluto Press.

Cowles, M., Caporaso, J. and Risse, T. (eds) (2001) *Transforming Europe: Europeanization and Domestic Change*, Ithaca: Cornell University Press.

Cox, J.K. (2005) *Slovenia*, London: Routledge.

CPRM (2007) *The Macedonian Accession to the European Union*, Occasional Paper No. 10, Skopje: Center for Research and Policy Making.

Creveld, M. van (1999) *The Rise and Decline of the State*, Cambridge: Cambridge University Press.

Curtin, D. and Wessel, R.A. (2005) *Good Governance and the European Union: Reflections on Concepts, Institutions and Substance*, Antwerp: Intersentia.

Cuvalo, A. (1990) *The Croatian National Movement, 1966–1972*, New York: Columbia University Press.

Cyert, R.M. and March, J.G. (1963) *A Behavioral Theory of the Firm*, Englewood Cliffs, NJ: Prentice Hall.

David, P.A. (2000) 'Path Dependence, Its Critics and the Quest for "Historical Economics"', in P. Garrouste and S. Ioannides (eds) *Evolution and Path Dependence in Economic Ideas: Past and Present*, Cheltenham: Edward Elgar.

Detlef, J. and Müller-Rommel, F. (2010) 'Political Institutions and Policy Preferences: A Comparative Analysis of Central and Eastern Europe', *Journal of Public Policy*, 30: 23–44.

Dowding, K.A. (1995) 'Model or Metaphor? A Critical Review of the Policy Network Approach', *Political Studies*, 43: 136–58.

ECORYS (2003) *Strategy and Capacity Building for Regional Development: CARDS 2002 Programme for Croatia. Inception Report*, Zagreb and Brussels: EC Delegation in Croatia/Ministry for Public Works, Reconstruction and Construction, 7 December.

Euractiv (2010) 'A Step in the Right Direction: Frontex, Greece and the Fight against Irregular Migration', *Euractiv*. Available at: www.euractiv.com/en/east-mediterranean/step-right-direction-frontex-greece-fight-against-irregular-migration-a nalysis-49 (accessed 22 July 2010).

Eurobarometer (2008) *Standard Eurobarometer 69*, Brussels: Directorate General for Communication.

European Policies Research Centre (2008) *Ex Post Evaluation of Cohesion Policy Programmes 2000–2006 Co-Financed by the ERDF (Objective 1 and 2). Work Package 11: Management and Implementation Systems for Cohesion Policy. Overview of Management and Implementation Systems of Cohesion Policy in 2002–06 Slovenia*, Glasgow: University of Strathclyde.

European Stability Initiative (2005a) *Moment of Truth: Macedonia, the EU Budget and the Destabilization of the Balkans*, Berlin, Brussels and Istanbul: European Stability Initiative.

European Stability Initiative (2005b) *The Helsinki Moment: European Member-State Building in the Balkans*, Berlin, Brussels and Istanbul: European Stability Initiative.

Eurostat (2009) *Citizens of European Countries Account for the Majority of the Foreign Population in EU-27 in 2008*, Brussels: Eurostat.

Fairbrass, J. and Jordan, A. (2004) 'Multi-level Governance and Environmental Policy', in I. Bache and M. Flinders (eds) *Multi-level Governance*, Oxford: Oxford University Press.

Farley, B. (2007) 'King Aleksandar and the Royal Dictatorship in Yugoslavia', in B.J. Fischer (ed.) *Balkan Strongmen: Dictators and Authoritarian Rulers of South Eastern Europe*, London: Hurst.

Faro, J. (2004) *Europeanization as Regionalisation: Forecasting the Impact of EU Regional-Policy Export upon the Governance Structure of Slovenia*, unpublished paper delivered at Harvard University, MA.

Featherstone, K. (1998) 'Europeanization and the Centre-Periphery: The Case of Greece in the 1990s', *South European Society and Politics*, 3: 23–39.

Featherstone, K. (2005) 'Introduction: "Modernisation" and the Structural Constraints of Greek Politics', *West European Politics*, 28: 223–41.

Featherstone, K. and Papadimitriou, G. (2008) *The Limits of Europeanization: Reform Capacity and Policy Conflict in Greece*, Houndmills: Palgrave Macmillan.

Featherstone, K. and Yannopoulos, G. (1995) 'The European Community and Greece: Integration and the Challenge to Centralism', in B. Jones and M. Keating (eds) *The European Union and the Regions*, Oxford: Clarendon Press.

Ferrera, M. (2005) *The Boundaries of Welfare: European Integration and the New Spatial Politics of Social Protection*, Oxford: Oxford University Press.

Fine, J.V.A. (2007), 'Strongmen Can Be Beneficial: The Exceptional Case of Josip Broz Tito', in B. Fischer (ed.) *Balkan Strongmen: Dictators and Authoritarian Rulers of South Eastern Europe*, London: Hurst.

Fink-Hafner, D. (1998) 'Organised Interests in the Policy-making Process in Slovenia', *Journal of European Public Policy*, 5: 285–302.

Fink-Hafner, D. and Robbins, J.R. (eds) (1997) *Making a New Nation: The Formation of Slovenia*, Aldershot: Dartmouth.

Finotelli, C. and Sciortino, G. (2009) 'The Importance of Being Southern: The Making of Policies of Immigration Control in Italy', *European Journal of Migration and Law*, 11: 119–38.

Fisher, S. (2006) *Political Change in Post-Communist Slovakia and Croatia: From Nationalist to Europeanist*, Houndmills: Palgrave Macmillan.

Flora, P. (ed., with S. Kuhnle and D. Urwin) (1999) *State Formation, Nation-Building and Mass Politics in Europe: The Theory of Stein Rokkan*, Oxford: Oxford University Press.

Flynn, B. (1997) 'Subsidiarity and the Rise of Soft Law', *Human Capital and Mobility Network*, Occasional Paper 40, Colchester: University of Essex.

Frane, A., Hafner-Fink, M. and Uhan, S. (2002) 'Public Conceptions and Images of the EU: The Case of Slovenia', *Innovations*, 15: 133–47.

Freeman, L. (2004) *The Development of Social Network Analysis: A Study in the Sociology of Science*, Vancouver: Empirical Press.

Fröhlich, Z. (2006) *Croatian Regional Strategy in the Framework of the EU Accession Process*, unpublished paper, 46th Congress of the European Regional Science Association, Volos, Greece, 30 August–3 September.

FRONTEX (2009) *General Report*, Warsaw: FRONTEX.

Gallagher, T. (2001) *Outcast Europe: Balkans 1789–1989: From the Ottomans to Milosevic*, London: Routledge.

Gallagher, T. (2003) *The Balkans after the Cold War: From Tyranny to Tragedy*, London: Routledge.

Gallagher, T. (2005) *The Balkans in the New Millennium: In the Shadow of War and Peace*, London: Routledge.

Gallup (2009) *Balkan Monitor: Perceptions of the EU in the Western Balkans*. Available at: www.balkan-monitor.eu/ (accessed 1 September 2010).

Geddes, A. (2011), 'Regions and Regionalism', in M. Rosenblum and D. Tichenor (eds) *The Oxford Handbook on International Migration*, Oxford: Oxford University Press.

Getimis, P. and Demetropolou, L. (2004) 'Towards New Forms of Regional Governance in Greece: The Southern Aegean Islands', *Regional and Federal Studies*, 14: 355–78.

Glenn, J.K. (2004) 'From Nation-States to Member States: Accesssion Negotiations as an Instrument of Europeanization', *Comparative European Politics*, 2 (1): 3–28.

Glenny, M. (2000) *The Balkans 1804–1999: Nationalism, War and the Great Powers*, London: Granta Books.

Goetz, K. (2000) 'European Integration and National Executives: A Cause in Search of An Effect', *West European Politics*, 23: 211–31.

Goetz, K. (2002) *Four Worlds of Europeanization*, unpublished paper prepared for the ECPR Joint Sessions, Turin, 22–27 March.

Goetz, K.H. and Meyerr-Sahling, J.-H. (2009) 'Political Time in the EU: Dimensions, Perspectives, Theories', *Journal of European Public Policy*, 16: 180–201.

Golub, J. (1996) 'Sovereignty and Subsidiarity in EU Environmental Policy,' *Political Studies*, 44: 686–703.

Gournev, P. (2003) 'Stabilizing Macedonia: Conflict Prevention, Development and Organized Crime', *Journal of International Affairs*, 57: 229–40.

Government of Slovenia (2007) *National Strategic Reference Framework 2007–2013. Unofficial translation approved 18 June*, Ljubljana: Government Office for Local Self-Government and Regional Policy.

Gow, J. and Carmichael, C. (2000) *Slovenia and the Slovenes: A Small State and the New Europe*, London: Hurst.

Grabbe, H. (2001) 'How Does Europeanization Affect CEE Governance? Conditionality, Diffusion and Diversity', *Journal of European Public Policy*, 8: 1013–31.

Grabbe, H. (2002) 'Stabilising the East While Keeping Out the Easterners: Internal and External Security Logics in Conflict', in S. Lavenex and E. Ucarer (eds) *Migration and the Externalities of European Integration*, Lanham, MD: Lexington Books.

Grabbe, H. (2003) 'Europeanization Goes East: Power and Uncertainty in the EU Accession Process', in K. Featherstone and C. Radaelli (eds) *The Politics of Europeanization*, Oxford: Oxford University Press.

Grams, I. (1991) 'The Republic of Slovenia: Geographical Constants of the New Central-European State', *Geojournal*, 24: 331–40.

Grasse, A. (2001) 'The Myth of Regionalisation in Europe: Rhetoric and Reality of an Ambivalent Concept', *Journal of European Area Studies*, 9: 79–92.

Graziano, P. and Vink, M.P. (eds) (2007) *Europeanization: New Research Agendas*, Houndmills: Palgrave Macmillan.

Haigh, N. (1999) 'European Union Environmental Policy at 25: Retrospect and Prospect', *Environment and Planning C: Government and Policy*, 17: 109–12.

Hall, P. (1989) *The Power of Economic Ideas*, Princeton, NJ: Princeton University Press.

Hardin, R. (1995) *One for All: The National Question in Yugoslavia: Origins, History, Politics*, Ithaca, New York and London: Cornell University Press.

Harmsen, R. (1999) 'The Europeanization of National Administrations', *Governance*, 12: 81–113.

Haughton, T. (2007) 'When Does the EU Make a Difference? Conditionality and the Accession Process in Central and Eastern Europe', *Political Studies Review*, 5: 233–46.

Haverland, M. (2003) 'The Impact of the European Union on Environmental Policies', in K. Featherstone and C. Radaelli (eds) *The Politics of Europeanization*, Oxford: Oxford University Press.

Hechter, M. (2000) *Containing Nationalism*, Oxford: Oxford University Press.

Hellenic Republic (2007) *National Strategic Reference Framework 2007–2013*, Athens: Ministry of Economy and Finance.

Héritier, A. (2005) 'Europeanization Research East and West: A Comparative Assessment', in F. Schimmlefennig and U. Sedelmeier (eds) *The Europeanization of Central and Eastern Europe*, Ithaca, NY: Cornell University Press.

Hirschmann, A.O. (1970) *Exit, Voice and Loyalty: Responses to Decline in Firms, Organizations and States*, Harvard, MA: Harvard University Press.

Hix, S. and Goetz, K. (2000) 'Introduction: European Integration and National Political Systems', *West European Politics*, 23: 1–26.

Holzinger, K., Knill, C. and Schäfer, A. (2006) 'Rhetoric or Reality? "New Governance" in EU Environmental Policy', *European Law Journal*, 12: 403–20.

Hooghe, L. (1996) 'Introduction: Reconciling EU-wide Policy and National Diversity', in L. Hooghe (ed.) *Cohesion Policy and European Integration: Building Multi-level Governance*, Oxford: Oxford University Press.

Hooghe, L. and Marks, G. (2001) *Multi-level Governance and European Integration*, Boulder, CO: Rowman & Littlefield.

Hooghe, L. and Marks, G. (2003) 'Unravelling the Central State, But How?', *American Political Science Review*, 97: 233–43.

Hooghe, L. and Marks, G. (2004) 'Contrasting Visions of Multi-level Governance', in I. Bache and M. Flinders (eds) *Multi-Level Governance*, Oxford: Oxford University Press.

House of Lords (2008) *FRONTEX: The EU External Borders Agency*, European Union Committee, 9th Report of Session 2007–8, HL Paper 60, London: The Stationery Office.

Hribar, T. (1993) 'Slovene Statehood', *Nationalities Papers*, 21: 43–9.

Hughes, J., Sasse, G. and Gordon, C. (2004) 'Conditionality and Compliance in the EU's eastwards Enlargement', *Journal of Common Market Studies*, 42: 523–51.

Hughes, J., Sasse, G. and Gordon, C. (2005) *Europeanization and Regionalization in the EU's Enlargement To East and Central Europe: The Myth of Conditionality*, Houndmills: Palgrave Macmillan.

Huliaris, A. and Tsardanidis, C. (2006) '(Mis)understanding the Balkans: Greek Geopolitical Codes of the Post-communist Era', *Geopolitics*, 11: 1–19.

Huysmans, J. (2006) *The Politics of Insecurity: Fear, Migration and Asylum in the European Union*, London: Routledge.

Inotai, A. and Stanovnik, P. (2004) 'EU Membership: Rationale, Costs and Benefits', in M. Mrak, M. Rojec and C. Sila-Jáuregi (eds) *Slovenia: From Yugoslavia to the European Union*, Washington, DC: The World Bank.

International Crisis Group (2001) *Macedonia: The Last Chance for Peace*, Berlin, Brussels and Istanbul: International Crisis Group.

International Crisis Group (2006) *Macedonia: Wobbling Toward Europe*, European Briefing No. 41, Skopje and Brussels: International Crisis Group.

International Crisis Group (2011) *Macedonia: Ten Years After the Conflict*, Europe Report No. 212, Skopje and Brussels: International Crisis Group.

Ioakimidis, P.C. (1996) 'EU Cohesion Policy in Greece: The Tension between Bureaucratic Centralism and Regionalism', in L. Hooghe (ed.) *Cohesion Policy and European Integration: Building Multi-level Governance*, Oxford: Oxford University Press.

Iotrides, J.O. and Wrigley, A. (1995) *Greece at the Crossroads: The Greek Civil War and Its Legacy*, Philadelphia, PA: Pennsylvania State University Press.

Jacoby, W. (1999) 'Priest and Penitent: The European Union as a Force in the Domestic Politics of Eastern Europe', *East European Constitutional Review*, 8: 62–7.

Jacoby, W. (2002) 'Walking the Walk and Talking the Talk: The Cultural and Institutional Effects of Western Models', in F. Bönker, K. Müller and A. Pickel (eds) *Postcommunist Transformation and the Social Sciences: Cross-disciplinary Approaches*, Boulder, CO: Rowman & Littlefield.

Jacoby, W. (2004) *The Enlargement of the European Union and NATO: Ordering from the Menu in Central Europe*, Cambridge: Cambridge University Press.

Jelavich, B. (1983a) *History of the Balkans: Volume 1, Eighteenth and Nineteenth Centuries*, Cambridge: Cambridge University Press.

Jelavich, B. (1983b) *History of the Balkans: Volume 2, Twentieth Century*, Cambridge: Cambridge University Press.

Jelavich, C. and Jelavich, B. (eds) (1977) *The Establishment of the Balkan National States 1804–1920*, Seattle, WA: University of Washington Press.

Jordan, A. (1999a) 'Editorial Introduction: The Construction of a Multilevel Environmental Governance System', *Environment and Planning C: Government and Policy*, 17: 1–17.

Jordan, A. (1999b) 'The Implementation of EU Environmental Policy: A Problem without a Political Solution', *Environment and Planning C: Government and Policy*, 17: 69–90.

Jordan, A. (2005) 'Policy Convergence: Passing Fad or a New Integrating Focus in European Union Studies?', *Journal of European Public Policy*, 12: 944–53.

Jordan, A. and Breukner, L. (2003) 'European Governance and the Transfer of "New" Environmental Policy Instruments', *Public Administration*, 81: 555–74.

Jordan, A. and Liefferink, D. (2003) 'The Europeanization of Public Policy', in K. Featherstone and C. Radaelli (eds) *The Politics of Europeanization*, Oxford: Oxford University Press.

Jordan, A. and Liefferink, D. (eds) (2004) *Environmental Policy in Europe: The Europeanization of National Environmental Policy*, London: Routledge.

Kajnč, S. and Svetličič, M. (2009) *Slovenian European Policy and a European State Administration for an Active, Successful and Efficient EU Membership*, Ljubljana: Centre for International Relations, University of Ljubljana.

Kalyvas, S.N. (2008) 'Why Athens is Burning', *International Herald Tribune*, 11 December.

Karajkov, R. (2007) *The Challenge of Regional Development in the Republic of Macedonia: The State of the Matter, Issues and Considerations*, The Fiscal Decentralization Initiative for Central and Eastern Europe, Local Government and Public Service Reform Initiative. Available at: http://lgi.osi.hu/publications (accessed 23 November 2009).

Kardelj, E. (1982) *Reminiscences: The Struggle for Recognition and Independence: The New Yuoglsavia, 1944–1957*, London: Blond & Briggs.

Kassim, H. (2003a) 'The European Administration: Between Europeanization and Domestication', in J. Hayward and A. Menon (eds) *Governing Europe*, Oxford: Oxford University Press.

Kassim, H. (2003b) 'Meeting the Demands of EU Membership: The Europeanization of National Administrative Systems', in K. Featherstone and C. Radaelli (eds) *The Politics of Europeanisation*, Oxford: Oxford University Press.

Kassim, H. (2005) 'The Europeanisation of Member State Institutions', in S. Bulmer and C. Lesquesne (eds) *The Member States of the European Union*, Oxford: Oxford University Press.

Kassim, H., Peters, B.G. and Wright, V. (eds) (2000) *The National Co-ordination of EU Policy: The European Level*, Oxford: Oxford University Press.

Kaufmann, D., Kraay, A. and Mastruzzi, M. (2007a) 'Growth and Governance: A Reply', *Journal of Politics*, 69: 555–62.

Kaufmann, D., Kraay, A. and Mastruzzi, M. (2007b) 'Growth and Governance: A Rejoinder', *Journal of Politics*, 69: 570–72.

Kaufmann, D., Kraay, A. and Mastruzzi, M. (2008) *Governance Matters VII: Aggregate and Individual Governance Indicators 1996–2007*, Policy Research Working Paper 4654, Washington, DC: The World Bank.

Kazakos, P. and Iokamidis, P.C. (eds) (1994) *Greece and EU Membership Evaluated*, London: Pinter.

Keohane, R., Macedo, S. and Moravcsik, A. (2009) 'Democracy Enhancing Multilateralism', *International Organization*, 63: 1–31.

Kettunen, P. and Kungla, T. (2005) 'Europeanization of Sub-national Governance in Unitary States: Estonia and Finland', *Regional and Federal Studies*, 15 (3): 353–78.

Kitromilides, P. (1983) 'The Enlightenment East and West: A Comparative Perspective on the Ideological Origins of the Balkan Political Traditions', *Canadian Review of Studies in Nationalism*, 10: 51–70.

Kitromilides, P. (1989) 'Imagined Communities and the Origins of the National Question in the Balkans', *European History Quarterly*, 19: 149–92.

Kitromilides, P. (1996) '"Balkan Mentality": History, Legend, Imagination', *Nations and Nationalism*, 2: 163–91.

Knill, C. (1998) 'European Policies: The Impact of National Administrative Traditions', *Journal of Public Policy*, 18: 1–28.

Knill, C. (2001) *The Europeanisation of National Administrations*, Cambridge: Cambridge University Press.

Knill, C. (2005) 'Introduction: Cross-national Policy Convergence: Concepts, Approaches and Explanatory Factors', *Journal of European Public Policy*, 12: 764–74.

Knill, C. (2007) *Environmental Politics in the EU: Policy-making, Implementation and Patterns of Multi-level Governance*, Manchester: Manchester University Press.

Knill, C. (2009) 'Hierarchy, Networks or Markets? How Does the EU Shape Environment Policy Adaptations Within and Beyond its Borders?', *Journal of European Public Policy*, 16: 873–94.

Knill, C. and Lehmkuhl, D. (1999) *How European Matters: Different Mechanisms of Europeanization*, European Integration Online Papers, 3 (7).

Knill, C. and Lenschow, A. (1998) 'Coping with Europe: The Implementation of EU Environmental Policy and Administrative Traditions in Britain and Germany', *Journal of European Public Policy*, 5 (4): 595–614.

Knill, C. and Tosun, J. (2008) 'Emerging Patterns of Multi-level Governance in the EU Environmental Policy', in T. Conzelmann and R. Smith (eds) *Multi-Level Governance in the European Union: Taking Stock and Looking Ahead*, Baden-Baden: Nomos.

Kofas, J.V. (1989) *Intervention and Underdevelopment: Greece During the Cold War*, Philadelphia, PA: Pennsylvania State University Press.

Kohler-Koch, B. (1996) 'Catching-up with Change: The Transformation of Governance in the EU', *Journal of European Public Policy*, 3: 359–80.

Kohler-Koch, B. (1999) 'The Evolution and Transformation of European Governance', in B. Kohler-Koch and R. Eising (eds) *The Transformation of Governance in the European Union*, London: Routledge.

Koliopoulos, J.S. (2002) 'Greece and the Balkans: A Historical Perspective', *Journal of South Eastern Europe and Black Sea Studies*, 2: 25–38.

Kooiman, J. (ed.) (1993) *Modern Governance: New Government-Society Interactions*, London: Sage.

Krasner, S. (1988) 'Approaches to the State: Alternative Conceptions and Historical Dynamics', *Comparative Political Studies*, 21: 223–46.

Krastev, I. (2002) *The Inflexibility Trap: Frustrated Societies, Weak States and Democracy*, Report on the State of Democracy in the Balkans, Sofia: Centre for Liberal Strategies.

Kurtz, J.M. and Schrank, A. (2007a) 'Growth and Governance: Models, Measures and Mechanisms', *Journal of Politics*, 69: 538–54.

Kurtz, J.M. and Schrank, A. (2007b) 'Growth and Governance: A Defense', *Journal of Politics*, 69: 563–69.

Ladrech, R. (1994) 'Europeanization of Domestic Politics and Institutions: The Case of France', *Journal of Common Market Studies*, 32: 69–88.

Ladrech, R. (2010) *Europeanization and National Politics*, Houndmills: Palgrave Macmillan.

Lajh, D. (2003) 'The Europeanisation of Regionalization: Building a Multi-level Institutional Setting in Slovenia', *Central European Political Science Review*, 4: 89–111.

Lajh, D. (2004) *Europeanisation and Regionalisation: Domestic Change(s) and Structural Networks in Slovenia*, unpublished paper prepared for the ECPR 2004 Joint Sessions of Workshops, Uppsala, 14–18 April.

Lees, C. (2000) *The Red Green Coalition in Germany: Politics, Personalities, and Power*, Manchester: Manchester University Press.

Lees, C. (2005) 'The Law of Diminishing Returns? Environmental Policy in the Federal Republic of Germany', in S. Green and W. Paterson (eds) *The Semi-Sovereign State Re-Visited*, Cambridge: Cambridge University Press.

Lees, C. (2007) 'Environmental Policy in the UK and Germany', *German Politics*, 16: 164–83.

Lenschow, A. (1999) 'Transformation in European Environmental Governance', in B. Kohlet-Koch and R. Eising (eds) *The Transformation of Governance in the European Union*, London: Routledge.

Lenschow, A. (2005) 'Environmental Policy: Contending Dynamics of Policy Change', in H. Wallace, W. Wallace and M. Pollack (eds) *Policy-Making in the European Union* (4th edn), Oxford: Oxford University Press.

Liefferink, D. and Anderson, M.S. (1998) 'Strategies of the "Green" Member States in EU Environmental Policy-making', *Journal of European Public Policy*, 5: 245–70.

Liefferink, D., Asts, B., Kamstow, J. and Ooijevaar, J. (2009) 'Leaders and Laggards in Environmental Policy: A Quantitative Analysis of Domestic Policy and Outputs', *Journal of European Public Policy*, 16: 677–700.

Lind, M. (1992) 'The Catalytic State', *National Interest* (July–August): 3–14.

Lindstrom, N. (2005) *Europeanization and Sub-national Governance in Slovenia*, paper prepared for the ECPR Joint Sessions of Workshops, Granada 15–19 April, published as 'Europeanization and Sub-national Governance in Slovenia', *Südoesteuropa*, 53: 500–19.

Lodge, M. (2000) 'Isomorphism of National Policies', *West European Politics*, 23: 89–107.

Long, J. (2003) 'Policy Implementation in a Multi-level System: The Dynamics of Domestic Response', in B. Kohler-Koch (ed.) *Linking EU and National Governance*, Oxford: Oxford University Press.

Lowi, T.W. (1964) 'American Business, Public Policies, Case Studies, and Political Theory', *World Politics*, 16: 677–715.

Magas, B. (2007) *Croatia Through History: The Making of a European State*, London, San Francisco, CA and Beirut: Saqi Books.

Maleković, S., Puljiz, J. and Froehlich, Z. (2010) *New Role for Regional Actors in Supporting Development in Croatia*, unpublished paper to the Regional Studies

Association. Available at: www.regional-studies-assoc.ac.uk/events/2010/may-pecs/papers/Malekovic.pdf (accessed 3 January 2011).

Mann, M. (1984) 'The Autonomous Power of the State: Its Origins, Mechanisms and Results', *Archives Européenes de Sociologie*, 25: 185–213.

Mann, M. (1993) *The Sources of Social Power: Volume II, The Rise of Classes and Nation-States, 1760–1914*, Cambridge: Cambridge University Press.

Mann, M. (2005) *The Dark Side of Democracy: Explaining Ethnic Cleansing*, Cambridge: Cambridge University Press.

March, J.G. and Olsen, J.P. (1984) 'The New Institutionalism: Organisational Factors in Political Life', *American Political Science Review*, 78: 734–49.

March, J. and Olsen, J.P. (1989) *Rediscovering Institutions: The Organizational Basis of Politics*, New York: The Free Press.

Marek, D. and Baun, M. (2002) 'The EU as Regional Actor: The Case of the Czech Republic', *Journal of Common Market Studies*, 40: 895–919.

Marenin, O. (2010) *Challenges for Integrated Border Management in the European Union*, Geneva: Geneva Centre for the Democratic Control of Armed Forces.

Marko, J. (2005) 'The Referendum on Decentralization in Macedonia in 2004: A Litmus Test for Macedonia's Interethnic Relations', *European Yearbook for Minority Issues*, 4: 695–721.

Marks, G. (1992) 'Structural Policy in the European Community', in A. Sbragia (ed.) *Euro-Politics: Institutions and Policymaking in the 'New' European Community*, Washington, DC: The Brooking Institution.

Marks, G. and Hooghe, L. (2004) 'Contrasting Visions of Multi-level Governance', in I. Bache and M. Flinders (eds) *Multi-level Governance*, Oxford: Oxford University Press.

Marks, G., Hooghe, E. and Blank, K. (1996) 'European Integration from the 1980s', *Journal of Common Market Studies*, 34: 341–78.

Massey, D. and Espinosa, K. (1997) 'What's Driving Mexican Migration? A Theoretical, Empirical and Policy Analysis', *American Journal of Sociology*, 102: 939–99.

Mattli, W. (1999a) 'Explaining Regional Integration Outcomes', *Journal of European Public Policy*, 6: 1–27.

Mattli, W. (1999b) *The Logic of Regional Integration: Europe and Beyond*, Cambridge: Cambridge University Press.

Mattli, W. (2002) 'Sovereignty Bargains in Regional Integration', *International Studies Review*, 2: 149–80.

Mazower, M. (2001) *The Balkans: From the End of Byzantium to the Present Day*, London: Phoenix Books.

Menon, A. and Weatherill, S. (2006) 'Transnational Legitimacy in a Globalising World: How the European Union Rescues its State', *West European Politics*, 31: 397–16.

Meško, G., Dimitrijević, D. and Fields, C.B. (eds) 2010 'Introduction', in G. Meško, D. Dimitrijević and C.B. Fields (eds) *Understanding and Managing Threats to the Environment in South Eastern Europe*, Dordrecht: Springer.

Meurs, W. van and Mungiu-Pippidi, A. (eds) (2010) *Ottomans into Europeans: State and Institutions in South Eastern Europe*, London: C. Hurst & Co.

Milward, A. (2000) *The European Rescue of the Nation-State* (2nd edn), London: Routledge.

Monastiriotis, V. and Tsamis, A. (2007) *Greece's New Balkan Relations: Policy Shifts but No Structural Change*, GreeSE Paper No. 1, Hellenic Observatory Papers on Greece and Southeast Europe, London: London School of Economic and Political Science.

Moravcsik, A. (1991) 'Negotiating the Single European Act: National Interests and Conventional Statecraft in the European Community', *International Organization*, 45: 19–56.

Moravcsik, A. (1993) 'Preferences and Power in the European Community: A Liberal Intergovernmentalist Approach', *Journal of Common Market Studies*, 31: 473–524.

Moravcsik, A. (1994) *Why the European Community Strengthens the State: Domestic Politics and International Cooperation*, Working Paper Series 52, Center for European Studies, University of Harvard.

Moravcsik, A. (1998) *The Choice for Europe: Social Purpose and State Power from Messina to Maastricht*, Ithaca, NY: Cornell University Press.

Morrison, J. and Crosland, B. (2000) *The Trafficking and Smuggling of Refugees: The End Game of European Asylum Policies*, Working Paper No. 39, Geneva: UNHCR.

Neal, A. (2009) 'Securitization and Risk at the EU Border: The Origins of FRONTEX', *Journal of Common Market Studies*, 47: 333–56.

North, D.C. (1990) *Institutions, Institutional Change and Economic Performance*, Cambridge: Cambridge University Press.

Noutcheva, G. (2006) *EU Conditionality, State Sovereignty and the Compliance Patterns of Balkan States*, unpublished paper for the 3rd Pan-European Conference on EU Politics, ECPR, Bilgi University, Istanbul, 21–23 September.

O'Dwyer, C. (2006) 'Reforming Regional Governance in East Central Europe: Europeanization or Domestic Politics as Usual', *East European Politics and Societies*, 20 (2): 219–53.

Olsen, J.P. (2002) *Towards a European Administrative Space*, ARENA Working Paper WP 02/06.

Olsen, J.P. (2003) 'Towards a European Administrative Space', *Journal of European Public Policy*, 10: 506–31.

Olsen, J.P. (2007) *Europe in Search of Political Order*, Oxford: Oxford University Press.

O'Neill, M. (1997) *Green Parties and Political Change in Contemporary Europe: New Politics, Old Predicaments*, Aldershot: Ashgate.

Pajnik, M., Kogovšek, N. and Zupanc, S. (2006) *Mapping of Policies Affecting Female Migrants and Policy Analysis: The Slovenian Case*, Working Paper No. 8 – WP1, Ljubljana Peace Institute, Institute for Contemporary Social and Political Studies.

Papacosma, V.S. (2007) 'Ioannis Metaxas and the "Fourth of August" Dictatorship in Greece', in B.J. Fischer (ed.) *Balkan Strongmen: Dictators and Authoritarian Rulers of South Eastern Europe*, London: Hurst.

Papadimitriou, D. (2001) 'The EU's Strategy in the Post-Communist Balkans', *Journal of South Eastern Europe and Black Sea Studies*, 1: 69–94.

Papadimitriou, D. (2007) 'George Papadopoulos and the Dictatorship of the Colonels', in B.J. Fischer (ed.) *Balkan Strongmen: Dictators and Authoritarian Rulers of South Eastern Europe*, London: Hurst.

Papageorgiou, F. and Verney, S. (1992) 'Regional Planning and the Integrated Mediterranean Programmes in Greece', *Regional Politics and Policy*, 2: 139–61.

Paraskevopoulos, C. (2005) 'Developing Infrastructure as a Learning Process in Greece', *West European Politics*, 28: 445–70.

Paraskevopoulos, C., Paangiotis, G., Rees, N., and Szlachta, J. (eds) (2005) *Adapting EU Multi-level Governance in Public Policy: Regional and Environmental Policy in Cohesion and Central and East European Countries*, Aldershot: Ashgate.

Pettifer, J. (2001) *The New Macedonian Question* (new edn), Houndmills: Palgrave Macmillan.

Philips, J. (2004) *Macedonia: Warlords and Rebels in the Balkans*, New Haven, CT and London: Yale University Press.

Piattoni, S. (2010) *The Theory of Multi-level Governance: Conceptual, Empirical, and Normative Challenges*, Oxford: Oxford University Press.

Pierson, P. (2004) *Politics in Time*, Princeton, NJ: Princeton University Press.

Polsby, N.W. (1980) *Community Power and Political Theory: A Further Look at Problems of Evidence and Inference* (2nd enlarged edn), New Haven, CT and London: Yale University Press.

Pond, E. (2006) *Endgame in the Balkans: Regime Change, European Style*, Washington, DC: Brookings.

Popetrevski, V. and Latifi, V. (2004) 'The Ohrid Framework Negotiations', in *The 2001 Conflict in FYROM–Reflections*, Skopje and London: Institute for War and Peace Reporting.

Potocnik, J. and Garcia Lombardero, J. (2004) 'Slovenia's Road to Membership in the European Union', in M. Mrak, M. Rojec and C. Sila-Jáuregi (eds) *Slovenia: From Yugoslavia to the European Union*, Washington, DC: The World Bank.

Poulton, H. (2000) *Who Are the Macedonians?*, Bloomington, IN: Indiana University Press.

Pressman, J.L. and Wildavsky, A. (1984) *Implementation* (3rd edn, expanded), Berkeley, CA: University of California Press.

Pridham, G., Verney, S. and Konstadakopoulos, D. (1995) 'Environmental Policy in Greece: Evolution, Structure and Process', *Environmental Politics*, 4: 244–70.

Purcell, M. and Nevins, J. (2005) 'Pushing the Boundary: State Restructuring, State Theory, and the Case of U.S.–Mexico Border Enforcement in the 1990s', *Political Geography*, 24: 211–35.

Pusić, V. (1994) 'Constitutional Politics in Croatia', *Praxis*, 13: 389–404.

Radaelli, C. (2003) 'The Europeanization of Public Policy', in K. Featherstone and C. Radaelli (eds) *The Politics of Europeanization*, Oxford: Oxford University Press.

Radaelli, C. (2004) 'Europeanisation: Solution or Problem?', *European Integration Online Papers*, 8 (4).

Radaelli, C. (2005) 'Europeanisation: Solution or Problem?', in M. Cini and A. Bourne (eds) *The Palgrave Guide to European Studies*, Houndmills: Palgrave Macmillan.

Rae, H. (2002) *State Identities and the Homogenisation of Peoples*, Cambridge: Cambridge University Press.

Ramet, S. (1993) 'Slovenia's Road to Democracy', *Europe-Asia Studies*, 45: 869–96.

Ramet, S. (1997) 'Democratisation in Slovenia: The Second Stage', in K. Dawisha and B. Parrott (eds) *Politics, Power, and the Struggle for Democracy in Southeast Europe*, Cambridge: Cambridge University Press.

Ramet, S. (1998) 'The Slovenian Success Story', *Current History*, 97: 113–18.

Ramet, S. (2005) *Thinking about Yugoslavia: Scholarly Debates about the Yugoslav Breakup and the Wars in Bosnia and Kosovo*, Cambridge: Cambridge University Press.

Ramet, S. (2006) *The Three Yugoslavias: State-building and Legitimation, 1918–2005*, Bloomington, IN: Indiana University Press.

Ramet, S. (2007) *The Independent State of Croatia*, London: Routledge.

Rehn, O. (2007) *Ohrid Agreement: Vital for European Path*, Conference on the Ohrid Framework Agreement, Skopje, 8 February. Speech/07/69, Brussels: European Commission.

Renner, S. and Trauner, F. (2009) 'Creeping EU Membership in South-east Europe: Dynamics of EU Rule Transfer to the Western Balkans', *Journal of European Integration*, 31: 449–65.

Republic of Croatia (2006a) *Strategic Development Framework for 2006–2013*, Zagreb: Republic of Croatia, Central Office for Development Strategy and Coordination of EU Funds.

Republic of Croatia (2006b) *Strategic Coherence Framework 2007–2013: Instrument for Pre-Accession Assistance*, Zagreb: Republic of Croatia, Central Office for Development Strategy and Coordination of EU Funds.

Republic of Croatia (2010) *National Strategic Reference Framework 2012–2013 Draft*, Zagreb: Republic of Croatia, Central Office for Development Strategy and Coordination of EU Funds.

Republic of Macedonia (1997) *National Environmental Action Plan: Synthesis Report*, Skopje, Ministry of Environment and Physical Planning.

Republic of Macedonia (2004) *National Environmental Action Plan: Synthesis Report*, Skopje, Ministry of Environment and Physical Planning.

Republic of Macedonia (2007) The National Programme for the Adoption of the Acquis, Skopje, Ljubljana: Government Office for Local Self-Government and Regional Policy.

Republic of Slovenia (2007) The National Strategic Reference Framework 2007–2013, Ljubljana: Government Office for Local Self-Government.

Republic of Slovenia (2008) *Programme of the Slovenian Presidency of the EU Council: What We Have Achieved*. Available at: www.eu2008.si/en/News_and_ Documents (accessed 23 October 2010).

Republic of Slovenia (2010) *Government Adopts Bill on Balanced Regional Development, 28 October*. Available at: www.svlr.gov.si/nc/en/splosno/cns/news/ article/582/ (accessed 12 December 2010).

Rhodes, R.A.W. (1988) *Beyond Westminster and Whitehall*, London: Unwin-Hyman.

Rhodes, R.A.W. (1997) *Understanding Governance: Policy Networks, Governance, Reflexivity and Accountability*, Milton Keynes: Open University Press.

Rizman, R.M. (2006) *Uncertain Path: Democratic Transition and Consolidation in Slovenia*, College Station, TX: Texas A & M University Press.

Rokkan, S. (1975) 'Dimensions of State Formation and Nation-Building: A Possible Paradigm for Research on Variations within Europe', in C. Tilly (ed.) *The Formation of National States in Western Europe*, Princeton, NJ: Princeton University Press.

Rokkan, S. (1982) 'Centres and Peripheries in Western Europe', in S. Rokkan and D. Urwin (eds) *The Politics of Territorial Identity: Studies in European Regionalism*, Beverley Hills, CA and London: Sage.

Rometsch, D. and Wessels, W. (eds) (1996) *The European Union and Member States: Towards Institutional Fusion?*, Manchester: Manchester University Press.

Rossos, A. (2008) *Macedonia and the Macedonians: A History*, Stanford, CA: The Hoover Institution.

Roudmetov, V. (2000) *The Macedonian Question: Culture, Historiography, Politics*, New York: Columbia University Press.

Ruggie, J. (1993) 'Territoriality and Beyond: Problematizing Modernity in International Relations', *International Organization*, 47: 139–74.

Rusi, I. (2004) 'From Army to Party – the Politics of the NLA', in *The 2001 Conflict in FYROM–Reflections*, Skopje and London: Institute for War and Peace Reporting.

Sack, R.D. (1986) *Human Territoriality: Its Theory and History*, Cambridge: Cambridge University Press.

Sassen, S. (2007) *A Sociology of Globalization*, New York: W.W. Norton.

Saurugger, S. (2005) 'Europeanisation as a Methodological Challenge: The Case of Interest Groups', *Journal of Comparative Political Analysis*, 7: 291–312.

Sbragia, A. (2000) 'Environmental Policy', in H. and W. Wallace (eds) *Policymaking in the European Union*, Oxford: Oxford University Press.

Scharpf, F.W. (1988) 'The Joint Decision Trap: Lessons from German Federalism and European Integration', *Public Administration*, 66: 239–78.

Scharpf, F. (1997) 'European Integration, Democracy and the Welfare State', *Journal of European Public Policy*, 4: 18–36.

Scharpf, F.W. (2001) *European Governance: Common Concern vs. the Challenge of Diversity*, Jean Monnet Working Paper No. 6/01, New York: New York University School of Law.

Scharpf, F.W. (2003) 'Legitate Diversity: The New Challenge of European Integration', *Zeitschrift fur Staats – und Europawissenschaften*, 1 (1): 32–60.

Scheider, F. (2004) *The Size of the Shadow Economies of 145 Countries all over the World: First Results over the Period 1999 to 2003*. DP No. 1431, December, Institute for the Study of Labour, Bonn: IZA.

Scherpereel, J.A. (2007) 'Sub-National Authorities in the EU's Post-Socialist States: Joining the Multi-level Polity?', *Journal of European Integration*, 29: 23–46.

Schimmelfennig, F. and Sedelmeier, U. (2005) 'Conclusions: The Impact of the EU on Accession Countries', in F. Schimmelfennig and U. Sedelmeier (eds) *The Europeanization of Central and Eastern Europe*, Ithaca, NY: Cornell University Press.

Schimmelfennig, F. and Sedelmeier, U. (2004) 'Governance by Conditionality: EU Rule Transfer to the Candidate Countries of Central and Eastern Europe', *Journal of European Public Policy*, 11: 661–79.

Schmidt, V.A. (2006) *Democracy in Europe: The EU and National Polities*, Oxford: Oxford University Press.

Schöpflin, G. (1973) 'The Ideology of Croat Nationalism', *Survey*, 19: 123–46.

Sciortino, G. (2010) 'The Regulation of Undocumented Migration', in M. Martiniello and J. Rath (eds) *International Migration and Immigrant Incorporation: The Dynamics of Globalization and Ethnic Diversity in European Life*, Amsterdam: Amsterdam University Press.

Scott, J. (1991) *Social Network Analysis*, London: Sage.

Scott, J.C. (1998) *Seeing Like a State: How Certain Schemes to Improve the Human Condition Have Failed*, New Haven, CT and London: Yale University Press.

Shea, J. (2008) *Macedonia and Greece: The Struggle to Define a New Nation*, Jefferson, NC: McFarland & Co.

SIGMA (1998a) *Sustainable Institutions for European Union Membership*, SIGMA Paper 26, Paris: OECD.

SIGMA (1998b) *Preparing Public Administrations for the European Administrative Space*, SIGMA Book 23, Paris: OECD.

SIGMA (1999) *European Principles of Public Administration*, SIGMA Book 25, Paris: OECD.

SIGMA (2002) *Slovenia: Public Service and the Administrative Framework Assessment*, Paris: OECD.

SIGMA (2008) *DG Admin's Perspective on Public Administration Reform in Enlargement Countries*, 2nd SIGMA Networking Seminar, 27–28 November, OECD: Paris.

SIGMA (2009a) *Former Yugoslav Republic of Macedonia: Administrative Legal Framework Assessment*, Paris: OECD.

SIGMA (2009b) *Preparing Public Administrations for the European Administrative Space*, SIGMA Book 44, Paris: OECD.

Skocpol, T. (1992) *Protecting Soldiers and Mothers: The Political Origins of Social Policy in the United States*, Newbury Park: Sage.

Skordas, A. (2002) 'The New Immigration Law in Greece: Modernization on the Wrong Track', *European Journal of Migration and Law*, 4: 23–48.

Sloat, A. (2003) 'The Preparation of the Governance White Paper', *Politics*, 23: 128–36.

Sotlar, A., Tičar, B. and Tominc, B. (2011) 'Slovenian Environmental Policy Analysis – from Institutional Declarations to Instrumental Legal Regulation', in A. Sotlar, B. Tičar and B. Tominc (eds) *Understanding and Managing Threats to the Environment in South East Europe*, Brussels: NATO Science for Peace and Security Series.

Spanou, C. (1998) 'European Integration in Administrative Terms: A Framework for Analysis and the Greek Case', *Journal of European Public Policy*, 5: 467–84.

Spanou, C. (2000) 'A Truncated Pyramid? Domestic Co-ordination of EU Policy in Greece', in H. Kassim, G. Peters, and V. Wright (eds) *Policy Co-ordination in the European Union: The National Level*, Oxford: Oxford University Press.

Stephenson, P. (2010) 'Let's Get Physical: The European Commission and Cultivated Spillover in Completing the Single Market's Transport Infrastructure', *Journal of European Public Policy*, 17: 1039–57.

Stritih, J., Quirjo, M., Spasojević, D., Stavrić, V., Marković, M., Simić, D. and Shkipe, D. (2007) *Environmental Policy in South Eastern Europe*, Belgrade: UNDP Working Paper.

Stubbs, P. (2005) 'Stretching Concepts Too Far? Multi-level Governance and Policy Transfer in the Politics of Scale in South East Europe', *Southeast European Politics*, 6: 66–87.

Sturm, R. and Dieringer, J. (2005) 'The Europeanization of Regions in Eastern and Western Europe: Theoretical Perspectives', *Regional and Federal Studies*, 15 (3): 279–94.

Surtees, R. (2005) *Second Annual Report on Victims of Trafficking in South Eastern Europe*, Geneva: International Organization for Migration.

Szajkowski, B. (2009) *Macedonia*, London: Routledge.

Tanner, M. (2010) *Croatia: A Nation Forged in War* (3rd edn), New Haven, CT and London: Yale University Press.

Taylor, A. (2002) 'Governance', in G. Blakeley and V. Bryson (eds) *Contemporary Political Concepts: A Critical Introduction*, London: Pluto Press.

Taylor, P.J. (1994) 'The State as Container: Territoriality in the Modern World System', *Progress in Human Geography*, 18: 151–62.

Tews, K. (2009) 'From Law-taking to Policy-making: The Environmental Dimension of the EU Accession Process – Challenges, Risks and Choices for the SEE countries', *Environmental Policy and Governance*, 19: 130–9.

Thielemann, E.R. (2000) 'Institutional Change and European Governance: An Analysis of Partnership', *Current Politics and Economics of Europe*, 9: 181–98.

Thomson, M. (2006) *Migrants on the Edge of Europe: Perspectives from Malta, Cyrpus and Slovenia*, Working Paper 35, Brighton: Sussex Centre for Migration Research.

Tilly, C. (1975) 'Western-state Making and Theories of Political Transformation', in C. Tilly (ed.) *The Formation of National States in Western Europe*, Princeton, NJ: Princeton University Press.

Tilly, C. (1984) *Big Structures, Large Processes, Huge Comparisons*, New York: The Russell Sage Foundation.

Tilly, C. (2005) *Identities, Boundaries, and Social Ties*, Boulder, CO: Paradigm Press.

Tilly, C. (2006) 'Why and How History Matters', in R.E. Goodin and C. Tilly (eds) *The Oxford Handbook of Contextual Political Theory*, Oxford: Oxford University Press.

Todorova, M. (1997) *Imagining the Balkans*, New York and Oxford: Oxford University Press.

Toplak, J. (2006) 'The Parliamentary Election in Slovenia, October 2004', *Electoral Studies*, 25: 825–31.

Trauner, F. (2009) 'Deconstructing the EU's Routes of Influence in Justice and Home Affairs in the Western Balkans', *Journal of European Integration*, 31: 65–82.

Tsalikoglou, I.S. (1995) *Negotiating for Entry: The Accession of Greece to the European Union*, Aldershot: Dartmouth.

Tsebelis, G. (2002) *Veto Players: How Political Institutions Work*, Princeton, NJ: Princeton University Press/The Russell Sage Foundation.

US State Department (2008) *Trafficking in Persons Report*, Washington, DC: State Department.

Uzelac, G. (2006) *The Development of the Croatian Nation: An Historical and Sociological Analysis*, Bangor: Edwin Mellen Press.

Vachudova, M. (2005) *Europe Undivided: Democracy, Leverage, and Integration after Communism*, Oxford: Oxford University Press.

Van Meurs, W.P. and Mungiu-Pippidi, A. (2010) *Ottomans into Europeans: State and Institution Building in South-Eastern Europe*, London: C. Hurst & Co.

Vaughan-Williams, N. (2008) 'Borderwork Beyond Inside/Outside: FRONTEX, the Citizen-detective and the War on Terror', *Space and Polity*, 12: 63–79.

Verney, S. (1994) 'Central State – Local Government Relations', in P. Kazakos and P.C. Ioakimidis (eds) *Greece and EU Membership Evaluated*, London: Pinter.

Vink, A. (2003) 'What is Europeanisation? And Other Questions on a New Research Agenda', *European Political Science*, 3: 63–74.

Vlašić, I. and Feketija, M.V. (2006) *The Importance of Environmental Protection: Croatia in the European Union Accession Process*. Available at: www.fes.hr/E-books/pdf/Croation_accession_to_EU4/12.pdf.

Vodopine, P. (1992) 'Slovenes and Yugoslavia', *East European Politics and Society*, 6: 220–41.

Wachtel, A.B. (2008) *The Balkans in World History*, Oxford: Oxford University Press.

Wallace, H. (2004) 'An Institutional Anatomy and Five Policy Models', in H. Wallace, W. Wallace and M. Pollack (eds) *Policy-Making in the EU* (5th edn), Oxford: Oxford University Press.

Wasserman, S. and Faust, K. (1994) *Social Network Analysis: Methods and Applications*, Cambridge: Cambridge University Press.

Wätli, S. (2004) 'How Multi-level Structures Affect Environmental Policy in Industrialized Countries', *European Journal of Political Research*, 43: 599–34.

Weale, A. (1996) 'Environmental Rules and Rule-making in the European Union', *Journal of European Public Policy*, 3: 594–611.

Weale, A. (1999) 'European Environmental Policy by Stealth: The Dysfunctionality of Functionalism?', *Environment and Planning C: Government and Policy*, 17: 37–51.

Weale, A., Pridham, G., Cini, M., Konstadakopoulos, D., Porter, M. and Flynn, B. (2000) *Environmental Governance in Europe: An Ever Greener Ecological Union?*, Oxford: Oxford University Press.

Weiss, L. (1998) *The Myth of the Powerless State: Governing the Economy in a Global Era*, Oxford: Polity Press.

Wellman, B. (1988) 'Structural Analysis: From Method and Metaphor to Theory and Substance', in B. Wellman and S.D. Berkowitz (eds) *Social Structures: A Network Approach*, Cambridge: Cambridge University Press.

Wessels, W. (1996) 'The Modern West European State and the European Union: Democratic Erosion or a New Kind of Polity?', in S.S. Anderson and K.A. Eliassen (eds) *The European Union: How Democratic Is It?*, London: Sage.

Wessels, W., Maurer, A. and Mittag, J. (eds) (2003) *Fifteen into One? The European Union and Its Member States*, Manchester: Manchester University Press.

Woodhouse, C.M. (1985) *The Rise and Fall of the Greek Colonels*, London: Granada Books.

Woodward, S. (2001) *Milošević Who? Origins of the New Balkans*, Discussion Paper No. 5, The Hellenic Observatory/The European Institute: London School of Economics and Political Science.

World Bank (2011) *Migration and Remittances Factbook 2011*, Washington, DC: World Bank.

Zito, A. (1998) 'Comparing Environmental Policy-making in Transnational Institutions', *Journal of European Public Policy*, 5: 671–90.

Zolberg, A. (1987) 'Wanted, but not Welcome: Alien Labor in Western Development', in W. Alonso (ed.) *Population in an Interacting World*, Cambridge, MA: Harvard University Press.

Zolberg, A. (1989) 'The Next Waves: Migration Theory for a Changing World', *International Migration Review*, 23: 403–30.

Index

Note: Page numbers in *italic* type refer to figures; those in **bold** type to tables.

For Product Safety Concerns and Information please contact our EU
representative GPSR@taylorandfrancis.com
Taylor & Francis Verlag GmbH, Kaufingerstraße 24, 80331 München, Germany